Hard Like Water

Hard Like Water

❖

Ethics in Business

Vincent Di Norcia

Water goes with the flow, bending with the turns in the riverbed, but it carved out the Grand Canyon. Water is soft and takes the shape of its container, but water can carry the load of a thousand-ton ship.

L. Copeland and L. Griggs, *Going International*

Toronto New York Oxford
Oxford University Press
1998

Oxford University Press
70 Wynford Drive, Don Mills, Ontario M3C 1J9
http://www.oupcan.com

Oxford New York
Athens Auckland Bangkok Calcutta
Cape Town Chennai Dar es Salaam Delhi
Florence Hong Kong Istanbul Karachi
Kuala Lumpur Madrid Melbourne Mexico City
Mumbai Nairobi Paris Singapore
Taipei Tokyo Toronto Warsaw

and associated companies in
Berlin Ibadan

Oxford is a trade mark of Oxford University Press

Canadian Cataloguing in Publication Data

Di Norcia, Vincent, 1937–
  Hard like water : ethics in business

Includes bibliographical references and index.
ISBN 0-19-541210-9

1. Business ethics. I. Title.

HF5387D558 1997   174'.4   C97-932551-X

Front Cover Image: J. Fuste Raga / First Light
Back Cover Image: S. Miller / First Light
Cover & Text Design: Brett Miller
Formatting: George Kirkpatrick

To the memory of my mother, Mary Lattrulo, a businesswoman before her time,
my father, Jimmy Di Norcia, her sociable partner,
and my father-in-law, David W.M. Ross, an engineer of hidden depths.

Contents

Acknowledgements

I would like to thank my wife, Linda, my in-house editor, for her support, and Andrea and Alex, my children. They have always been patient and helpful, and never lost for words. And Linda beats me in both number-crunching and wordsmithing. Thanks also to a host of friends who have helped in myriad ways: Mark Baetz, Norm Bowie, David Braide, Colin Boyd, Len Brooks, Jane Butler, Max Clarkson, David Conrath, Rupert Cook, Barry Cotton, Frank Cunningham, Alice Dickson, John Dodge, Brian Donohue, Sally Gunz, May Jarvie, Henry Knowles, Sophie Landry, Claire Lecoupe, Mike Magazine, Mike Malkoski, Cash Matthews, Bob Michelutti, Jacques Monet, Graeme Mount, Graeme Nicholson, David Nitkin, Paul Reid, Mike Ross, Darla Scott, Gordon Sharwood, Joyce Tigner, Mark Wiseman, and David Wood, my colleagues at the University of Sudbury, the Laurentian University School of Commerce and Administration, the Sudbury Chamber of Commerce, and the Department of Government of the London School of Economics; and, at Oxford University Press: Monica Meehan, Euan White, and Phyllis Wilson, and my copy editor, Richard Tallman.

Vincent Di Norcia
Sudbury, June 1997

Prologue

Ethics in Business

It was the best of times, it was the worst of times.

Charles Dickens, *A Tale of Two Cities*

Our morality tales are increasingly at odds with the challenges we confront. The prevailing versions have limited relevance to the relationships that frame our lives—with other peoples of the earth, within our firms, toward our poor, toward our leaders.

Robert Reich, *Tales of a New America*[1]

Changing Times, Changing Tales

One hundred fifty years ago Charles Dickens told horror stories about the hard life that befell millions in the industrial cities of England. Today, unfortunately, his words still ring true. The 1980s, like the 1960s, were the best of times. But then came the recession of the 1990s. Today, news of rising stock prices competes with stories of joblessness. From Toronto to London abject poverty stalks the streets side by side with obscene wealth. A new kind of bank is growing, the food bank. Business is not the engine of social plenty that it once promised to be; Charles Dickens would not have been surprised.

The first aim of *Hard Like Water* is to show the extent to which ethical values penetrate into business. To this end each chapter moves from old tales about amoral or unethical business to new tales about ethical values in business. The second goal is to stress the social character of business. Accordingly, the adjective 'social' appears often in the coming chapters, as in 'socially inclusive ownership', 'social management', the 'social market', and 'social trade' (in Chapters 1, 2, 8, and 9). The two aims are interlinked, for 'ethics' comes from '*ethos*', the Greek for social customs, just as 'morality' reflects the Latin '*mores*'.[2] Social values are the starting point of morality and ethics. Ethics build on care for the quality of social relationships. This explains the development of subjects through the chapters. *Hard Like Water* moves from inside the firm in Chapters 1 to 6 to outside it in the last four chapters, to relations with nature, society, and foreign nations, and, finally, the future.

As the amoral old ways of doing business still persist, each chapter of *Hard Like Water* begins by telling an old tale about the conflict between hard-headed business realism and soft-hearted moral idealism, and then expands on that story as appropriate to that area of business. But we need new and better tales about ethics in business—

hence the subtitle of the book. So the second part of each chapter concludes with new tales in which ethical values are seen at work in specific business contexts. The aim of the Prologue is to introduce the concept of ethics used in *Hard Like Water*, to show their economic connotations, and to sketch their roots in classic moral theory.

I: Business vs Ethics, The Hard Old Tale

Perhaps the oldest tale of all is to say business ethics is an oxymoron. Business and morality, the old story goes, are two separate worlds. My interests are separate from, or even opposed to, yours. Greed and the bottom line govern business. Maximizing my gains matters more than minimizing your pains. Since doing good is hard, unpleasant, and doesn't pay well, business is constantly at odds with morality. It is no wonder then that many see business and morality as separate compartments, or even irreconcilable opposites, as in the diagram below:

Business	vs	Morality

Unfortunately, there has been no shortage of moral scandals in business, and they support the old tale. For decades Johns-Manville put the health of thousands at serious risk from exposure to asbestos. In 1984 Union Carbide's pesticide plant in Bhopal, India, broke down, leaking tons of poison gas into the neighbouring community, and over 3,000 people died. In 1989 the *Exxon Valdez* ran aground in Prince William Sound, Alaska, devastating the local ecosystem (see Chapter 7). In 1992 an explosion ripped through the Westray coal mine in Pictou, Nova Scotia, killing 26 miners (see Chapter 4). Today, stock prices soar as thousands of managers and workers lose their jobs; and when employment increases share prices dive. In the 1980s numerous banks and trust companies made bad loans to dubious developers, dictators, and criminals, putting their depositors' capital at risk; many went bankrupt. After letting Nick Leeson gamble $1.5 billion on the Asian derivatives market, Barings Bank finally went bankrupt in 1995 (see Chapter 2).

Oxymoronic Thinking

You set up an absurd dichotomy between ethical absolutism and the so-called real world and then you wonder how ethics can possibly be at home in business.

Robert Solomon and Kristin Hansen, *It's Good Business*[3]

The solution to the moral problems caused by bad business practices is not to luxuriate in fulminations of self-righteous moralizing. Nor will moralistic talk about altruistic self-sacrifice sit well with business values. Rather, we need to tell different stories that transcend such absurd dichotomies.

II: Soft New Tales

Ethics in Business

Today, new tales are being told, especially in North America. In the last two decades the 'applied ethics' field has grown rapidly. Since 1989 EthicScan, an ethics consulting firm, has published a business ethics newsletter, the *Corporate Ethics Monitor*.[4] Most business schools now have ethics courses. And ethics are increasingly accepted as a normal part of doing business; many companies already have ethics codes. So many businesses are themselves discussing ethics that it is becoming an accepted part of business life.

But, many ask, what are ethics? The first answer is social. Moral values are commonplace, familiar, and pervasive. They are found in all social spheres, from the home and family to the workplace and the marketplace. They have evolved, like the species, over the millennia. One result of that long history is that a few core values have been found to be fundamental to the survival, health, and development of civilizations across the world.[5] Accordingly, *Hard Like Water* works with a set of such values, termed the *core ethic*. It consists of four core values: *life, welfare, honest communication*, and *civil rights*, supplemented by five performance maxims. All are presented in Table 0.1.

I speak of a core ethic because these values and maxims are a subset of moral values. There are others: happiness, self-realization, integrity, trust, wisdom. 'Core' means substantive practical centre, most fundamental values, the heart of actual moral conduct. These values are found across the world, in varying forms. Ethics begin with care—care for humans and nature, for the welfare of others, for communication, and for civil rights. That care takes practical form in the four positive and negative norms and the five performance maxims. The aim of the core ethic is to make it easier to identify and discuss ethical values in business and thereby improve its ethical performance. Now to explain each core value and maxim, noting its relevance to business and economics.

1. *Care for life*. The first core value reflects the teaching of Buddha, Christ, and Francis of Assisi. Quality of life is also the purpose of an economy. A main function of business and markets is to help people live and live well (see Chapter 5). That is why people produce and exchange the goods they need and want. No business therefore may deliberately put the life of employees, customers, or others at risk, or wantonly destroy natural habitats and life forms (see Chapters 4 to 7). Unfortunately, businesses do not always choose to do the right thing, as we will see in the stories of the Westray mine, the tobacco industry, the *Exxon Valdez*, and others. But there are also new tales to tell, about firms that make better choices, such as Northern Telecom, The Body Shop, Levi Strauss, 3M, and others.

Table 0.1: **The Core Ethic**		
Core Values		
The Norms→ **The Values↓**	**The Positive** **Norms: Do . . .**	**The Negative** **Norms: Don't . . .**
Life	Care for Life	Kill
Welfare	Care for Welfare	Steal
Honest / Open Communication	Care for Communication	Lie
Civil Rights	Care for Civil Rights	Violate Civil Rights
Ethical Performance Maxims		
1st	Do No Harm	
2nd	Solve the Problem	
3rd	Enable Informed Choice	
4th	Act, Learn, Improve	
5th	Seek the Common Good	

2. *Welfare*. This value pervades every chapter of *Hard Like Water*, for it easily takes on economic significance. Here ethics and economics are close companions. Welfare is much broader than utility, as the next section explains. Welfare ranges from material, psychological, social and cultural well-being, and a healthy environment, to happiness, pleasure, economic gain, and, of course, the avoidance of associated harms. Welfare is not a static good so much as a dynamic relationship, of reciprocity and mutual benefit and support, which has evolved and developed over the millennia.[6] It is an ancient, widely understood human value. 'All human organization', Robert Reich remarks, 'depends on reciprocal obligations and mutual trust that others' obligations will be fulfilled.'[7] Reciprocity lies at the foundation of social life, in kinship relations, family property, gift-giving, and, certainly, trade.

Welfare is not merely a stock of moral goods; it also denotes reciprocity, those forms of social relations that benefit the parties involved. It signifies that people's interests typically are interlinked and interdependent, that each benefits in and through bringing benefits (or reducing harms) to or with others. Thus markets grow because they rest on mutually beneficial exchanges in which both sellers and buyers gain. Productive enterprises represent communities of interest, characterized by reciprocity among, for example, shareholders, management, and employees, and, externally, in the market relations between the enterprise and its customers and suppliers. So understood, reciprocal welfare is the ethical foundation of business (see Chapters 3 to 5).

Mutual Support and the Evolution of Welfare

There is, [Darwin] showed, in Nature itself, another set of facts, parallel to those of mutual struggle, but having a quite a different meaning: the facts of mutual support within the species [and among species], which are even more important . . . on account of their significance for the welfare of the species and its maintenance.

Peter Kropotkin, *Ethics*

The core value of reciprocal welfare also implies a more socially inclusive concept of ownership than the old restrictive notion of private property (see Chapter 1). In *Hard Like Water* different property systems are found to be appropriate to different kinds of socio-economic system. Common property notions are not only appropriate to employee-owned companies like Algoma Steel but also for sharing information in communication networks. In contrast, Aboriginal peoples favour a much looser, almost free, tribal property system. Nature, however, is not an infinite resource or a 'free good' (see Chapters 1, 4, 6, 7, 8).

3. *Honest communication.* The third core value is fundamental in markets as well as in social life. Honest and open communication means trust and informality. It slashes the costs of everyday social interactions and business transactions, often to zero. Open, free, honest communication makes life enjoyable, and it pays off handsomely. It is a fundamental factor in modern democracy, science, and markets, and is especially important in the information age (see Chapter 6). The more we can trust people, the easier and freer our social and economic life is and the less we have to police transaction and social exchanges and to worry about the privacy and security of our information systems.

On the other hand, the more untrustworthy a person or organization, the more we have to be on our guard with them and police all information and economic exchanges. Relations turn formal, bureaucratic, and legalistic; and all communications are in writing, in triplicate. Where communication is not trustworthy, as in the corrupt markets of central Africa and eastern Europe, markets fail and affluence declines.

4. *Civil rights.* The fourth core value refers to the key democratic values: individual and group freedoms, basic political and legal rights, equality and justice, and voluntary, private, civil associations. These values are epitomized in the famous slogan of the French Revolution, *liberté, égalité et fraternité* (freedom, equality, and brotherhood or community). Western capitalism has developed largely in association with liberal or civil democratic values; but their relationship is uneven and problematic, as shown in the amoral *laissez-faire* notions of free trade and markets, the corrupt capitalist systems in eastern Europe, and foreign investments in corrupt regimes like Nigeria (see Chapters 8 and 9).

The value of fair treatment or equity, a concomitant of reciprocity, is implicit in the negotiations, contracts, and exchanges on which business rests. It is explicit in fair treatment of employees and customers and in society's calls for a fairer distribution of the benefits of a productive economy (see Chapters 4, 5, 8). Egalitarian values pervade both market economies and nations. The Canadian constitution, for instance, enshrines both individual and group rights: the fundamental freedoms and regional, cultural, and gender equality rights. Fairness or equity is important, for example, in employment and marketing and international business (see Chapters 4, 5, 9). Canadian businesses have learned to respect French-Canadian and Aboriginal cultures (see Chapter 8). Recognizing various stakeholder interests, at first a fundamental of pluralist democracy, now has become an accepted norm in business. The obligation to recognize stakeholder welfare structures the development of this book; the chapters move from internal stakeholders—owners, management, and employees (Chapters 1–4)—to external stakeholders such as customers, suppliers, the environment, social interests and governments, and foreign nations (Chapters 5–9). An excessive stress on the law and rights, however, tends to legalize ethical values and economic activity. In contrast to the law, the power of which comes from sanctions and threats, exchange values rest on reciprocity and informed choice, as do ethics.

Espousing care for moral values may reflect idealistic goals or good intentions. But mere good intentions can pave the road to the wrong place. One must walk one's talk. When interviewing managers at Falconbridge Mining in Sudbury, Ontario, as part of an environmental research project, I was struck by managers' frequent reference to 'doing the right thing'. Actions do speak louder than words; but where immediate action is not possible, credible commitment to constructive specific actions in an acceptable time frame is to be expected. Results count in ethics, as in business. In their codes many Canadian companies express a commitment to numerous values: integrity, worker health and safety, honesty, customer service, respect for privacy and intellectual property, equity in employee relations, and environmental protection. Such statements are not meant to describe actual firm practice, but to espouse the values and commitments that should infuse the organization and guide practice. At least that is how they are interpreted here.

The core ethic is a performance ethic. A business that cares for life, for instance, acts to reduce the health and safety risks to workers and consumers and to protect neighbouring ecosystems. For these reasons, five performance maxims are added to the four core values: *do no harm*; *solve the problem*; *enable informed choice*; *act, learn, improve*; and *seek the common good*. The maxims facilitate the move from verbally espousing care for ethics to commitments to realizing those values and putting them into practice. The maxims are only guidelines. There are no ethical algorithms. There is no rule book for good conduct, for performance is complex and dynamic. It varies with the situation, the person, the resources available, etc.

1. *Do no harm*. The concept of doing no harm, our first performance maxim, has been part of medical ethics since Hippocrates. It relates directly to the negative norms

in the core ethic, indicating that there are unacceptable choices and actions. There is, it suggests, a fundamental duty not to kill or maim people, rob them, violate their rights, or destroy ecosystems. Since no choice is free of risk, as business people know, one should minimize the risks to oneself and others and balance them against the possible rewards (see Chapters 1 and 2). Nor should one's actions make things worse. In effect, one should try to add to the general welfare, to bring about more benefits than harm. As one manager, concerned about an ethical problem, said to Barbara Toffler, 'Goodness for me is helping your fellow man. . . . Bad is doing anything that would harm other people.'[8]

2. *Solve the problem*. Central to this second maxim are three things: (1) identify the ethical problem; (2) search for possible solutions; and finally, (3) implement the best achievable solution (see Chapter 2). Problem-solving requires social intelligence as well as technical and economic rationality, for business problems are socio-economic in character. Problem-solving is a widely accepted technique in medicine, engineering, science, education, and management, and it is a constructive way of understanding ethical performance in business. This is important, for there are many difficult problems with no easy solution.[9] In contrast, interpreting ethical problems as moral dilemmas is not all that helpful. It is a typical product of abstract moral theory, as the next section will explain.

3. *Enable informed choices*. The third maxim emphasizes that accessing the best available information is essential to good performance. Informed choice links communicating appropriate information with free choice. Freedom, the maxim implies, is not very helpful if one is ignorant of the information relevant to making a choice. Informed, voluntary choice lies at the foundation of both democracy and markets. Informed consent, too, is a long-standing rule of contract and a maxim in professional/client relations. Physicians, engineers, and lawyers and other professionals are all obliged to inform their clients of any risks involved in their services, just as businesses are required to communicate material information about workplace and product risks to their employees and consumers, respectively (see Chapters 4 and 5). These are powerful maxims. If most organizations followed the 'do no harm' and 'informed choice' maxims alone, they would radically transform society for the better.

4. *Act, learn, improve*. This maxim stresses the need to ensure that the problems are solved, that predictable consequences are anticipated, and that the right thing is done well. The aim of the core ethic is improvement, to move from avoiding the bad to practising the good, and thence to attaining excellence, the best achievable level of performance. This reflects the need to learn continually. Ethical management is therefore like continuous improvement. Managers should listen to problem reports, respond to early signs of trouble, and continually improve. On this reading ethical performance is open to indirect quantitative measurement. Employment equity means that the proportion of women, ethnics, visible minorities, etc. found at various levels of an organization reflects that in the available workforce; and reducing stakeholder risks and improving quality both involve statistical measurement (see Chapters 4–7). The goal is excellence,

not perfection, for the latter sets the goalposts so high as to be unreachable. So one must monitor, learn from mistakes, practise, tinker, experiment, and refine one's performance. One must also remain sensitive to new problems as they arise. And one must do one's best, as Mill suggested.

Do Your Best

Men should act to the best of their ability. There is no . . . absolute certainty, but there is assurance sufficient for the purposes of human life.

John Stuart Mill, *On Liberty*

To learn and improve requires openness to feedback, negative as well as positive. Problem-solving calls on organizations to encourage problem reports, enhance sensitivity to early warnings, and try to foresee the consequences of their actions. Unfortunately, many bureaucratic and autocratic organizations prefer unquestioning loyalty and groupthink (see Chapter 3). The result is that small problems can fester into large crises (see Chapter 8). For Johns-Manville and A.H. Robin, refusal to listen to feedback about health risks in their products meant bankruptcy. On the other hand, firms like Procter & Gamble and Johnson & Johnson responded immediately to reported problems about their products. The result was both to save lives and protect their markets. This unwillingness to learn is especially dysfunctional in today's technological society and knowledge economy (see Chapter 6).

5. *Seek the common good.* This imperative, our fifth and final maxim, originated in traditional political theory, where it defined the ethical role of the State as securing the good of the whole society. Today it has currency in reminding executives and directors of their duty to care diligently for the good of the whole corporation, and not just one small group within it, such as shareholders (see Chapter 1). From an ethical perspective at least, if not in law, they must look to the interests of various stakeholders in the firm: its employees, customers, and suppliers. This may even extend to relations with external stakeholders in society and with governments, as talk of 'social responsibility' implies (see Chapters 8 and 9). Since stakeholders' perceptions and interests often clash, owners and executives often find themselves balancing a variety of competing interests. None the less, John Donne's famous poetic phrase still rings true: 'No man is an island entire of itself; every man is a piece of the continent, a part of the main.'

Hard Like Water is divided into two parts. Part One, Exploring the Core, introduces and further articulates the elements of the core ethic in connection with three key aspects of business: ownership, management, and organization. A few more tools are added to the core ethic: a stakeholder map, a risk matrix, the ethical problem-solving method, and two approaches to organizational values and cultures. In Part Two, Journeying Further, those elements are used to interpret ethics in other areas of business: employee and customer relations, technology and environmental management, social issues management, international business, and planning for the future.

In Chapters 1–3 some implicit elements of the core ethic are made more explicit, such as its implications for risk management, stakeholder relations, and reciprocity in exchange. By the end of Chapter 3 the general elements of the core ethic will have been articulated. Throughout the book ethics are shown to evolve from within business itself. The first six chapters explore internal concerns about ownership, management, organizational values, employees, technology, and markets. The last four chapters deal with more external matters—the natural environment, government, foreign operations, and the future. Various elements of the core ethic are examined in each chapter, when and as needed, for, as the next section explains, it is a concrete performance-oriented ethic, not an abstract formal theory.

Theory and Practice

This excursus into moral theory may interest the philosophically inclined reader. The aim is to explain the pragmatic approach envisioned by the core ethic in *Hard Like Water* and its links with classic moral theory. Why bother? some might ask. Everyone knows what morality is. Life, welfare, and communication, after all, are widely shared values and the performance maxims are practical common sense. Indeed, a central aim of the human quest for a universal moral theory was to show that moral reasoning is the same everywhere, regardless of persons, interests, organizations, cultures, situations, or the times. To do this, different moral theories linked practical moral judgement with various universal norms and formal models of practical reasoning. That quest, dating back millennia, has settled on a small set of candidates for universal moral norms. I will focus on four—virtue, duty, utility, and care—noting their links with the core ethic.

    1. *Virtue*. The first candidate for a universal moral value was *virtue*. Plato and Aristotle both argued that a few key virtues constituted the heart of the good life: self-control, courage, justice, friendship, and wisdom.[10] Each ranked his set of virtues in a moral hierarchy. To both authors, political, military, and cultural virtues mattered more than such economic virtues as productivity, efficiency, trade, quality, and creating or distributing wealth. In this they merely reflected the moral presuppositions of fourth-century BC classical culture.

    This was an aristocratic culture in which religion, politics, law, and the arts ruled. Trade for profit was not virtuous, and work was for slaves. The higher moral goals (which only the nobles could be trusted to achieve) centred on self-mastery, justice, friendship, knowledge, and cultivated leisure. The great thinkers were well born and well placed. Socrates opposed democracy and favoured élitism. Plato came from an aristocratic family, and Aristotle was an adviser to Alexander the Great. All disdained the merchant class and devalued their contributions to the wealth and vitality of classical civilization. None the less, Aristotle did acknowledge a few quasi-economic values: community self-sufficiency (a reflection of the agricultural economy), justice in exchange, and 'large-souled' liberality (a reflection of the importance of gifts and reciprocity in traditional cultures). The core ethic and the business ethos preserve the latter insight in the concept of reciprocal exchange. A society's list of virtues and the related moral hierarchy would then seem to vary with one's society, culture, and economy.

The economic virtues had been devalued in pre-modern cultures because people had no experience of economic growth and widespread affluence.

Sixteen hundred years later, in the fourteenth century, modern Renaissance capitalism was born and a different value system emerged. The new business partnerships shared the risks, the responsibilities, and the rewards. The new economy was based on partnerships, contracts, investments, and loans. People soon learned that not only work and money but agreement and trust were required to conduct a business successfully.[11] The world has not been the same since. In sixteenth-century Europe, however, philosophy still moved in the highest circles. Michel Montaigne, the founder of modern philosophy, was a close friend of King Henry III. René Descartes debated philosophy with Jean de Silhon, the secretary to Cardinal Richelieu in the court of Louis XIII. Yet at the height of the European Renaissance, 400 years ago, John Calvin originated the 'Protestant work ethic' by declaring the respectability of productive work and approving of interest-paying loans for enterprise investment purposes (but no interest, he added, should be charged on loans to the poor). A century later John Locke associated rationality with productive work and proclaimed that the chief end of government was to protect private property.[12] The first signs of a new, economic ethic were now dimly visible.

2. *Duty.* The second universal moral norm was *duty.* It was the product of Immanuel Kant's new theory about the moral power of reason, which evolved out of the revolutionary turbulence of the eighteenth-century Enlightenment. Kant was a religiously devout professor of philosophy at the University of Königsberg in Prussia.[13] For Kant, morality rested on a pure sense of duty, derived, he argued, from the rational motivation of goodwill. It is signalled by modal verbs like 'should' or 'ought to'. This spiritual rationality ultimately led to faith in God. In many ways Kantian theory represented a secularized Protestantism.

In seeking a purely rational foundation for duty, Kant formulated his famous 'categorical imperative' of an unqualified (i.e., 'categorical') moral duty: one ought to act as if the principle guiding one's action were a universal law of action in an ideal rational world. In effect, one should universalize the core value in one's action. One should universalize one's duty. Moral reasoning thus meant generating, or applying, universal moral laws to specific situations. Kant modelled moral judgement in terms of a legal judgement, e.g., as subsuming a specific case under the appropriate law. But a law court is a special place, with access to a written legal code containing ready-made laws from which one can select the appropriate moral rule. One also enjoys 20/20 hindsight about the specifics of the case. Such practical and cognitive luxuries are not available to persons in real-life decision-making situations, such as managers, enterpreneurs, employees, and customers. Furthermore, Kant's expectation that one could successfully project the moral choices of persons of totally different cultures and backgrounds is abstract and naïve, for it does not assume any obligation to understand the cultural and social background of other persons. Here universal duty conflicts with respect for persons.

Kant offered another version of his imperative: one ought to respect rational free beings or persons as having intrinsic value in themselves. We should treat persons as ends, not merely as means to our ends. Here Kant gave eloquent expression to the Enlightenment value of the dignity of the human person, the foundation for liberal belief in human rights. It takes contemporary form in requiring business (and other organizations) to treat employees, consumers, investors, and other stakeholders fairly regardless of their race, gender, religion, etc. Respect for persons underlies the core value of care for civil rights. The other values in the core ethic can each be redefined in rights terms, too, that is, of a fundamental right to life, property, and communication.

While many situations require us to treat others instrumentally as in part a means to our ends, this reflects a prudential or practical imperative of everyday life. None the less, Kant's devaluation of practical decision-making, like his low view of inclination, reflects the low place economic and social practicality have in his moral hierarchy. In this sense the duty ethic remains traditional.

For Kant, moreover, one is obliged to act only to the extent that one can so act. 'Ought' follows 'can'. Here, *duty* approaches the much more complex notion of moral responsibility. Kant certainly believed that moral responsibility should begin with pure goodwill or an appropriately moral motive or intention. But responsibility also involves other elements. As Kant said, one should be able to act. One should have adequate resources, preferably access to the best available knowledge or information. Also, one must enjoy the appropriate social or organizational authority to act, and one should try to foresee the outcomes of one's choices. All these considerations are relevant to business decisions. *Hard Like Water* considers responsibility in several places, in the discussion of the problem-solving and informed-choice maxims of the core ethic, of moral agency in Chapter 3, of social accountability or responsiveness in Chapter 8, and of legal liability in Chapters 5 and 6.

Kant not only gave duty a purely rational explanation, he also stripped duty of its traditional connotations. The notion of duty originated in traditional, pre-modern Western and Eastern cultures, where it denoted the obligations of one's position in the social hierarchy. One had duties to one's inferiors, superiors, family, community, nation, and gods. This concept of duty is still prominent in Indian, Confucian, and Japanese cultures.[14] It also lives on in the obligations of subordinates to superiors in modern corporations.

3. *Utility.* For Kant, moral duty was opposed to the sensory inclinations of pleasure, desire, and worldly goods. Or, as many observed, if it's hard it's good. From this it is a short step to the classic dichotomy of altruistic moral duty versus utilitarian economic self-interest. And in fact, in 1789 Jeremy Bentham proclaimed a new universal, but quantitative, moral norm, *utility*. For once philosophy was ahead of the times and the economy; for a few decades later the new industrial market economy based on scientific and technical knowledge had taken centre stage. Only in 1895 did Alfred Marshall apply it to modern market economics, basing rational economic choice on marginal utility.

In effect Bentham favoured inclination over duty, reversing the austere Kantian moral hierarchy; and he did so in the same half decade in which Kant published his own works on moral theory. Bentham defined utility as pleasure (or pain). This covered 'benefit, advantage, pleasure, good, or happiness', and, one might add, economic benefits and costs. Utilitarian morality seeks to maximize utilities and minimize disutilities. Inasmuch as Bentham saw pleasure (and pain) as a homogeneous, measurable good, he expected that a quantitative moral calculus was possible. Indeed, he saw utility in Enlightenment terms, too, for the greatest good of the greatest number represented a moral rationale for social reform.

The Principle of Utility

... is that principle which approves, or disapproves, of every action, according to its tendency ... to augment or diminish the happiness of the party whose interest is in question.

Jeremy Bentham, *Principles of Legislation and Morals*, 1789

The new economy soon became a controversial topic of moral debate. Social critics like Charles Dickens and John Stuart Mill and enlightened capitalists like Josiah Wedgwood were all concerned about socio-economic problems of rural depopulation, a nearly impoverished working class, and urban slums and crime. They argued that sufficient wealth was being generated to enable a decent life for the majority of people, and decried the immorality of the unjust distribution of wealth. Their moral crusade rested on economic values of reciprocity and equity in the allocation of society's resources—in a word, on the core value of welfare. Because of their achievement any attempt to define virtues today would have to give prominence to economic values.[15] Hence, the growing affinity of economic and ethical values and the rise of business ethics.

In 1861 John Stuart Mill published his own critical re-evaluation of utilitarianism.[16] He argued that there is no way of measuring the amount of utility produced by an action or policy. Also, there is a variety of human goods, which are not reducible to any single utilitarian notion such as pleasure (or money). Nor can human goods be aggregated and evaluated in a single moral calculus. Nor can one validate any ranking of these different utilities in some definitive utilitarian version of a moral hierarchy.

In Mill's spirit, welfare, the second core value, incorporates the kernel of truth in utilitarianism without implying a commitment to any single type of moral good. The performance maxims of 'do no harm', 'improve', and 'common good' all stress the results of one's choices. Welfare is a broad normative concept. It includes social, cultural, and spiritual well-being as well as material utility. In addition, welfare is best defined in terms of reciprocity, or the fair exchange of goods. Civil rights notions of equity and fairness, for example, raise questions of justice in market exchanges and the distribution of goods. Thus markets are dynamic welfare exchange systems. In these ways the core ethic expands the otherwise narrow economic values used in business.

Finally, Mill distinguished between the utility or overall good produced by a specific act and the increased good resulting from generalizing that act into a rule of action or policy. Rule utilitarianism is similar to duty theory in tending to assimilate good moral reasoning to following the right rules. But this is a very problematic view of moral judgement. Decisions, like the persons who make them, involve much more than following a few pre-set rules. To argue that moral choice is the result of logical, deductive reasoning is to demean practical intelligence to the level of a computer program. That is the stuff of science fiction, e.g., *Star Trek*'s Mr Spock of planet Vulcan. Moral judgement is too complex and creative to be perfectly simulated by a logic machine.

An Ethic of Care

Just as the language of responsibilities provides a weblike imagery of relationships to replace a hierarchical ordering that dissolves with the coming of equality, so the language of rights underlines the importance of including in the network of care not only the other but also the self.

Carol Gilligan, *In a Different Voice*[17]

---

4. *Care*. Carol Gilligan listened carefully to the distinctive moral note in women's voices and heard in them the end of abstract moral theory. Women, she found, talked about social connectedness, listening, and not harming people; in a word, about *care*. This led her to propose a more concrete social ethic of *care*, especially care for persons. Care is central to the core ethic; for it begins with the positive norm of care for life, welfare, etc. One might reinterpret Kantian morality as care for persons, and utilitarianism as care for the welfare of others. However, if it is to be credible, care should lead to commitment and performance. So interpreted the core ethic is a care ethic.

A warning is in order. None of these theories have been impartially tested and proven valid to the satisfaction of independent inquirers, as is normal practice in scientific research. There is no consensus on any of these theoretical notions or on any ranking of moral values; nor is there agreement on how to resolve conflicts among competing norms and values. The quest for a universal moral theory has failed. The core values and performance maxims, it is true, are stated in general terms. The norms, Care for Life and Do Not Kill, are not restricted to particular situations, problems, decisions, or persons. The appearance of universality, however, is deceiving. In contrast to the quest for universality and logical/quantitative certainty in moral theory, the core ethic is presented as a set of helpful values and maxims to guide people searching for morally satisfactory solutions to their problems and trying to make better decisions. The core ethic's norms and values are presented as guidelines for making decisions and solving problems in the midst of actual, complex, changing situations, where uncertainty and ambiguity are the norm. Life is not as simple as theory.

To move away from universal rules or absolute norms may appear to some moral theorists as an invitation to relativism. If relativity denotes the importance of context to one's actual choices, no problem. In real life one must interpret general norms and values in terms of complex, dynamic situations. As persons, groups, situations, times, and problems differ, so do the choices one makes, even when using the same set of values and norms. So all general rules are practical maxims, performance guidelines. The practical difficulty of applying any general rule to complex, changing, particular situations is well known. On the other hand, the generality of the prescriptions of the core ethic is indeed intended to suggest that ethical performance is not completely relativistic.

The core ethic, moreover, incorporates key insights of classic moral theory and relates them to performance. The core values and maxims can be seen as bases for different virtues. The core norms and performance maxims embody various duties or responsibilities, e.g., to respect life, do no harm, etc. Welfare clearly has a utilitarian flavour. The notion of rights is implicit in civil rights values.

Nor are the core values or performance maxims purely arbitrary. They are not a matter of personal or social preference or caprice. Rather, they reflect shared values, across different individuals, regions, classes, genders, religions, cultures, and histories. Values like mutual support and reciprocity, as Kropotkin argued in his masterpiece on evolutionary ethics, *Mutual Aid*, have evolved over the millennia. The core values do suggest a tentative moral hierarchy in which the value of life comes first, then welfare, communication, and civil rights; but hierarchies shift as contexts and problems change. These values are rooted deeply in our evolutionary past.

The Complexities of Ethical Performance

Moral problems must be resolved within the interpretive complexities of concrete circumstances, by appeal to relevant historical and cultural traditions, ... institutional and professional norms, and by relying on ... comparative case analysis.

Earl Winkler and Jerrold Combs, *Applied Ethics: A Reader*

Actual situations are often so complex that small contextual differences often lead one to quite different moral judgements. But the interpretation of moral values and norms may vary with the person, the situation, the organization, the culture, and the times. (Indeed, empirical research into shared values across times, cultures, etc. should be a main thrust of future theorizing about ethics.) Outside of routine or 'black and white' cases where the right choice is obvious, the interpretation of any general rule (technical, financial, or ethical) in a specific situation is a complex, highly contextual, and variable matter. The 'problem-solving' and 'act, learn, improve' maxims both assume that actual decision-making is complex, uncertain, and difficult. Hence, one always needs to search for the best available knowledge, the best possible solutions.

A shift to more practical social concerns has been discernible in ethics. Business ethics is itself part of that return of philosophy to reality. A bottom-up, empirical, and concrete approach to interpreting ethical performance increasingly seems more productive than top-down, abstract moral theory. So *Hard Like Water* tells tales about the old and new ways of performing ethically in business. One hopes it will be more helpful in solving ethical problems in business contexts.

One hopes the performance ethic presented in the chapters to come will be *Hard Like Water*. Water can be both soft and hard, gentle and powerful. A soft rain helps crops grow, but flooding and raging torrents destroy homes and buildings, and rivers eventually reduce mountains to valleys. You can freeze to death in a Canadian winter, but you can also use snow to build a home. Just as the right amount of 'clean' water is appropriate for drinking or swimming, so ethical practices should be appropriate to the situation. Impurities can go too far, however. All organisms need natural waters to live, but chemicals can poison our lakes and oceans.

Impure Waters

One knows that if the water is too pure the fish won't swim in it. No honesty is complete that does not weigh consequences. It does not matter that the man who signs the cheque is a hypocrite; what matters is that the bill is paid.

Ivan Alexander, *The Foundations of Business*

Just as water is rich in nutrients and other substances, so ethical performance in business is complex. In business, ethical values like care for life, the environment, the employee, and stakeholder welfare are usually found in association with business values like efficiency, productivity, and profitability. Such linkages are to be expected in a diverse, evolving social sphere like the business world and the marketplace. But, as Ivan Alexander observed, what really matters are results, ethical and economic. This is the assumption that guides the discussion of ethics in business in the chapters of *Hard Like Water*.

Part One

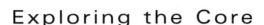

Exploring the Core

The aim of Part One of *Hard Like Water* is to explore and expand on the core ethic in connection with three key aspects of business: ownership, management, and organizational values. Each chapter explicitly articulates one or two otherwise implicit elements of the core ethic. Thus:

❖ Chapter 1, Owning Values, includes a *stakeholder map*, to help businesses identify their stakeholders and develop good relations with them. Owners and managers are not only key internal stakeholders but also constitute the core business partnership.

❖ Chapter 2, Managing Values, introduces a *risk matrix* and an *ethical problem-solving* model. The risk matrix classifies risks and also shows what minimizing risks to an acceptable level involves. Ethical problem-solving shows how one identifies and solves ethical problems in business.

❖ Chapter 3, Organizing Values, first presents *values as social organizers*, which stresses the importance of win/win reciprocal exchange values in business. Then a *risk/feedback* model of ethical corporate culture is offered, which highlights the need to encourage feedback and minimize risk in organizations.

Chapter 1

Owning Values

A corporation represents far more than its current stock price; it embodies obligations to employees, customers, suppliers and communities.

Robert S. Saul, Peters Merchant Bank

The maximization of profit [is] simply a complicated way of phrasing the old saw of 'buying cheap and selling dear'. Profitability is not the purpose of business enterprise . . . but a limiting factor on it. . . . Its purpose must lie in society since a business enterprise is an organ of society.

Peter Drucker, The Practice of Management[1]

The Partners' Ship

It was 1390. In Genoa at a small dockside trattoria, Aldo Rossi, a merchant from Florence, was discussing a business venture with Sandro Puccini, a ship's owner and captain. Into his third glass of Alpine wine, Sandro kept complaining about storms, pirates, and dishonest foreign traders. His ships carried foods, dyes, leather, sugar, ceramics, iron, rough wool, slaves along the trade routes from Italy to England, the Black Sea, and Africa.[2] Rossi would pay the usual half-price of the shipment of fine Italian woollens, silks, silver, and paintings to Spain and Africa. Cosmo Gorassi, Rossi's cousin and a Milan banker, helped them to finalize the terms for financing the voyage, insuring the compagnia against losses and sharing the profit. Four hours later, full of wine, fish, and pasta, they agreed on all the details and shook hands. Then Andrea Lattrulo, Rossi's notary and his wife's niece, wrote up a contract for all to sign. Their partnership was afloat, again. It might take another year before they could realize a profit. Once before it took Aldo three years to sell everything off, and he netted 9 per cent profit on his capital. To say business can be hard like water would not have surprised any one of them.

Chapter 1 seeks to answer the questions, what are the ethical values involved in owning a business? And how should the risks and returns (or welfare) from a business partnership, or company, be distributed? Modern business partnerships began in the early years of the Italian Renaissance. And following the old Italian usage, we still call businesses 'companies' (or '*sociétés*' in French). Both terms recognize the social character of business ownership. Property systems enable owners to create or destroy and buy or sell companies. They define who has the right to make enterprise *ownership* decisions, who has what controls over its assets and operations, and how the risks and returns (i.e., *welfare*) are to be distributed among the partners and other internal stakeholders. A company's assets are its capital, real estate, plant, and technologies, e.g., Aldo's goods,

Cosmo's money, Sandro's ship, and their skills; but not Aldo, Cosmo, and Sandro themselves. Different property systems vary in the ways they exclude (or include) different stakeholders from (or in) ownership and control of the assets owned by a business. They also vary in the ways they distribute the costs and benefits of managing the firm's assets. The old private property approach, for instance, restricts ownership, control, and gain-sharing to a small group of owners and executives, that is, the core decision-making business partnership. Other stakeholders are excluded from sharing in ownership or control, and often are excluded from an equitable share in the resultant benefits. A common property system, on the other hand, includes a wide range of stakeholders in owning and controlling common assets, and distributes costs and benefits more equitably. In both private and common property systems the assets are fairly well defined and formally controlled, in contrast to tribal property. Not only is the latter a more open and inclusive property system, but tribal assets such as land are less clearly defined and are regulated by unwritten social customs.

Chapter 1 is divided into two parts. Part I starts with a major ownership decision: the biggest corporate deal of the 1980s, the out-of-control auction for R.J.R. Nabisco. It raises ethical concerns about the modern business partnership, such as the tendency to high-risk financing, its narrowly financial business values, and increasingly adversarial relations between owners and management. Implicit in these concerns are further questions about the old private property system, its restrictive view of board reform, and its tendency to distribute risks inequitably among the company's stakeholders, as shown in the final act of ownership, declaring bankruptcy.

Part II, in contrast, tells new tales about franchises whose structural tensions show the need to make business ownership more inclusive of its internal stakeholders. The core welfare and property values suggest a more socially inclusive approach to corporate ownership. The chapter thus concludes by suggesting that, by using a new ethics tool, a stakeholder map, companies can and should identify and invite other internal stakeholders—notably, but not exclusively, their employees—to share in their partnership.

I Old Tales about Ownershp

Auctioning the Company

Ross Johnson, the new CEO, wanted to bring some fresh air into the stale old bureaucratic ways of R.J.R. Nabisco (or RJR).[3] In Johnson's view management took control. It was not merely the agent of the shareholders. He wanted to diversify R.J.R. Nabisco away from the long-declining cigarette market (the R.J. Reynolds side of the company) into more promising food markets (the Nabisco side). He wanted to move the head office from Winston-Salem, North Carolina, to New York. To keep the board happy Johnson increased compensation and perks for the directors as well as the executives. He also bought a corporate jet.

Since Johnson thought the stock was undervalued, on 21 October 1988 he came to the board and proposed an unprecedented US$17.6 billion buy-out of R.J.R. Nabisco at $75 a share, financed mostly in cash. This was about $20 over the current share price. Johnson would retain management control over the company, and executives would continue to enjoy a large share of the profits. Since Johnson thought this was close to the top price for the company, he did not expect a bidding war. But some directors feared that his move would put the company 'in play' on Wall Street. They were right. Four days later, on 25 October, Kohlberg Kravis and Roberts, a large Wall Street investment banker, made its move, offering $90 per share for R.J.R. Nabisco; but only $79 was in cash, just $4 more than Johnson's bid. The whole transaction cost $19 billion, of which $2.5 billion was for fees to bankers, lawyers, and bridge financing. Ross Johnson did not know it, but he had just lost control of his company.

By the end of October a bidding war for RJR had broken out, as the board had feared. The auction logic of the trading floor began to prevail. There was no way to limit the competitive bidding or the financial leverage. In mid-November Kohlberg Kravis and Roberts upped its bid to $94 per share. Johnson followed with $100 per share. By 1 December the final bids were in. Johnson offered $112 per share; Kohlberg Kravis and Roberts, $109. The board opted for the Kohlberg Kravis and Roberts offer. Johnson had bet, and lost, the company.

As was the Wall Street custom, the buy-out was highly leveraged. The total amount paid for the company was $24.9 billion. RJR's top executives got golden parachutes, but middle management and the employees did not. Managers were upset because many had surrendered their stock options to the company months ago at $53.50 a share, well under the final bid. Johnson's bid took note of employee concerns by proposing generous severance packages and medical and moving benefits. All were accepted by Kohlberg Kravis and Roberts.

Kohlberg Kravis and Roberts's offer totalled US$24.9 billion, making the R.J.R. Nabisco leveraged buy-out (LBO) the largest to date. There were $561 million in fees; $336 million for investment banker bridge financing; $324 million to various banks; and $75 million for Kohlberg Kravis and Roberts. The bid was highly leveraged, for it followed the usual Wall Street financing ratio of 10 per cent cash to 90 per cent debt. The full financing took months, and was not completed until late March 1989. The immense debt involved would be financed by $11.5 billion in high-interest 'junk' bonds, underwritten by Drexel Burnham Lambert.[4]

R.J.R. Nabisco was now run by Kohlberg Kravis and Roberts and company. To pay back the debt and the fees, they sold the corporate jets and cut all the perks. Seven hundred employees took early retirement, and 1,600 middle managers and factory workers were laid off. Two divisions were sold off, for about $5 billion; but a third division did not reap the hoped-for price. In 1989 Nabisco's profits increased 40 per cent; but the R.J. Reynolds Tobacco division lost sales volume to Phillip Morris. As time went by RJR found it difficult to pay bondholders the high interest owed on its junk bonds. In the spring of 1990 Kohlberg Kravis and Roberts had to infuse another $1.7 billion of its own money in RJR stock and renegotiate $7 billion in bank loans, all to reduce the company's debt and improve its finances. By early 1995 Kohlberg Kravis and Roberts had unloaded its 35 per cent stake in R.J.R. Nabisco, reaping a minimal profit of about $0.11 per share.

Financing Games

The high-stakes poker game for R.J.R. Nabisco revealed a deep, ethical split between the traditional business community and financiers in their views of the risk of debt-based financing, the related tendency to erect short-term financial gains into a primary criterion of business performance, and the underlying battle between shareholders and management over the governance of the corporation. Underlying them all is the old tale of private property as the basis of corporate ownership and governance.

First to the financing. Kohlberg Kravis and Roberts preferred highly leveraged financing of corporate acquisitions. They had a $5.6 billion war chest, which could be leveraged to $45 billion following the usual Wall Street 1:9 ratio. They issued high interest-paying junk bonds to obtain the needed capital, underwritten by Drexel Burnham Lambert. They also exacted a 1.5 per cent management fee on their LBOs and took 20 per cent of profits from the new company. Having borrowed so heavily to buy a firm, Kohlberg Kravis and Roberts needed relatively high future earnings and cash flows to pay off the resultant debt load. Because of the high financial leverage the new owners had to cut costs radically in their newly acquired firms. As a result they ruthlessly downsized operations and sold off divisions and assets. Only such a strategy would yield the efficiencies and profits that would raise the stock price sufficiently; and selling the stock at these higher prices would make the leveraged buy-out profitable.

Through LBOs, argues Michael Jensen, the dean of financial economics, privately held debt becomes the main source of capital for business and the basis of corporate ownership.[5] Since only financial markets can discipline firms, LBOs shift the capital structure of the firms away from equities or securities markets. The high debt load, for instance, inhibits take-over bids. For these reasons, Jensen concludes, 'Equity is soft; debt is hard.'

But does the theory work? The reality, as the outcome of the RJR buy-out showed, was often different from the financial economist's theory.[6] The financing assumptions underlying the buy-out involved a high-stakes gamble on the future. Cost-cutting often weakened productive operations. Indeed, R.J.R. Nabisco had to sell off its healthy and profitable Del Monte division to reduce its high debt because weaker business units would not attract a high enough price. Defaults on junk bonds were higher than their promoters acknowledged. Sometimes the result of highly leveraged buy-outs and acquisitions was to increase corporate debt and lose market value. The immediate requirement to pay back bondholders or reward investors often could not be reconciled with the equally pressing need to reinvest in new technology, employee training, and product development, or to increase sales and market share. Furthermore, the rosy share price guestimates that financiers assumed in the heat of an LBO auction so as to rationalize the high debt financing did not always pan out; or they did not stay high for long when they did rise.

On the other hand, equity is soft. For many people stocks are financial commodities and stock markets are markets in shares rather than companies. They are, Robert Reich feels, paper markets.[7] They do not create wealth. They merely rearrange assets. And securities markets are notoriously volatile. In October 1987 Wall Street collapsed, while through 1996 and early 1997 it was probably flying notably higher than the economy. Markets so easily prone to fluctuation are hardly reliable economic indicators. And for long periods low stock prices did not reflect the value of solid firms like Hewlett-Packard and Boeing. Financial markets are a world of their own. Their fluctuations, warns Michael Lewis, who worked on the trading floor at Salomon Brothers on Wall Street, often reflect rumours, promoters' interests, greed, panic, and investor perceptions.

Rumours, Gambling, and Financial Markets

Rumors moved markets. The rumors bore an uncanny resemblance to whatever people feared most. Often the most unlikely . . . rumor caused panic in the markets. . . . Options and futures have no equivalent in the world of professional gambling, because real casinos would consider the leverage they afford imprudent.

Michael Lewis, *Liar's Poker* [8]

It is a trite observation that most shareholders invest money in stocks to gain high, short-term financial returns. For many people stocks are just one investment vehicle, alongside bonds, investment certificates, art, accounts, mortgages, gold, diamonds, futures, etc. Canadian stock markets have had numerous problems: insufficient disclosure of information, dubious promotions, conflicts of interest, and insider trading.[9] There is much room therefore, for doubt about the ability of ordinary people to make informed financial investment choices.

Business Values

Two opposed views of business and its values were at stake in the R.J.R. Nabisco auction. On the one hand the preferred take-over or LBO targets, financiers claimed, were fat, cash-rich firms with bureaucratic management that was unresponsive to market forces. On the other hand, highly leveraged buy-outs or hostile acquisitions may not be the best solution for poor administration, low productivity, or declining sales. You don't use a missile to hunt rabbits. The more leveraged a corporate acquisition the more likely the rewards would not justify the risks. Incurring an excessive debt load on overly rosy payback assumptions could be a high road to ruin. No company should get so highly leveraged as to endanger its profitability or survival. Instead, it is important to keep debt low and lower the cost of capital.[10] In that way rewards are more likely to outweigh the risks.

While Ross Johnson had argued that the shares were undervalued, he also financed his initial bid on a mainly cash basis, with minimal debt. It seems reasonable that corporate restructuring be financed without incurring a high debt load that would inhibit the organization's future growth. Wall Street's penchant for high leverage and junk bonds raised serious concerns for conservative investment bankers like Ted Forstmann of Forstmann Little, an unsuccessful bidder for R.J.R. Nabisco.

Barbarians on Wall Street

Today's financial age has become a period of unbridled excess with accepted risk soaring out of proportion to possible reward. Every week with ever-increasing levels of irresponsibility, many billions of dollars in American assets are being saddled with debt that has virtually no chance of being repaid. Most of this is happening for the short-term benefit of Wall Street's investment bankers, lawyers, leveraged-buyout firms and junk bond dealers at the long-term expense of Main Street's employees, communities, companies and investors.

Ted Forstmann[11]

Sound business values were in question. One should not, for instance, confuse transient stock market prices with long-term business performance. The primarily financial values of securities markets are not reliable measures of all-round business performance. Nor are financial norms such as short-term profits, share prices, debt load, or cash flow the only measures of business performance. Indeed, many long-term R.J.R. Nabisco shareholders were concerned that Wall Street financiers like Kohlberg Kravis and Roberts did little to build plants, employ people, improve sales or products, or support local communities. Short-term share price gains, in their minds, were no substitute for healthy long-term development of the business.

Many institutional investors, such as pension funds and large mutual funds, act more like owners and keep a watchful eye on a wide variety of business performance indicators.[12] A wide range of economic indicators, only some of which are financial, are used to evaluate business performance: financial returns, long-term profitability, productivity, sales growth, market share, customer loyalty, employee morale, product development, environmental protection, and technological innovation. No one indicator is absolute. Each measure is relative to the industry average and to previous performance. To avoid short-term fluctuations all indicators should be measured for several years, preferably over the appropriate business cycle.

The Battle for Corporate Control

Since the 1930s corporate ownership and control have become increasingly differentiated, largely in response to the increase in size of firms and the fevered financial speculation of the 1920s and the resultant Depression. By the 1940s management had gained control of the large modern corporation. In the 1980s, as we saw, shareholder activism, hostile take-overs, LBOs, competitiveness, and globalization reignited the struggle for power in the corporation and worked to reverse the long-term managerialist trend. The RJR buy-out epitomized the power struggle between investors and management for the control of the corporation. All too often the battle for corporate power put the welfare of middle managers, employees, and suppliers unnecessarily at risk. Another ethical problem is the tendency of the private property ownership system to exacerbate owner and board/management relations

Jerry Kohlberg, who had founded Kohlberg Kravis and Roberts in 1975, favoured a reciprocity-based view of the relationship between financiers and management. He believed that investment banking should be done with integrity and should not charge any fees or incur excessive debt. In 1987 Kohlberg quit the company he had founded, unhappy with the direction Kravis and Roberts were taking it. He pointedly referred to his co-operative vision of financiers' role in his retirement speech. Notwithstanding his admonition, a little over a year later Kravis and Roberts moved away from Kohlberg's ethical approach and entered the auction for R.J.R. Nabisco.

Financiers as Partners of Management

Investments could be made in undervalued businesses where we, as financiers, would put our money, time and effort right alongside management. We would do everything in our power to ensure that our investment *and theirs* turned out well.

Jerry Kohlberg, 1987 retirement speech

In fact, soon after the RJR buy-out, hostile take-overs and LBOs declined. By 1995 friendly corporate mergers were on the rise.[13] More companies are handling acquisitions in-house without relying on high-priced investment bankers for advice. They are working with pension funds and banks with long-term interests rather than with highly leveraged financiers and corporate raiders. There is more awareness that any merger requires minimal debt, responsible management, and good planning. Even friendly mergers can fail, due to the numerous difficulties of meshing different corporate cultures and management systems. Hostile acquisitions remain justified in cases where the target firm has been a dog for years and only outsiders can revitalize it.

Instead of putting their firms on the auction block, boards might be wiser to install new, more entrepreneurial executive teams. Fat, bureaucratic organizations often may need a new entrepreneurial approach as well as sharp, surgical cost-cutting. Increasing sales and returns can also improve profitability and, one hopes, share price. Intensifying hostility and increasing risk in the search for short-term financial gain is not the ethically preferred path to business renewal. After all, such imprudence has often led to bankruptcy.

Bankrupt Partnerships

Highly leveraged, overly speculative investments, driven by short-term expectations of high gains, wreaked economic havoc in the 1980s. Such an approach led to the failures of several Canadian banks and trust companies; US$600 billion was lost when hundreds of US savings and loans firms went under. Declaring bankruptcy is the ultimate act of ownership. It raises several ethically significant questions about the practice of ownership: the need for responsible business management and corporate governance, and the fairness of the distribution of control and risk among the firm's internal stakeholders in ownership decisions.

A few years ago I served on the board of a small for-profit local concert series. When the market shifted beyond our resources to respond, we realized we had to fold the company. We did so prudently, while we were still in the black. Ours was a very serious ownership decision, one that none took lightly, quite unlike merely holding shares in a firm. When larger companies are bankrupt and close down, not only money is lost, but people lose their jobs. Their lives are shattered and their talents go to waste. Often whole communities are devastated, and the public foots the bill in growing social assistance costs. So a wide group of interests is at risk when a firm goes bankrupt.

The risk of bankruptcy remains a real economic concern in Canada. Business and consumer failures are on the rise. In 1996 total bankruptcies were 19.2 per cent higher than in 1995, and 72.5 per cent over the 1990 total, exceeding the previous peak in 1992, as shown in Table 1.1. Business failures increased 7.3 per cent over 1995 and consumer bankruptcies were up 21.7 per cent. The net liability, or moneys owed to creditors, exceeded $8 billion (a guestimate), more than double the 1990 total of $3 billion. As with consumers, the larger firm and the greater the number of failures, the greater the losses. Contrast these numbers with 1968, which had just 1,308 consumer bankruptcies, 1/50th the current total and the lowest on record. The Canadian bankruptcy numbers, however, are nearly one-third those of the US, even though the population is only one-tenth the size. This suggests a weaker Canadian economy, a view reinforced by unemployment rates that hovered around 10 per cent since 1980, unlike much lower levels in the US.

Table 1.1: **Canadian Bankruptcy Data**				
	1990	**1992**	**1995**	**1996**
Business	11,642	14,317	13,258	14,229
Consumer	42,782	61,822	65,432	79,631
Total	54,424	76,139	78,690	93,860
Net debt ($bn)	$2.97	$7.6	$5.2	$6.5+

Bankruptcies are often the result of overly risky investments and overly leveraged or speculative financing. Risk is part of running a business, 'but this does not make [businesspeople] gamblers', Ivan Alexander warns. 'More business failures are due to overtrading, overextension, overexpansion, too many hopes, than have ever been caused by economic recession.'[14] This cautionary advice is often ignored. Owners gamble their capital and lose. And creditors rarely get back more than 3 per cent on the dollar.

In 1979 US bankruptcy law was reformed, moving away from the old punitive debtor's prison model towards a more conciliatory problem-solving approach. Canadian law is moving in the same direction. Chapter 11 of the US bankruptcy law enables the courts to help a firm reorganize, delay liquidation for as long as 18 months, and perhaps recover. The aim was to give the company time to recover and avoid shutting it down if possible. But the reform may have gone too far and allowed firms to avoid their social responsibilities. Litigation over unacceptable health risks from their products forced both Johns-Manville, the main asbestos producer, and A.H. Robin, the maker of the critically defective Dalkon Shield birth control device, into bankruptcy. It allowed each firm to avoid paying full awards to those harmed by their products.

Sharing the remaining assets of the firm in a bankruptcy intensifies tensions among the company's stakeholders. Creditors want the firm to be liquidated as soon as possible so that they can get some money back, while shareholders and employees want to keep a sick enterprise alive as long as possible. US law, Walter Stewart argues, tends to favour shareholders over other creditors. Chapter 11 gives shareholders a veto over any rescue plan, thereby favouring them over other creditors.[15] This reinforces the financier's view of the firm and the old private property system. The result of recent North American legal reforms has been to redistribute the bankruptcy risk. In addition, as John Grisham observed, the courts can be lenient in extending litigation and court hearings. The increased court costs and lawyers' and accountants' fees reduce the balance available to the creditors.

A Growth Field

The bankruptcy Code has a marvelous provision which grants an automatic stay in all legal proceedings against a debtor. That's why you see big rich corporations, including Texaco, run into bankruptcy court when they need temporary protection. . . . Bankruptcy [is] the growth area of the future, what with uncertain economic times and all, job cutbacks, corporate downsizing. . . . It sure looks lucrative today. Bankruptcy petitions are being filed left and right. Everybody's going broke.

John Grisham, *The Rainmaker*[16]

Other countries enforce earlier payments to creditors and other stakeholders. In Japan equity and employees come first, along with informal rescues of weak firms. Germany stresses preserving equity and keeping the company alive, usually with the help of its supervisory board and bankers. Making employees creditors, too, helps discourage boards from using bankruptcy as a means of evading their obligations to them. In Canada the board of a bankrupt firm must guarantee six months' back wages to employees. In 1995, for example, the court ordered the former directors of the bankrupt STN company to pay $567,000 in vacation, severance, and termination pay to the 316 employees who lost their jobs.

Further reforms seem to be in order. One needs to find the right trade-off between helping a company to turn itself around and, where this is not possible, repaying creditors the maximum amount possible within a reasonable time. The courts should require proof of insolvency and set relatively short reorganization deadlines. It should be easier for businesses and consumers to pay off their debts than to evade them by declaring bankruptcy. There should be tougher enforcement on cheaters, fuller financial disclosure, and improved severance for employees. Bankruptcy law, like the property system, needs to find a better balance among the responsibilities of business to its various stakeholders: notably, employees and suppliers as well as investors and lenders. Similar tensions afflict corporate governance.

Board Games

From the perspective of the ongoing battle for corporate control, shareholders have been encouraged to see the board as the adversary of management. The traditional view is that directors represent the interests of the owners and all shareholders in ensuring the continuance and growth of the organization.[17] But holding shares in a company is not the same as owning it (except perhaps in the abstract world of the law). On the contrary, shareholders should be treated for what they commonly are, short-term investors and sources of capital, along with banks and bondholders. This does not justify their near-exclusive monopoly on ownership powers. They certainly should enjoy the one right they really want, namely to hold the stock so as to sell it, hopefully for a gain.

Exercising the powers of ownership, moreover, is far more demanding of one's energy and time, more complex in its practices, and more challenging in its responsibilities than investing in stocks or bonds. Part-time investors cannot, and usually do not want to, take on the full governance responsibilities of ownership. However, a key weakness in most corporate governance reform proposals has been their continuing restriction to the relatively small group of shareholders, owners, and senior executives and their exclusion of any role for other internal stakeholders, notably middle management and employees. The result is to put their welfare at excessive risk when major ownership decisions, such as acquisitions, buy-outs, mergers, and bankruptcy, are being deliberated by the board.

Nor can the directors run the firm. Most corporations are governed by small boards of directors nominated by a much larger body of shareholders. Average board size for the 472 Canadian firms surveyed in the *Corporate Ethics Monitor* is 14, but it ranges from three to 40; only about one in seven directors is female. And usually, wherever you find shareholders, you also find a large corporation with a significant, and necessary, management structure.[18]

Certainly boards today have their problems. Indeed, corporate governance reforms are currently being debated by the Toronto Stock Exchange, the Ontario Securities Commission, and the Canadian Senate. These are all mainstream discussions, set within the old model of ownership. Thus the proposals for reforming corporate governance assume that the directors' primary obligation is to the shareholders. This is the context for reform proposals to alleviate problems of inadequate diligence and resources for directors, conflicts of interest, and self-dealing (especially in large holding companies), and for calls for directors to be more independent of management. There are also concerns that boards are not taking their responsibilities for strategic planning and risk management seriously enough. Critics like Donald Thain find the Toronto Stock Exchange's recent proposals too weak to put a stop to the dubious games directors play.

Board Shenanigans

The reader should be under no illusions about the incompetence, stupidity, power politics, legal shenanigans, high stakes, nasty problems, scandals, immorality and dirty tricks to be found in the goings-on of corporate governance.

Donald H. Thain, TSE Corporate Governance Report: Disappointing[19]

To reform boards properly we need to clarify their core ethical and business responsibilities. Directors already have many obligations, over and above ensuring satisfactory returns to investors. They are responsible for overseeing the general governance and strategic direction of the organization. Directors therefore need to exercise good business judgement in governing the firm, that is, in making major capital investments, watching the finances, minimizing business risks, hiring and evaluating executives, and ensuring legal and regulatory compliance—often in several political jurisdictions.

The board's, and owners', primary mandate is to care for the best interests of the company as a whole. It is to keep the whole enterprise afloat and, hopefully, growing. In ethical terms, it is to articulate the common good of the company over time. Directors should therefore deliberate carefully about key decisions like selling their company or buying another one. The board, again in concert with the firm's executives, periodically needs to evaluate the company's overall performance. To this end a wide variety of performance measures should be used and not merely financial indicators.

From this perspective the battle between Ross Johnson and Kohlberg Kravis and Roberts over the ownership and control of R.J.R. Nabisco became an out-of-control auction, driven primarily by financial concerns. The result was to force share values to unrealistic heights. One could reasonably argue that the RJR board made a serious error in not stopping the auction after the second round of bidding, say with a share price somewhere in the $80 to $90 range. This may have been better for the good of the company as a whole, and not only the shareholders. But under the old system of shareholder primacy, most boards would hesitate to exercise this kind of business judgement for fear of litigation. On the other hand, an acquisition at a lower price would have involved less debt and therefore required less cost-cutting merely to finance the debt. That would have probably meant many managers and employees would still be at work at RJR, and its healthy Del Monte division might have been kept, without drastically lowering the pressure for needed efficiencies and increased returns.

The RJR buy-out also exemplified the contest between shareholders and management for the control of the corporation. But surely it is a strange view of corporate governance to set owners and management at war with each other. While the board should not be the uncritical accomplice to powerful, bloated, or incompetent management, owners and management remain key partners in the business. They share a common interest in its welfare. Nor should directors interfere in management; owning is not managing. Accordingly, developing a healthy board/management relationship is critical to the survival and future growth of the company.[20]

Directors should not hypercritically oppose management or uncritically accept their views. Nor should they try to micromanage the business themselves. Rather, they should practise due diligence. To that end directors should question management about the information and proposals presented, and about any potential problems. Directors who neglect their responsibilities may be held liable for their negligence if they have not been diligent. Such liabilities are increasingly being enforced.

A Director with an Attitude

My questions are direct. They are all due diligence questions. Basically, I say, 'My butt is hanging out to dry here, fellow.' You turn around to the auditors and say, 'Are you happy with these jokers? Are they giving you access to everything? Are the systems good?'

George Watson, CEO, TransCanada Pipelines

But if our assumptions about ownership of firms are outdated, the function of modern boards is not adequately grasped. The capitalist form of enterprise ownership is very old. It originated in the renaissance *compagnia*, such as the core decision-making partnership of Aldo, Sandro, and Cosmo. It evolved through international trading companies like the Hudson's Bay Company. In the nineteenth century the limited liability, joint stock company was invented. A century ago firms were very much smaller, so it was easier, albeit never uncontroversial, to see the firm as the exclusive possession of the owners, almost a personal asset.

Today's corporations are much too large and complex to be the privately owned asset of any individual or small group. The old private property/shareholder primacy model is an anachronistic ownership system for such large and complex organizations. It also unnecessarily constricts the options for corporate governance reform. The obligations of directors of large companies are extensive and daunting. Large institutional investors like pension funds and insurance companies know their limitations as directors. They take the long view and see themselves as the executive's partners in corporate governance, but they do not try to manage the firm themselves.[21] New directors especially need some training in exercising their responsibilities. Given the pace of change today, even experienced directors need refresher sessions. At Fonorola Canada, for example, each of the six annual board meetings involves a day's training on regulatory and technological matters and the like.

We cannot, it follows, continue to work with old, simplistic notions of private property in the (usually small) firm. To focus merely on the so-called fiduciary obligation of management solely or primarily to shareholders may be legally correct as a guiding rule of corporate governance; but it is not the best ethical norm, or even a good guide to optimal business performance of the enterprise as a whole. It is interesting to note that none of the 44 firms responding to a survey done for *Hard Like Water* ranked shareholders or profit-maximizing first in their list of organizational values. Stelco's *Code of Conduct and Ethics* notes the need for 'full and timely disclosure to shareholders'; and in its 1995 *Mission Statement* Quaker Oats commits itself to earning an 'above-average' return on equity and 'aggressive growth in quality earnings over time'.

There are other signs of awareness of a need for significant changes in corporate governance. Given board/management tensions and the complexity and scale of large corporations, Adam Zimmerman, former CEO of Noranda Forest, feels boards should be advisory. Directors would advise management on strategy, policy, and major decisions, evaluate their performance, and help prepare financial and other reports to shareholders and company stakeholders. Legal responsibility for the enterprise would rest with its executives, for they actually control the firm. Special attention should be given to two key board responsibilities, risk management and stakeholder relations. Each might be the responsibility of a special board/management committee. The risk management committee should have two special powers, to access all needed information and to stop or delay potentially catastrophic decisions.

Given their primarily money-lending role in the firm, shareholders probably should not enjoy ownership powers unless they have owned a significant block of shares, say 5 per cent or more, for at least a year. Small and short-term shareholders probably should not have voting rights or be eligible for nomination to the board. They should not be invited to join the core governing partnership until they have demonstrated a serious, long-term commitment to the firm. This is similar to the rear-end load requirement in some mutual funds, which ensures long-term investor commitment to the fund.

Just as shareholders have a right to a return from a profitable firm, so employees and managers have a right to a decent income from such a firm. One lends money; the other group contributes their skills and effort on a daily basis. In today's economy both are property rights, whatever the law may say; but the latter right is frequently at odds with the former. Employees and managers who have been with the company more than a few years have a major stake in its welfare. On this basis they have a morally cogent claim to participate in corporate governance.

The new tale, then, is that the board should care for the welfare of other long-standing internal stakeholders, that is, managers and employees. Also, from a welfare risk standpoint such stakeholders have a relatively equal claim to involvement in the core decision-making partnership and its governance councils as do shareholders and bondholders. Often their stake in the company is greater and more at risk in ownership decisions. The time has come, therefore, to tell new tales, about more inclusive forms of ownership.

II New Tales: Socially Inclusive Ownership

Franchising Ownership

Today franchises represent a significant growing sector of the economy, with over $40 billion in sales, hundreds of thousands of employees, and extensive supplier networks. We find franchises everywhere: fast-food outlets like Harvey's and Tim Horton's, retail stores like The Body Shop, M&M Meat Shops, and Canadian Tire.[22] There are also service franchises, for example, for temps, such as Drake Office Overload, and for tax filing, such as H. & R. Block and many others. On the surface, franchises seem to constitute an extended network of owner-partners. In reality, franchises stretch the notion of the core governing partnership much further than private ownership allows.

A franchise is a network of interlocked businesses based on the private property form of ownership. Most franchises are privately owned by the *franchisor*. This gives the franchisor the right to market and license the sale of its own brand of products or services through *franchisees*, who contract with the franchisor to operate franchise outlets. Franchisees typically are small entrepreneurs who invest their limited capital in a franchise and then work long, hard hours to make a go of it; they have a large stake in the franchise. Most franchisees want to run a successful enterprise and make a satisfactory return on their investment.

The franchisor/franchisee relationship, however, is neither simple nor unconflicted. Franchisors operate in two markets: that for their product/service, like the franchisee; and also that for selling franchises, unlike the franchisee. The franchisor's interest is to sell as many franchises as possible, get a good price for supplies sold to franchisees, enforce the franchise contract, and define a successful strategy for the franchise. The franchisor/franchisee relationship, unfortunately, is not a partnership of equals. Most of the risks lie with the franchisee, while the franchisor reaps most of the rewards. The result is significant tension in franchisor/franchisee relations.

Some of the problems that tend to arise in franchises are high franchise fees, hidden costs, inflated promises about returns, high prices for supplies, poor locations, no control over locations, unilateral franchisor decisions with little franchisee recourse. Some franchisors have been able to get franchisees to agree to costly contracts with harsh performance requirements without allowing franchisees any effective voice in the overall management of the franchises. Franchisees, for their part, often have inflated expectations of high short-term returns, of making a killing with little effort, and underestimate the work and the risks involved in developing a successful franchise. Many do not understand the changes and complexity of modern markets and are not skilled in business accounting, management, or employee or customer relations.

Franchisors sometimes ignore franchisee concerns and refuse to renegotiate arrangements, even though the original product or service market has significantly changed, because their ownership of the franchise allows them to run it without involving the franchisees as partners. The franchise business often is not responsive to market changes. This can lead to declines in sales and returns. The rising concern with health and fitness, for example, has meant less demand for fat-rich foods and problems of adjusting product offerings in many fast-food franchises. Two-thirds of grocery stores today are franchises, but the retail grocery business operates in a low-margin, highly competitive, and fast-changing market. As the Loeb's story shows, difficult market conditions can exacerbate tensions in franchisor/franchisee relations.

Franchise Tensions and Changing Markets at Loeb's

In June 1996, 22 Loeb store franchisees initiated a lawsuit against Loeb Inc. The franchisees were seeking compensation and damages for alleged violations of the franchise agreement. After some negotiations in the fall of 1996, Loeb terminated its agreements with 19 of the litigants and was considering running the stores itself. There are 111 Loeb supermarkets in the Ontario franchise, with annual sales of about $1.8 billion. The franchisees alleged that the franchise package they were given before buying the stores had misleading projections of sales and profits. They complained that it allowed Loeb to control the retail and wholesale price of goods sold in the stores and required them to operate in ways that keep their profits low. The low profits, responded Loeb's lawyer, Françoise Guenette, were a result of the tough Ontario market: 'We have to lower prices to get the sales volume we need and we have to reduce costs to compete in this market.' In November the courts upheld Loeb's franchise termination rights, the lawsuits were withdrawn, and the parties negotiated a settlement.

There have been many other problems over the years. Many franchisees have complained about non-disclosure of key contract elements, unfair business practices, kickbacks, rosy promotions, and a lack of accountability of franchisors to franchisees. In response to such problems the Canadian Franchise Association has developed an ethics code for franchises. It recommends 'full and accurate disclosure' in clear written agreements to franchisees of all matters affecting the franchisor/franchisee relationship. These contracts should cover such matters as supplies pricing, advertising costing, location decisions, and the franchisor's duty to disclose his/her accounts, etc. Each member of the association agrees to be bound by this code.

Government regulations follow similar lines. Alberta, for instance, requires a high standard of information disclosure: franchisors must show good faith and fair dealing in franchise promotion and agreements. They should provide material information to prospective franchisees, such as: assumptions regarding earnings claims and successful outlets, the names of former franchisees, clear explanations of franchise renewal, termination, sales volume requirements, and franchise transfer terms. Many US states require disclosure of company finances and information on key executives, including any criminal records and bankruptcies.

When the franchisor/franchisee relationship is a healthy partnership, both parties benefit. Some franchises, like M&M meats and Cara foods, have developed successful relations with franchisees. M&M, for instance, has a franchisee advisory council. The franchisor provides needed training and assistance in setting up and running the business, charges reasonable fees for the licence and supplies, and helps the franchisee to succeed and the franchise itself to respond to changing markets. The risks and rewards are equitably shared. In these ways the franchise approximates an extended business partnership, but the partners typically do not enjoy most of the key information access rights or decision-making powers.

To conclude, a root cause of franchise system tensions is the restrictive confinement of what should be an inclusive business partnership system within the hard shell of the private property system. The franchisor owns the franchise and franchisees own their outlets; but they are not equal partners with the franchisor. Rather, there is an imbalance in their ownership and control over the franchise. Inasmuch as franchises represent a new form of business network, and there are major tensions among their business partners, franchises demonstrate the need for a more inclusive ownership system.

Stakeholders as Partners

The modern company, we have seen, should not continue to rest on the outdated private property system in which shareholders are the dominant stakeholder. As this section will show, this constrictive form of ownership not only puts other stakeholders at unnecessarily excessive risk, it also is an overly exclusive form of governing partnership and rigid species of corporate governance. Its narrow restrictiveness misaligns the private property mode of ownership with the increasing size and complexity of the modern corporation. On these grounds a more inclusive and flexible ownership system is needed.

The R.J.R. Nabisco buy-out, paper markets, shareholder primacy, directors' difficulties, bankruptcy, and franchises all exemplify in their own way the epochal shift to large, managed organizations and away from the small firm. A modern company is a large, complex network of interacting interests, relatively structured inside the organization but also reaching outside it to take in customers, suppliers, competitors, communities, governments, and other publics. Corporations often employ hundreds and thousands of people in widely spread business units in several communities. They usually have several divisions and numerous products and markets, often in different nations.

Given such complex, expanding networks, the corporate ownership system needs to evolve, too. It can no longer be modelled on one individual's private ownership of his personal assets. Few would agree that a large modern corporation should be the personal possession of an individual, like a home or car, or even a small store.

Unfortunately, the private property system does precisely that. It allows a small core of business partners, sometimes a family, to exclude a much larger group of people from decisions that may put their welfare at significant risk.

Corporate ownership is becoming increasingly *corporate*, as are administration and management. The modern firm has expanded well beyond the original small base of owners, executives, and financiers. They own millions in corporate (decidedly not personal) assets. A more truly corporate ownership is needed, however. Large companies represent an extensive community of shared welfare, a growing network of reciprocal interlinked interests. The bigger the firm, the wider the welfare net it involves and the more people who share in its rewards, and its risks. Shareholders, managers, employees, suppliers, customers, and governments are interlinked in complex ethical and economic networks of reciprocal welfare, mutual obligation, and shared rights and risks.

Mergers and acquisitions, bankruptcies, board membership, and franchise problems all show the strains of the private property system, especially when it is applied to large, complex modern organizations. In mergers, acquisitions, and buy-outs, shareholders can and have traded firms like commodities. Similarly, many of the problems of franchises arise from excluding franchisees from access to information and making key decisions. And one of the main problems in bankruptcies is the clash between different creditor stakeholders: shareholders, lenders, employees, and suppliers.

But the welfare of employees, as well as that of other stakeholders such as suppliers, is caught up in that of the company. They are sometimes treated merely as corporate assets, like capital, plant, and technology. Private ownership decision-making excludes employees, suppliers, and other stakeholders from any say in the ownership decisions that affect their welfare. This approach increases the danger of treating the corporation as a commodity to be auctioned off in securities markets. Corporate buy-outs and auctions have commodified the corporation.[23] To buy and sell commodities like paper and metals is one thing, but it is quite another matter to buy and sell whole companies. It is to treat other stakeholders—that is, people—also like commodities.

And they are at significant risk. Just as franchisees are often at the mercy of franchisors, so middle managers and employees often find themselves on the losing end of ownership decisions, as we see in the tales about franchises, bankruptcies, the RJR buy-out, and the Goodyear take-over defence (see below).

6,700 Employees Lose Their Jobs at Goodyear

In early 1987 the CEO and board of Goodyear Tire decided to defend themselves against a hostile take-over attempt by the Anglo-French financier, Sir James Goldsmith. To finance that defence Goodyear had to buy back stock worth US$2.6 billion, close several plants, and lay off 6,700 employees—1,675 jobs alone were lost when Goodyear closed its aging Toronto plant. Goodyear also had to cut back a strategically important radial tire project. Even though his take-over bid was ultimately unsuccessful, Goldsmith did well. He made US$100 million.

The old private property system perpetuates an overly narrow model of the core business partnership consisting merely of shareholders, owners, and some executives. This ownership system excludes most internal stakeholders from involvement in any share in the ownership and control decisions of corporate governance. It also tends to concentrate the rewards and benefits of the company to the same small group, while shifting signficant risks and costs onto employees, often including middle managers. They have a strong claim to participate in the partnership; but they were not invited into the core business partnership.

Yet internal stakeholders have little or no say in decisions that put their own welfare seriously at risk. In effect, the private property system does not recognize the full community of interests in the company. It puts major internal stakeholders at significant risk and does not give them adequate voice. Such practices offend welfare values and the do-no-harm and informed-choice maxims. For these reasons, C.B. Macpherson maintained, 'the existence of private property . . . makes property a morally contentious issue.'[24]

Many North American businesses already recognize some obligations to all the company's stakeholders, at least rhetorically, in their corporate value statements. In the 1996 survey undertaken for this book, most of the 44 firms responding ranked their commitments to employees, suppliers, customers, and local communities as higher than those to shareholders (see Chapter 3). Northern Telecom's 1995 *Code of Business Conduct,* for example, lists employees, shareholders, customers, suppliers, governments, and even the scientific community as its stakeholders. While Nortel acknowledges the commitment to 'provide value to shareholders', this is qualified by the need for 'financial prudence'. And it goes on to say that 'shareholder value is delivered through satisfied and loyal customers.' Such statements indicate that the shift towards a more balanced and inclusive view of business as a community of reciprocal interests has already begun.

Firms, however, need to translate their new concern with stakeholders into more serious commitments. But classic stakeholder management theory offered a company little guidance on how to identify or rank its stakeholders.[25] The old private property system, for example, yields the following stakeholder ranking, as evidenced in the RJR buy-out, Goodyear take-over defence and other corporate acquisition decisions, the bankruptcy law, and franchise relationships. Owners, franchisors, and shareholders would come first, with executives and other advisers a near second. Depending on the decision or problem, other groups would follow in something like this order: lenders, employees, suppliers, customers, unions. On the other hand, the new ethical view of the community of interests involved in a modern business would rank stakeholders according to the relative degree of risk for each stakeholder group. Thus, for a corporate buy-out or acquisition decision, the old 'investors first' model and new stakeholder risk approach would generate contrasting rank orders:

Old: Owners & Investors	➔ Executives	➔ Employees	➔ Suppliers	
New: Employees	➔ Suppliers	➔ Executives	➔ Owners	➔ Investors

The new order rests on the following relative measures: the amount of capital each stakeholder has committed to the firm (where one assumes a job to be a capital asset), mobility, the time each has committed to the company, and total assets or wealth.[26] This new order discloses the obvious. Employees by and large are less mobile than investors and executives. They spend more of their time in the business and have more of their capital relative to their total assets tied up in the business.

The contrast in rankings shows the need for some method of identifying and ranking stakeholders. One clue is the impact on their welfare of the decision or problem under discussion. The risk-minimizing message of the first performance maxim, 'do no harm', suggests mapping stakeholders in terms of the extent to which they are at risk.[27] In this way we may be able to respect informed stakeholder choice and determine their claim to inclusion in exercising the governance powers of corporate ownership. If, in addition, we distinguish between internal and external stakeholders, the result is to produce the stakeholder map shown in Table 1.2. I use the RJR buy-out decision to illustrate how it works.

Table 1.2: A Stakeholder Map for the R.J.R.Nabisco Leveraged Buy-Out

	Internal	External
Directly Affected/ Involved	S1 • RJR owners/board • RJR management • RJR employees	S2 • Advisers to RJR & other bidders • Lenders, other financiers
Indirectly Affected/ Involved	S3 • RJR unions • RJR suppliers	S4 • Local communities • Governments • RJR customers

The vertical axis in Table 1.2 measures the extent to which each group's stake or welfare is directly at risk. Those stakeholders at direct or significant risk are placed in the top two quadrants, S1 and S2. Those at indirect risk, or at little risk, are placed in S3 and S4. Those who are members of the company, e.g., shareholders, managers and employees, are internal stakeholders and are placed in one of the left quadrants (S1 or S3). All decision-makers are usually direct internal stakeholders and placed in S1. External stakeholders are placed on the right-hand side, in S2 or S4. In S3 we find two groups affected by the LBO to a lesser degree, unions and suppliers. Local communities, governments, and customers, being indirectly affected external stakeholders, are put in S4. One value of this approach is to sort out self-proclaimed stakeholders from those genuinely at risk. Often the media, activists, and interest groups may claim to be, but their welfare is not clearly at risk.

Where one locates a stakeholder on the map varies over time with the problem and the organization. The map is flexible and relative to the situation and the context. The map also helps us extend the boundaries of the business partnership. It is made up of major internal decision-making stakeholders. They are normally located in S1. On the other hand, the wide community of interest in the company is much broader. It includes everyone with a direct stake in the company's operations—shareholders, executives, employees, suppliers, and customers. That community is usually located in S1 and S2, but it can extend to S3 and even S4, depending on the decision and the situation.

Another use for the map is to determine participation rights in the relevant decision. The general principle is that those groups most at risk from a problem or decision have the greatest claim to participate in making the decision or solving the problem. In effect, they have a right to informed choice in the deliberation/problem-solving process. They or their representatives should therefore be invited into the core business partnership. Those least at risk would seem to have the least right to consultation. Thus, as we move from S2 to S3 we move from stakeholders who should be invited to take an advisory role to those who merely have a right to be kept informed. Those in S4 would have a right to be informed, but not to share or be consulted for advice on a decision. The point of this exercise is to clarify two related matters: the degree of stakeholder risk and of stakeholder rights to involvement in the relevant decision. As one works with the stakeholder map one will increasingly see that the borders between the quadrants are artificial. After all, there are degrees of direct/indirect risk and involvement in the deliberative process.[28]

By clarifying the bases for expanding the business partnership and seeing the company as a wider community of interests, the stakeholder map makes the case for a more inclusive, common, and truly corporate property system of business ownership. A more inclusive common, or corporate, property system would invite middle managers and employees, and even suppliers and customer representatives, to participate in corporate policy-making, strategizing, and governance councils in consultative, advisory, and decision-making capacities.

German employees, for example, participate in management and enjoy representation on the supervisory boards of large public firms. Many are also long-term shareholders. Except for Volkswagen, where labour dominates, shareholders like banks and insurers hold the balance of power on boards. In Japan the large firm is governed by a network of cross-shareholding among banks, associated companies such as suppliers, and even customers. Franchisee owners and their representatives should be invited into a real, effective partnership with franchisors. Their participation can be effected in myriad ways at all levels of the organization. Suppliers and customers should also be invited into the appropriate councils of the firm.

Unions, too, can and should be involved in corporate acquisition and buy-out decisions so as to better protect their members, as the Hiram Walker story below suggests.

The CAW union local worked with Allied Lyons executives to help it acquire Hiram Walker and fend off the Reichmanns' take-over bid. The CAW's involvement in a corporate acquisition is a sign that more inclusive forms of corporate governance are being tried out.

Unions as Take-over Players

In 1986 the Reichmann brothers sought to acquire Hiram Walker, a Windsor, Ontario, holding company with gas, oil, and distillery divisions. Having watched how the Reichmanns dismembered Gulf Canada, the Canadian Auto Workers local was concerned for its 460 members' jobs. In preparing to resist the take-over they found a letter suggesting a plant rationalization agreement between the Reichmanns and Seagram's. This meant there would be lay-offs. So the union opposed the Reichmann take-over, despite a personal promise of no lay-offs from Paul Reichmann himself. Instead, the union local worked with Walker management to support Allied-Lyons PLC's bid for Walker. Allied-Lyons promised to maintain Walker's employment levels, list Walker as a separate Canadian distilling company, sell shares in Canada, give local management autonomy, and keep the corporate head office in Canada. With the help of the auto workers Allied-Lyons won the take-over battle and acquired the Walker distillery, and the CAW local kept its members' jobs. The employees' right to an income won a small battle in the merger wars. A new form of partnership, indeed.[29]

Summary

The aim of Chapter 1 has been, first, to show the ethical and functional limitations of the old private property system and to argue for a more inclusive, truly corporate, business ownership system to better reflect the size and complexity of large modern firms. Secondly, considering the welfare of all stakeholders affected by the firm's decisions and operations, we saw, would better reflect the broad community of interests a modern company represents, in contrast to the old concept of the business as a restrictive partnership of owners and shareholders alone. Thirdly, including a wider range of internal stakeholders in corporate governance not only expands the community of interests involved in the company. It also should facilitate stakeholder feedback and enhance the company's responsiveness to problems and change. Such more inclusive ownership systems should, one hopes, improve the quality not only of stakeholder relations but also of ownership decisions like those respecting acquisitions, buy-outs and bankruptcies, and franchisor/franchisee relations. It would also, one might expect, improve the company's profitability and growth. Management in today's large firms is at least as important as ownership, and it, too, needs to be examined from an ethical perspective. That is the subject of the next chapter.

Chapter Two

Managing Values

All courses of action involve risks.

Niccolo Machiavelli, *The Prince*, Chapter XXI

Ethical concerns are part of the routine practices of management. They are characterized by concerns about relationships and responsibility. . . . They frequently involve factors that make right and wrong less than patently clear.

Barbara Toffler, *Tough Choices*[1]

Ship's Executive

Sandro Puccini is chief executive on his ship, but Aldo Rossi owns the goods he is transporting, and Sandro, Aldo, and Cosmo are partners in the export business. Aldo, a clothmaker and a merchant, cannot sail a ship. That is Sandro's job. Sandro mans and stocks the ship and sails it to London and other ports, where he offloads Aldo's goods to the local merchants and then loads the ship with cloth and other supplies and goods for Aldo to sell in Italy. If Sandro is successful they can pay off Cosmo's loan and make some profit. In the meantime, Sandro has to do his job and manage the ship.

The aim of Chapter 2 is to identify some of the ethical values at work in managing companies. Part I begins by putting to rest the old tale about hard-headed amoral management. To this end we begin with the tale of appalling financial mismanagement at Barings Bank, only to find it echoed in many other firms. This discloses the tension between euphoria and prudence in financial management. Underlying that tension is the need for an ethical approach to managing risk. To that end a risk matrix is formulated, drawing on the 'do no harm' performance maxim. One's doubts about old-time management rationality are even more confirmed in the next section, which describes the extraordinary willingness of presumably rational executives to fall for soft-headed management fads. Part II, in contrast, begins by suggesting that managerial work is much more social in character than the hard old view of managerial rationality had presumed. Management is therefore presented as involving ethical problem-solving, which unpacks the mandate of the second performance maxim, 'solve the problem'. Ethical problem-solving is shown to involve a much broader socio-economic understanding of practical intelligence.

An Old Tale: Riskless Finance

Betting the Company

> Be careful . . . 'tis attended with risk. Many houses called considerable . . . have absolutely ruined those who have placed confidence in them. Let [the] example of grasping at too much and not being contented with a very handsome profit . . . be a warning to you.[2]

Thus in 1776 did Francis Baring's mother warn her son against developing a merchant bank. Francis, however, did not listen. In the nineteenth century Barings helped finance Canada's westward expansion; and in 1890 Barings almost failed due to bad South American loans.

More recently Barings had become a knowledgeable player in modern Asian financial markets. In 1988 Barings Securities expanded its Singapore operation under Chris Heath, an optimistic risk-taking trader. Heath expanded proprietary trading to increase revenues; but there was no 'Chinese wall' to separate it from client trading, as is normal practice. This raised client concerns about possible conflicts of interest, as the expansion in Singapore rested on rosy revenue projections to offset the high overhead costs. Barings needed more clarity about managerial responsibility and the organizational hierarchy, better reporting of revenues, and stricter financial controls. So in the early 1990s Barings management moved to develop more formal management structures and stricter financial controls to offset Heath's hands-off style and also to help the Singapore unit develop beyond the entrepreneurial phase.

Barings Securities was highly leveraged in relation to its capital base. One former director felt Barings management was not the best, for it had little understanding of the relations between management and risk. Peter Norris, who was sent out to assess the Singapore securities operation, remarked on the lack of appropriate controls. He created an Investors' Bank unit with a more prudent banking culture. In April 1992 Barings sent Nick Leeson, a young derivatives trader, to head the Singapore exchange office. The Singapore office chief, James Bax, had expressed serious reservations to London about Leeson; Leeson, Bax noted, reported directly to London, and was given responsibility for both making trades or sales and reconciling the accounts. To allow someone to both execute orders and settle them was, in writer Judith Rawnsley's view, 'like making a poacher into a game-keeper'. The year 1992 ended with £6 million in losses, partly due to a decline on Japan's Nikkei Exchange.

By 1994 floor traders were concerned about the accounting controls in Singapore. Risk analysis, they felt, was poorly understood by corporate management in London. The system for reconciling trading accounts at the end of the day was primitive. London's numbers and Singapore's did not match: 'It was a farce. You could have hidden anything in those books', one trader said.[3] Accounting methods were not consistent across business units, and a new complex management system was also causing problems. In August 1994 a routine internal audit queried Leeson's high returns. It concluded that there was a real risk that he could override normal controls because he ran both the front and back office. The auditors advised that Leeson no longer supervise the back office work of reconciling the books and signing cheques. If these changes had been accepted Leeson's deception would have been discovered and Barings would have survived. But they were not. London ignored both Bax and the auditors, for Leeson's trades were bringing in very high earnings, often US$10 million a week, and the Asian operation enabled Barings to declare high profits. London executives and the board were so heady with the high revenues from Singapore that they did not hear the warning bells ringing.

Derivatives are financial instruments whose price reflects anticipated changes in that of an underlying asset, such as stocks, currencies, and commodity futures. They are commonly used to protect firms engaged in international business against the risk of losses from volatile currency, interest rate, or commodity price shifts. Carefully managed derivatives can help stabilize returns and reduce risk. They only cost a small fraction of the assets they are used to purchase. Thus a small rise in asset value can yield an exceptional gain. On the other hand, when asset prices decline, the results can be equally calamitous.

Barings management never did separate Leeson's conflicting front and back office duties. Thus, no one was making sure that the £742 million Barings sent to fund Leeson's derivative account (twice its capital base) was balanced by revenues from such sources as client accounts and trades executed. Leeson's huge profits were almost treated as risk-free arbitrage, which conflicted with well-established risk/reward ratios in investment banking.

From the beginning, however, Nick Leeson's speculative trading had reaped losses. Since he controlled the books, he was able to hide his reckless gambles, unauthorized trades, and high losses. Leeson buried his losses in account 8888 and in forged documents—8888 showed losses of £2 million in 1992, £13 million in 1993, £116 million by June 1993, and £108 million by December 1994. In response to the massive Kobe earthquake on 17 January 1995 the Nikkei Exchange dived 1,000 points. On 30 January 1995 Leeson gambled, desperately, that the Nikkei would shift upwards. He lost £253 million. Then he doubled his bet. On 23 February he lost £63 million. That day he left Barings. Four days later the Nikkei went down 800 more points. Leeson had lost £827 million. Barings was ruined. Mother was right after all.

There had been warnings from outside sources, too. In early 1995 the Singapore stock exchange had contacted Barings about its trading. There were rumours that Barings was critically exposed on the Nikkei trades. But Barings London chose not to listen, (over)confidently assuming they were hedged against any losses. So Barings executives let Leeson bet the company. They lost their bet.

In its subsequent inquiry into Barings collapse, the Singapore financial police criticized Barings for mismanagement. Not only did they charge Leeson, they also alleged that in early 1995 top Barings executives suppressed information about shortfalls in Leeson's trading account and encouraged Leeson to deceive auditors. They indirectly criticized Coopers and Lybrand, the auditors, for failing to detect the fraud.[4] They also criticized the lax regulatory oversight of the Bank of England. Not everyone got the message. One day after Barings collapsed, Deutsche Bank engaged in a US$48 million currency swap with Barings![5] But the crux of the Barings collapse was poor management. Later, in a BBC interview, Leeson denied he was a crook:

> I don't think of myself as a criminal. I didn't steal any money. I've certainly misled people. . . . There are a lot of similarities with gamblers, but unfortunately I lost more than I won. . . . But it never entered my mind that Barings would fold as a result. . . . As stupid as it may sound, none of this is really real money. It's not as if you have cash sitting in front of you.[6]

Financial Euphoria

Barings was but one of many cases of speculative fever in the euphoric 1980s. The decade was strewn with the corpses of banks done in by go-go, high-risk financing, such as the Canadian Commercial and Northland banks and several trust companies. In his report on the Northland Bank's demise, Mr Justice Willard Estey observed that at these banks, 'The financial statements became gold fillings covering cavities in the assets and in the earnings of the bank.'[7]

'Where were the accountants?' in the bank and S&L failures, Len Brooks wonders. He adds, 'The paramount duty of a professional accountant . . . is really to ensure the accuracy and reliability of his work for the benefit of the end user—the public.'[8] It is noteworthy that auditors' warnings to Barings of problems in Leeson's trading went unheeded. Auditors act as an early warning system for owners, managers, and the investing public. But they are often in a difficult situation, inasmuch as they are paid by the company on whom they report and its management sometimes deceives them. Furthermore, there is a catch-22. The disclosure of even small problems in financial institutions can lead to a loss of confidence and a run on deposits. It can become a self-fulfilling prophecy. The comments of Estey and Brooks also apply to the failures of numerous North American savings and loan S&L or trust companies, like the one in Seminole, Oklahoma (pop. 10,000).

James Wesley Mooty II

In the mid-1980s the Seminole Savings and Loan company took on James Wesley Mooty II, a former commodities trader, as a financial adviser. Mooty suggested they invest in highly risky interest rate hedges. That advice cost the Seminole S&L $10 million of its $18 million asset base. Like Nick Leeson, Mooty then advised another gamble to pay off the losses, namely leveraging an investment of $1.4 billion in financial futures by $439,997 in cash, or a 31:1 loan to cash ratio (versus the usual 10:1 ratio). Seminole soon went belly up.

The reason Mooty was able to ruin the Seminole s&l lay in the 1982 deregulation of s&ls. Washington allowed an s&l with, say, $3 million on deposit to lend out $100 million. It also allowed the owners of an s&l to use it to lend money to a friend for real estate speculation and pay themselves high management fees for the transaction.[9] To hedge against the loan default risk s&ls also had to offer depositors high interest rates. When interest rates declined and many real estate loans failed, the s&ls were whipsawed between the high loan losses and high deposit pay-outs. Hundreds of them failed. The losses suffered by shareholders, depositors, and s&ls approached US$600 billion.

How could such irrational mismanagement have transpired in what are normally deemed conservative institutions like banks, trust companies, and s&ls? The economist John Kenneth Galbraith has discerned the same highly infectious capacity for delusion in the Dutch tulip bulb mania of the 1630s, the eighteenth-century South Sea bubble, the over-leveraged US canal-building spree of the 1830s, the feverish stock market of the 1920s, and the highly leveraged growth of the 1980s. In classically sardonic fashion he terms this recurrent syndrome of mass irrationality 'financial euphoria'.[10] In each case the euphoria of boom times led to fear and panic as the bubble burst. The result was a recession, like the terrible crisis of the 1930s and, more recently, the restructurings and downsizings of the 1990s. The harsh impact of the most recent economic downturn was softened, fortunately, by the public support systems of the modern welfare state—which were created in the aftermath of the depression 60 years ago.

In each of these periods, as in the Barings collapse and the bank failures, speculators ingeniously invented new paper financial devices: stock promotions, highly leveraged investments and bonds, overly optimistic loans, derivative hedges, etc. They assumed a misplaced confidence in the future, an unquestioning faith in the market, and a weak memory for previous crashes. The result, Galbraith observes, is a 'serious commitment to error'. Financial euphoria, moreover, can infect management, too, as shown by the story of Mike Williams, an executive in an international financial firm.[11]

Free-wheeling Ralph

Mike's company allowed managers a great deal of discretion. His boss asked him to monitor Ralph, an older free-wheeling manager of a lending office in the Far East whose credit practice was somewhat informal. Ralph, an alcoholic, had approved around $90 million in risky loans on an informal word-of-mouth basis without a proper evaluation of creditworthiness or written approval. Mike's job was to stop Ralph from ruining the company. So he went in and saved the operation. As he told author Barbara Toffler, 'I walked in—there were no credit files, . . . no financial statements, . . . no information on the borrowers at all [except for loan payment billings]. There had been no credit discipline whatsoever. . . . Ralph [still] could not believe anything was wrong.'

Ultimately, the company lost $14 million from Ralph's bad loans. Even after Mike Williams cleaned up the mess, his boss did not support him. So Mike spent a few years in the organizational wilderness before his career got back on track. All these cases suggest that financial euphoria degrades a company's capacity to manage the business of risk.

The Executive Fashion File

Modern management also seems vulnerable to irrational euphoria over the latest nostrum for corporate ills, especially when hyped by a consultant. Otherwise hard-nosed executives are seduced by the softest types of high-priced snake oil. Eileen Shapiro, in her book-length critique of corporate 'fad-surfing', raises numerous questions about many trendy programs: excellence, mission statements, visioning, re-engineering, restructuring, low-cost production, the flat organization, total quality/continuous improvement, open environments, customer satisfaction, empowerment (and, I should add, business ethics). She offers many examples of consultants' jargon in her witty *Fad Surfing in the Boardroom*. For example:

> *Change Management*: The process of paying outsiders to create the pain that will motivate insiders to change, thereby transferring the change from the company's coffers into those of the consultants.

Some consultants, it seems, peddle some very dubious programs.

Hidden within most fads is a good idea, but it is overblown and made into a panacea. Or a program leader pushes it too far and coerces people to accept his nostrums uncritically. Furthermore, consultants tend to stress process over outcomes, partly for the reason that they know a lot about 'management' but little about the substantive details of running a specific business. For instance, the aim of re-engineering, Michael Hammer and John Champy tell us, is to reduce radically the work time needed for administration as well as production.[12] This is usually done with the help of new information and communication technologies. But Hammer and Champy also demand total change: 'Re-engineering means starting all over, starting from scratch. [It] is an all-or-nothing proposition that produces dramatically impressive results. Most companies have no choice but to muster the courage to do it.'

The core ethic, in contrast, only enjoins one to improve one's performance. It does not demand total transformation in six weeks or six months. Being a performance ethic it stresses substantive outcomes more than process. Indeed, when I hear anyone talk about an approach that will totally change an organization overnight, I am reminded of a favourite saying of an old friend: 'There's no such thing as instant coffee.' As an incurable coffee addict, I have strong doubts that instant coffee is coffee in any important sense of the word. Similarly for calls for instant and total change in management. The 'informed choice' maxim, moreover, is incompatible with high-pressure, psychologically intimidating tactics. So executives who allow an outside consultant to override their own business judgement are in effect saying that outside expertise matters more than inside knowledge.

Shapiro points out that most of these approaches can be powerful management tools when appropriately designed and used. Different techniques can be combined to craft solutions tailored to a company's unique problems. But managers should decide on the tools to be used and how to adapt them to their organization to solve the problems facing them. In effect, management remains responsible for reducing the risks of failure and enhancing the chances of success. Management must solve its own problems.

The Business of Risk

At bottom, these stories are different tales about risk. The old tale is that a euphoric focus on high short-term gains can seduce one into a high-risk gamble. Every investment and business decision, indeed every choice, involves some degree of risk. As engineers like to say, there is no zero risk. So the newer and better tale is to call for *responsible risk judgement*. One should not let the prospect of gain lead one to neglect the risk of loss. Instead, sound risk judgement involves management minimizing the risks, that is, reducing them to an acceptable level.

Another lesson from these tales is the need for the disclosure of information that affects risk judgements, for example, through independent audits of the company's records. It is the auditor's professional responsibility to report any such problems and risks, both to management and to the investor community. Timely disclosure can prevent financial disasters like the bank failures. This needs to be done in a balanced fashion that neither exaggerates nor underplays the problems in a company. Problem reports should be set within the context of the company's strengths and related to comparable industry performance in the same time period.

There is a further wrinkle to risk judgement, for these sorry tales suggest that the players confuse two different types of risk, *capital risks* and *pay-off risks*. In a capital risk the stakes are very high. One is putting most or all of one's assets, one's capital base, at risk. One therefore cannot afford to lose. In a pay-off risk, in contrast, one gambles a relatively small amount of one's income in hope of a much greater gain. Usually one can afford the bet and take the losses. Overly speculative investors, however, driven by greed, tend euphorically to focus on high short-term pay-offs and downplay the all-too-real risk of losses. Such overly optimistic pay-off assumptions often lead to excessive leverage, as we saw in the R.J.R. Nabisco and Barings stories. But when one's bet is large relative to one's total assets the gamble changes into a capital risk. Where there is a real likelihood of high capital loss the gamble approaches an unacceptably high loss level. A key cautionary maxim respecting capital risks is, *Never bet the company*. Excessive capital risks may lead to losing the company and bankruptcy, as Ross Johnson, Nick Leeson, and James Wesley Mooty II all discovered.

Such major capital losses in a company also put the welfare of many investors, employees, and other stakeholders at unacceptable risk, but, as we saw, they often have no choice in the matter. So prudence is even more required in capital risk judgement.

Otherwise, catastrophe may be the outcome, not only for oneself but for the company and its stakeholders. No investment should be so blinded by the promise of pay-offs as to put one's capital base at significant risk (outside of crisis situations where capital risk is the only alternative).

Both pay-off and capital risks should, of course, be kept to acceptable levels. Yet there is no precise way of measuring risk levels. The caution against speculative gambles and capital risks suggests that the likely rewards should outweigh the likely risks. Obversely, the greater the risk the less one should gamble on the gain. This is the clue to determining an acceptable level of risk, for risk is defined as the probability of a hazard, loss, or harm occurring. In effect, then, the more serious the hazard or harm (e.g., high capital loss) and the more probable its occurrence, the less acceptable the risk. On the other hand, where there is a relatively high probability of a minimal harm occurring (e.g., losing $1 on a 6/49 lottery ticket), the risk is acceptable. One is—relatively—secure. This suggests the four-level risk classification, as shown in the risk matrix in Table 2.1.

Table 2.1 **Risk Matrix**		
	High Probability of Occurrence (+P)	**Low Probability of Occurrence (-P)**
Serious Hazards (+H)	R1 Unacceptable (+P x +H)➡	R2 Worrying (-P x +H)➡
Lesser Hazards (-H)	R3 Minimal (+P x -H)➡	R4 Optimal (-P x -H)

The principle is relatively simple. The greater the harm and the more likely its occurrence, the more unacceptable the risk. This insight suggests a rule for minimizing risk. As the direction of the arrows suggests, good risk judgement means rejecting unacceptable risks (R1) and reducing one's risks to as close to optimal as possible (move from R1, R2, or R3 to R4). One may have to tolerate more risk than one prefers (R3), and, if absolutely necessary, accept a worrying risk (R2). The less choice one has, of course, the higher the risk level one may have to tolerate. The more control one has, the more one should act to lower the probability of harm and reduce the extent of that harm (e.g., reducing the amount one bets). This is the substance of responsible risk-minimizing management. Since the probability of risk is offset by that of gains, a new tale needs to be told of the social character of management, its purpose, the ethic of problem-solving, and the diverse socio-economic intelligence on which it rests.

II A New Tale:
Socially Intelligent Management

Profit and Purpose

Perhaps the oldest and hardest business tale is that the main purpose of management (and ownership) is to maximize the firm's profits. Certainly that is the view of David Roderick, a former chairman of US Steel: 'The duty of management is to make money. Our primary objective is not to make steel.'[13] Not to mention Milton Friedman's famous words:

Friedman on Social Responsibility

There is one and only one social responsibility of business . . . to increase its profits . . . to make as much money as possible while conforming to the basic rules of the society, [namely] those embodied in law and in ethical custom.[14]

To demand constant increase of profits every quarter is unrealistic and risky. It ranks pay-offs over risks. Such a gain-maximizing mind-set approaches financial euphoria. Under the debate about profit lie different views of the purpose of management. Most would agree that management should seek a satisfactory or reasonable rate of return on the firm's capital. Table 2.2 shows what average financial returns looked like for large North American firms in 1995:[15]

Table 2.2 **Comparative Annual Returns**			
	1 yr Profit (%)	**Return on Assets (%)**	**Return on Equity (%)**
Top 500 Canadian Firms (Mean)	5.11	23.2	24.4
Top 500 Canadian Firms (Median)	3.23	13.6	11.6
Top 1000 U.S. Firms (Mean)	6.0	na	16.3

In the table, profit is net earnings after taxes, stated as a percentage of sales or revenue. (The median is stated for the Canadian firms to mitigate the skewing effect of a few unusually high returns on the mean.) To give a fuller picture of financial returns the table also presents return on assets and shareholders' equity. While profits are relatively low, returns on assets and equity are much higher. One might rephrase Friedman and say that, in the old conventional view, increasing the firm's financial returns is the main responsibility of management.

Financial measures, moreover, are paper returns. They are susceptible to creative manipulation. Management can increase quarterly profits by shifting expenses and revenues from one quarter to another, or can artificially inflate short-term returns by starving a plant, deferring maintenance and capital expenditures. Reliable numbers therefore assume ethical management, integrity of records, sound accounting, and full disclosure to the auditors and financial community. Nor is profit a purely financial or capitalist notion. It is expected even in State enterprises in China, James O'Toole reports, but there it is managed differently.[16] Profit was seen as a means to other enterprise and social ends.

A Chinese Communist Factory Manager's View of Profit

Without profit, we must lay off workers, it is difficult to borrow working capital, we must cease production, our retirees' pension fund cannot be replenished, we cannot support community schools. The State needs some measure by which to evaluate if we are meeting the needs of consumers. . . . Profits are like breathing. You must breathe to live; but you don't live to breathe.

Financial returns, we saw in Chapter 1, are only one set of business performance measures. Profit, similarly, is but one test of business performance. Taken alone, it does not tell us enough about a business. Indeed, a wide body of business opinion dissents from the profit-maximizing view. The real question about profit, Peter Drucker contends, is not, "'What is the maximum profit this business can yield?" It is "what is the minimum profitability needed to cover the future risks of this business?'" On this reading a primary purpose of management is to avoid losses and survive. It is to minimize the company's risks. In effect, to do no harm. As Drucker adds, 'If we want to know what a business is we have to start with its *purpose*. . . . it must lie in society since business enterprise is an organ of society. There is only one valid definition of business purpose: *to create a customer*.'[17]

In Drucker's view, the task of increasing returns takes management well beyond financial investment into entrepreneurship. The firm cannot realize profits unless it sells its goods to consumers. Profit, as Peters and Waterman said, is a by-product of doing business well. It is through marketing, innovation, and sales that businesses gain revenues to pay the bills and sustain the enterprise over time. Placer Dome, a hard-nosed international mining company, defines its corporate objectives as increasing production and seizing base metal market opportunities that improve long-term cash flow.

Peters and Waterman also proposed a rich, multi-levelled concept of business performance stressing markets, innovation, strategy, culture, and stakeholders. As we saw in Chapter 1, a fuller picture of business performance gives us a better picture of the long-term health of the firm. This suggests that management's main overall responsibility is to help the company achieve a reasonable level of performance relative to the industry over several years on the major business performance indicators and to help it grow.

Profits, however, raise an important problem for management, that of determining the most productive allocation of the firm's earnings and resources. What is the best distribution of the company's financial returns? How should management allocate them in response to competing demands? These questions are central to the overall success of the business. Among the aspects of the business competing for a piece of the profit pie might be the following:

- higher employee wages
- increased share dividends
- improvement of products or marketing
- reduction of debt
- plant expansion
- investment in new technology.

Such tough choices put managerial judgement to a demanding, ethical test, for one of the most difficult of ethical problems is that of distributive justice. The conventional norms on which fair distribution rests are several: need, merit, potential benefit or return to the organization (or productivity), stakeholder choice, and stakeholder representation. There is no formula for resolving the many, often political, tensions among them, or for optimizing the whole set. Ultimately, then, resource allocation decisions are difficult and require good, informed, and experienced judgement.

Allocating Resources at Hewlett-Packard

At Hewlett-Packard people, materials, facilities, money, and time are the resources available to us for conducting our business. By applying our skills, we turn these resources into useful products and services. If we do a good job, customers pay us more for our products than the sum of our costs.

David Packard, *The HP Way*

Hewlett-Packard, David Packard comments, decided to use its profits to finance growth on a 'pay as you go basis . . . primarily out of earnings', rather than borrowing money.[18] In this way HP avoided long-term debt and did not have to sell healthy divisions or lay off good employees. This self-financing approach required good management of company assets as well as its profits.

The examination of risk and profit raises serious reservations about the old profit-maximizing, purely financial model of business, about vulnerability to trendy fads, and about management. In its place a newer, softer, and richer view is emerging, with the help of the values and maxims of the core ethic. It suggests that *the first responsibility of management is to ensure the survival of the enterprise over time*, that is, to minimize both the capital and pay-off risks of critical losses and bankruptcy. It is, in effect, to do no harm to the company. This further suggests that a core responsibility of management is to reduce the risks to the firm's stakeholder network—its management, employees, shareholders, suppliers, and customers. This is not an idle, abstract matter. On the contrary, it is especially important and challenging in a world of dynamic markets and high socio-economic turbulence.

The second positive responsibility of management builds on the first. Assuming survival is likely, management should work to secure the welfare of the company as a whole over time, including that of its stakeholders. To determine a satisfactory level of returns and rewards is a primary management objective. Minimizing risk is complemented by obtaining gains for the company and its stakeholders. Rather than maximizing one's gains, however, the aim is to ensure the overall welfare of the company, as defined by the full range of business performance measures. Management needs to determine what actual levels of sales, profitability, employment, productivity, and growth are possible for this company in this socio-economic environment over what time period. In effect, *the second responsibility of management is to determine and secure the common good of the company over time.* Given the complexity and large size of the modern firm, both responsibilities are difficult and challenging. The top 500 Canadian firms average about 4,800 employees in Canada. On the other hand, the workforces of international firms are much larger (about 24,000 for the 379 firms that supplied data in *Corporate Ethics Monitor* surveys).[19] In addition, markets are dynamic and constantly changing.

Underlying the management task of determining the most productive allocation of resources is the notion of productivity itself. The old view is that productivity is merely the ratio of labour inputs (costs) to production outputs (benefits). But this is too narrow a view. There are three fundamental factors of production: finance capital, technology, and people. These are the firm's key strategic resources.[20] Each is a potential benefit as well as cost. Management's job is to achieve an optimal productive balance among them all in relation to markets and to sustain that optimal mix over time. So one must manage people, employees, and the organization as well as money and technology. Management, that is, requires excellent social as well as economic problem-solving and skills. The coming chapters will extend our understanding of the profoundly social character of management and business.

Ethics in Problem-Solving

Minimizing risk puts a premium on problem-solving in management, especially when it is reinterpreted in ethical and social terms. Given the normal limitations of technical, economic, and human cognitive resources, one should be prepared for things to go wrong. They will, as a matter of course. One of the main tasks of a manager, Henry Mintzberg holds, is to handle disturbances (see the next section). Problem-solving is a widely accepted way of dealing with difficulties and quandaries in engineering, medicine, education, and business. A commitment to make good decisions and solve the company's problems is a core obligation of management responsibility. Indeed, Bell Canada's five-stage ethical decision model shows that companies are already aware of the value of problem-solving:

1.   How do I know there's a problem?
2.   Analyse the problem.
3.   Brainstorm the alternatives.
4.   Use available resources.
5.   Take the problem up line (i.e., to one's superior).[21]

All too often, moral issues are phrased in terms of accusatory blame. Yet, moralizing does not tell us what was wrong, what the options were, or how to remedy the problem. Rather, as Robert Reich says, 'Placing blame is among the most comforting cognitive acts, for it allows one to cast away responsibility.'[22] Problem-solving, in contrast, stresses a more intelligent, managerial approach to ethics. Ethical problem-solving means two things. Firstly, it means that the core ethic supports intelligent problem-solving. Secondly, problem-solving is also a good way to identify and handle ethical difficulties in business, e.g., problems involving the core values of care for life, welfare, honest communication, and civil rights. And such matters arise frequently enough in business. Generally speaking, problem-solving involves three steps: identifying the problem, searching for solutions, and monitoring the outcomes. We will take them in turn.

1. *Identify the real problem.* The first ethical requirement is to identify the real problem. If you don't ask the right question you won't get the correct answer. When, for instance, the local police told a warehouse manager for an English parcel service company that three of his employees had been caught selling 'stolen' pallets from his warehouse, he assumed that they were guilty of theft. In fact, his personnel manager told him that the pallets 'were just throwaways' and it was an accepted practice for employees to sell them.[23] From the first, therefore, it is very important to identify the problem correctly.

From the beginning, management needs to gather good information, and separate out irrelevant data so that the real problem can be discerned. This means evaluating the various perceptions of different stakeholders. In the parcel service story, an indirect external stakeholder, the police, had misunderstood an internal practice in a company and led a manager to the wrong conclusion. On gathering information from direct stakeholders, however, the real problem was identified and solved. Often problems are not what people believe them to be. While ethical problem-solving requires management to listen to the diverse concerns of various stakeholders, it does not require managers to accept uncritically everything they say. Indeed, stakeholder views often conflict, depending on their stake in solving the problem.

So problem identification is a very challenging task.[24] It requires good interpersonal, informational, investigative, and research skills. Often problems are mixed, being both economic and ethical in character. Sometimes they are purely administrative or technical. And sometimes there is no real problem at all. Each is an important finding. The earlier a problem is identified, moreover, the less chance it will grow worse. This shows the importance of the 'management by walking around' style employed at Hewlett-Packard. It is not only informal—it also keeps executives' ears to the ground. As a result, they are better able to detect early warning signals of a problem developing and to resolve it before it grows to critical proportions.

Let us take an example. Say there has been very costly downtime on the new, computerized, just-in-time production line at the Ontario plant of the fictitious Blakeley Appliance Company. It could endanger delivery of a major order to a new customer. Some engineers think it is operator error. Many workers blame the computer that manufactures the software and the robots. Some managers think the problem is the complex new software that the engineers insisted on. The union, as usual, blames management for speeding up production and bringing in the robots without much consultation. So the first problem is one of sorting out the informed guesses.

2. *Search for solutions.* The first requirement in any solution search is to ask the right question. Since Blakeley has a teamwork culture, an inclusive task force is created to search for a solution. The task force members include representatives of key direct internal stakeholders: a manager, an engineer, and a line operator. Their first job is to identify possible hypotheses about the problem. They at once decide to canvass a wide range of stakeholder opinion. Soon some leads turn up: a software bug, a hardware glitch in the robot, and/or an operator training deficiency. Now the task force begins to search out the most likely solution.

The company still faces an imminent contract delivery deadline. So a solution is needed fast. But a good solution search requires adequate time and resources.[25] The stress and pressure can be moderate but not excessive. The task force needs to canvass all solution options thoroughly and with an open mind. The time pressure is dangerous. It might harden external, activist stakeholder attitudes. If a struggle between various stakeholder interests dominates an issue there is a real danger of a solution search degenerating into an unproductive and interminable 'garbage can' process.[26] This can take many forms. A euphoric fixation on the 'solution' of high returns, for example, led Barings' management to ignore rising warnings of a critical problem.

In any large organization there are people who have their favourite pet solution for any problem. Some old favourites are:

❖   cut costs
❖   maximize profits
❖   get with the latest management fad
❖   bring in a consultant
❖   blame the workers
❖   invest in new technology
❖   give us more money.

Engineers, for example, favour technical fixes. Ideological and moral crusaders reframe all problems in terms of their pet concern, whether that concern is greedy owners, union bosses, radical feminists, or wasteful governments. Moralists want to blame someone or, alternatively, see noble self-sacrifice to some cause as the right solution for all that ails humankind. The classic macho demand to 'do something' can itself inhibit and derail the solution search process. 'Garbage can' is a fitting label for this cacophony of conflicting agendas. It has derailed many otherwise well-intentioned solution searches in both business and government.

Let us say, however, that despite the pressure our Blakeley task force works well and makes two key discoveries. (1) There are discrepancies in a small part in the robot. The problem is found to originate with the supplier, who substituted it for the right part due to delivery pressures, not thinking the small difference would matter; but it did. In addition, the software supplier tells the task force that (2) the operator training procedures could use updating.

3. *Act, observe, improve.* At a certain point in a solution search, usually sooner rather than later, one has to make an informed choice and opt for the best achievable solution option in the circumstances. The relatively unlimited time and resources for academic inquiry do not obtain in real-life problem-solving. The Blakeley plant task force gets the right part into the robots and calls for appropriate operator retraining. After 10 days of overtime the plant meets the delivery date for the contract, and the new customer is happy.

Afterwards, management and employees both felt that the task force should stay in place and continue monitoring production to sustain the increased productivity. As a result it uncovered some other minor technical and operator problems—just-in-time systems are very sensitive to minor glitches. So it began to work on these new problems. In addition, it discovered that one of the line operators is a software hacker and found a socio-technical systems expert at the local community college. The hacker now advises the committee, and the expert has been asked to design a better operator training program. Six months later things have improved so much that the Ontario plant is leading the whole company in productivity and task force members are being invited to talk to other Blakeley plants about their problem-solving process.

The plant task force met the ethical requirements of problem-solving. They involved affected stakeholders to help solve the problem and listened to their suggestions. They searched for and identified the problem, and, having gathered extensive information, were able to choose and implement the best achievable solution in the situation. They monitored the outcome over time and improved the system even more. They not only did the right thing, they observed the results and then did things better. That is what ethical problem-solving means. The task force process was ethical because it not only identified and solved the downtime problem, it also managed to reduce the unacceptable risk of losing the contract date and managed to advance stakeholder welfare. This was also because the task force deliberations were intelligent and reasonable and avoided organizational power trips, turf wars, and moralistic blame games.

Finally, one other important lesson is to be learned from the Blakeley plant story—management agreed both to create the task force and to keep it going, despite time and cost pressures. Even after it had implemented the solution the task force continued to monitor the operation and detected some new problems and prevented them from growing to critical proportions. This shows the importance of intelligent management, of keeping adequate resources in place to deal with current and future contingencies, which are notoriously unpredictable. Management vigilance is necessary because situations change, as Russell Ackoff warns. 'Few problems, once solved, stay that way. Changing conditions tend to unsolve previous problems.'[27] Thus problem-solving itself is an ethical achievement and demonstrates a broad socio-economic intelligence. Management, in other words, is a social practice.

Social Management

The old story of management values is epitomized in the hardball played to acquire R.J.R. Nabisco and other firms, and in the quantitative, unemotional values of bottom-line, profit-driven management. The manager, like the ship's captain of old, is the epitome of hard logical rationality. He is, as Marshall McLuhan observed, as dehumanized personally as his job is impersonally rational.

The Inhuman Executive

The successful executive has to strip himself of every human quality until he is nearly mad with boredom. Then he can work, work, work without distraction. The work is the narcotic for the boredom as the boredom is the spur to work.

Marshall McLuhan, *The Mechanical Bride*[28]

But this is a decidedly 'malestream' view of the separate, socially disconnected, and uncaring self. The RJR and Barings stories have shown the tensions and difficulties caused by this old model of management. In his classic study of managerial work, Henry Mintzberg offers a much different, softer, and more social tale.[29] Mintzberg discerned three fundamental management roles: interpersonal, informational, and decisional. The first, interpersonal, role is expressly social, as is the second, informational role. It is captured in the core value of communication. The final, decisional, role is not unlike ethical problem-solving.

Interpersonal roles: figurehead, leader, liaison
Informational roles: spokesman, monitor, disseminator
Decisional roles: resource allocator, entrepreneur,
                     negotiator, disturbance handler

Management responsibilities are much more intricate and social, as befits the organizational complexity of large firms. Much of a manager's time is taken up in meetings, in communicating, in receiving and assessing information, and in responding with decisions. To sort out that complexity we must distinguish between executive and administrative management. Executives are responsible for formulating the corporate mission and corporate policy, minimizing strategic risks, allocating resources, co-ordinating the wide-ranging operations of the whole organization, and identifying problems and preventing them from developing into major crises. They work at the highest level of the firm, in close collaboration with the board and owners. They have the ethical responsibility of defining the community of interests on which the business rests. Their leadership position, however, may make executives prone to overconfidence. As a recent study argues, many managers 'believe they can control the outcomes of decision better than they really can. Their illusions of superiority, favorable self-image, optimism, and control of situations are all threats to intelligent decision-making.'[30]

Executives, then, are the corporate figureheads, leaders, and spokespersons, and sometimes even entrepreneurs. As public spokespersons they play the distinctly political roles of representing the firm and negotiating with its stakeholders. Accordingly, Mintzberg likens an executive 'to the neck of an hourglass, standing between his organization and a network of outside contacts, linking them in a variety of ways.' Think of an hourglass with constant pressure from the bottom as well as the top, and his comment is true not only for executives but also for administrators.

The responsibility of administrative managers is to supervise employees and implement the policies and plans of the executives to whom they report. Administrators perform the more mundane, ongoing tasks of liaison with employees and between divisions, disseminating information, negotiating with staff, customers, and suppliers, monitoring operations, and, of course, handling disturbances. This last task requires responsiveness to barely perceptible early warnings to prevent small problems from blowing up. On a less harmonious note, administrative managers have been blamed for the problems of bureaucratic inefficiency and corporate waste. This is the hard view taken in the high finance battle for corporate control. For these reasons, administrators often find themselves at the losing end of corporate control battles. But without good everyday administration, complex modern organizations would become anarchic and soon cease to function, especially if they operate in different markets and diverse nations.

Given their position in the organizational hourglass, administrative managers play conflicting roles and are subject to myriad cross-pressures. Administrators must cope with pressures from executives to meet ever-increasing profit, output, or sales targets, and also must motivate employees to work productively and sell products to customers. If they take too coercive or adversarial an approach to employees, however, the result can be guerrilla warfare in the workplace. Managers must live up to their obligations to their superiors, employees, divisions, and customers. At the same time, they need to maintain good relations with suppliers, distributors, and retailers.

Such conflicts are a staple topic in business ethics research.[31] Managers face moral problems all the time. Unfortunately, ethical values are not an accepted part of the manager's vocabulary. But managers need to see discussions about ethical concerns as a familiar, comfortable part of the job, as has begun to happen in many companies with health, safety, and environmental issues, which have become accepted elements of good business.[32]

These descriptions of executive and administrative work suggest a different, more social and concrete model of managerial intelligence, especially when one adds the ethical notions of stakeholder relations, minimizing risks, and problem-solving. The Blakeley task force, for example, involved direct internal stakeholders in problem-solving. Managerial work thus goes beyond the narrow confines of conventional rationality. Management is not a matter of a quantitative calculus.

Instead, managerial work involves a full range of human skills:

❖ interpersonal relations
❖ communication
❖ negotiation
❖ decision-making.

As the core ethic implies, managerial work involves all the practical skills human intelligence has developed. Human intelligence, Howard Gardner has argued, involves 'multiple intelligences'.[33] His research in cognitive psychology led Gardner to conclude there are several different types of problem-solving intelligence: linguistic, logical-mathematical, musical (or auditory/temporal), spatial (or visual), bodily-kinesthetic (in manual work and sports), and intrapersonal (individual reflectiveness) and interpersonal (social). Each involves a distinctive practical know-how or intellectual competence and an appropriate set of problem-solving and information-processing skills. They help us avoid danger, respond appropriately to crisis, and reinforce our social perceptions. Different people show competence in different intelligences.

Managerial work is not restricted to linguistic and logical-mathematical skills, as traditional scientific, technical, and philosophical notions of rationality all implied. Managerial work is as socially 'soft' as it is financially 'hard'. But the whole theme of this book is that the softest of elements, water, can be hard and forbiddingly powerful and tough, as well as soft and refreshing. Soft is harder than it seems. Management is *hard like water*, for it calls on the full range of human intelligences. Management is a practical and social art. Ethical values, it follows, are not as irrelevant to management as many have thought. Indeed, Mintzberg says that managerial work involves 'a blend of duties and rights', to the point that the manager 'serves as focal point of the organization's value system'.[34]

Summary

Chapter 2 began with an old tale about financial mismanagement at Barings Bank. Instead of hard-headed rational management we found a euphoric disdain of risk, and then an equally disturbing tendency to surf the latest fads. In contrast, the 'do no harm' maxim suggested a risk matrix, supported by the distinction between capital and pay-off risks, to encourage a more prudent, risk-minimizing management style. The second part of the chapter began by suggesting that we should distinguish between executive and administrative management. In both instances managerial work, as Mintzberg has shown, is much more social in character than has been commonly assumed. To this end an ethical problem-solving approach, resting on Howard Gardner's notion of multiple problem-solving and information-processing intelligences, was then presented. This theme of the importance of social values in business is continued in the next chapter, on organizational values.

Chapter 3

Organizing Values

Loyalty to the corporation intensifies when it is perceived to be under attack from outsiders. The troops rally around the flag.

Brian Grossman, *Corporate Loyalty*

Organizations are complex, ambiguous, and paradoxical. The real challenge is to learn how to deal with this complexity.

Gareth Morgan, *Images of Organization*[1]

Values in Shipping

Aldo, Sandro, and Cosmo had been partners for a long time. They had negotiated many deals in which they shared the costs as well as the profits. Once they agreed they shook hands. That was it. Sure, Andrea, their notary, wrote it up and they all signed it, but it wasn't necessary. They knew what they'd said, and they never went back on their word. The only changes they ever made afterwards occurred when she pointed out a mistake they made. They grumbled a lot, they complained, and everyone was first to speak up about any problems he saw. Often they had to wait months before seeing any gains from their investment; and they sometimes lost out, from pirates, storms, and bad markets. But they stuck to their deals. They were loyal to each other; but the business was based on loyalty and trust. That did not preclude Aldo, Sandro, or Cosmo—or even Andrea—from voicing any concerns they had, often loudly and at length. Because of their trust, and their profits, their partnership had stood many tests over time: the pirates and the storms, dubious dealers, and the ups and downs of markets and tastes. If they hadn't trusted each other, their partnership would have shipwrecked a long time ago.

The main aim of Chapter 3 is to answer the question, how can organizations make moral decisions? Several difficulties afflict discussions of organizational values. Firstly, many confuse this question, whether an organization can be a moral agent, with the question whether an organization is a person, as it is in law. The legal fiction, however, is just that—fiction. So the real problem, then, is how can large modern organizations make moral decisions? It is easier to see how small partnerships such as the one binding Aldo, Sandro, and Cosmo together can act as one, but an organization of thousands of people is a very different kind of social and economic institution. They are, as Gareth Morgan comments, complex and ambiguous.

None the less, some answers to the questions about moral decision-making by organizations are possible. The first response, presented in the old tale in Part I about the conflicts between autocracy, loyalty, and voice, is negative. To the extent that autocratic organizations demand total loyalty, the result is 'groupthink'. Concerned members are discouraged from reporting any ethical problems, for such organizations suppress concerned voices inside the organization and force people outside the organization to blow the whistle. The new tales in Part II begin by noting that every organization has its own value system or culture. Businesses can and should build on their own natural foundation of win/win reciprocal *exchange values*, rather than win/lose *threat values*. Mutual benefit in exchange represents an implicitly ethical foundation for social integration in an organization. Corporate cultures, furthermore, are classified in risk and feedback terms, both of which reflect key aspects of the core ethic. Finally, organizations make moral decisions by effectively codifying their values and taking responsibility for ethical decision-making in an appropriately organized fashion. Chapter 3 begins with an old and all-too-familiar tale: the conflict between loyalty and voice in the autocratic corporation, followed by a discussion of the related problem of whistle-blowing.

I: Old Tales about 'Groupthink' and Whistle-Blowing

Corporate Autocracy

'An explicit system of accountability for subordinates would probably have to apply to top executives as well and would restrict their freedom.' Robert Jackall came to this opinion as a result of an extended look inside two large US companies, a chemical firm and a textile company.[2] Messengers bearing bad news, Jackall reported, are not welcome in the executive suites of many large corporations. Their critical voices are seen as distinctly disloyal. In these firms reporting problems is not the path to the top. It is more likely to lead to an invitation to exit the company. Positive feedback, not negative, is welcome. The result is that bureaucratic conformity and buck-passing are the expected norm in these organizations. Making accountability explicit would not only encourage messengers to report problems. It would require executives to listen to them. 'Ethics code' is not a favourite phrase in these executive suites.

In both firms studied by Jackall a quasi-feudal 'fealty to the king' overrode other obligations. Administrative managers were expected to show total loyalty to the CEO and his team. The CEO's word was law. Executives accepted responsibility for the firm's achievements, while blame for any problems was passed back down the organizational hierarchy to lower management levels. Instead of reporting or solving problems, the role of administrative management was to prevent the executives at the top from being held responsible for any mistakes or problems. An image of corporate harmony was to be created and preserved. The overall effect, Jackall writes, was to 'separate substance from appearances, action from responsibility, and language from meaning'.

Mid-level administrative managers were the point men. Being in the centre of the corporate hourglass, they bore most of the pressure. Advancement beyond middle management depended less on performance than on the ability to manipulate various corporate symbols, watchwords, and fads without being identified too closely with any one of them. Performance was subject to myriad, conflicting social interpretations. Appraisals were worded in code. Thus, if someone was 'exceptionally well qualified', this meant that the person in question 'has commited no major blunders to date'. Managers in one firm privately spoke of the CEO's managerial seminars as elaborate rituals without any hard results. They labelled his speeches 'incantations over the assembled multitude'.

Smothering feedback, however, had its risks. The chemical company management kept delaying replacement of old technology in one plant for over five years. It would cost US$6 million, which would have lowered the quarterly profits. So they kept delaying plant improvements, until government inspectors finally visited and found the plant to be in serious violation of environmental regulations. The resultant total repair bill, including litigation to stop the government order, came to about $150 million. Delaying needed technological innovations so long increased the costs nearly 25 times. This hardly fits the conventional image of management rationality in which business takes so much pride, and it makes one wonder about demands by business leaders that government be run as efficiently as a business. Indeed, within the company, government regulators were perceived as soft-headed idealists, lawyers as crooks, unionists as radical troublemakers, and the media as rabble-rousers.

Jackall's portraits offer evidence of the wasteful corporate bureaucracy of which Wall Street dealers and corporate raiders like Henry Kravis and George Roberts have often complained; but the responsibility for all the waste lay with the CEO and his executive team, not with the mid-level administrative 'bureaucrats'. If the reality of the executive suite is less than flattering, perhaps it is time to reconsider the efficiency and importance of mundane administrative managerial work. Who else, for example, can report to the top of the organization what is really going on at the bottom, in numerous offices and plants? Those in the executive suite usually do not know and cannot find out for themselves.

When the CEO of one firm announced his coming visit to a plant, over $100,000 was spent sprucing it up. A costly booklet was printed, complete with colour photos and fancy diagrams. Such a visit resembled a corporate version of the Potemkin village routine in former Communist states, not to forget the pre-revolutionary French monarchy. Long before the Ruler visited a small village, everything would be spruced up. The whole visit was elaborately staged. High expenditures for false corporate fronts thus rest on a centuries-old autocratic tradition.

Whenever the CEO resigned, Jackall reports, the transition to the rule of a new CEO began. The creation of a new, loyal executive team spread insecurity and uncertainty throughout the organization. It was not unlike the tensions among the military and courtiers whenever a Roman emperor died—often with some help from his friends. Everyone diplomatically and tensely sought to discern who the new Ruler might be, so as to ensure being hitched to the new rising star. When the new CEO took power, mistakes and problems were blamed on the previous team, for the key to managerial success was one's ability to outrun the mistakes of the previous regime.

Loyalty vs Voice

Autocratic organizations, Jackall's study shows, treat critical voices as disloyal to the extent that they discourage problem reports. Thus, they cannot make ethical decisions—and this often inhibits good business decisions, too. Similar problems arise when managers are deemed to be merely the agents of the shareholders, with a primary duty to increase their returns.[3] In both cases, expectations of unquestioning loyalty are passed down the organizational hierarchy. The result is that concerned managers are silenced, and forced to exit the firm and blow the whistle, often quite publicly. Take, for instance, the story of Raymond C. Quinn.[4]

Raymond C. Quinn, Whistle-blower

Raymond C. Quinn was a senior trader at Merrill Lynch. In 1992 he became concerned about the Dallas operation. Traders were raising bond prices more than 5 per cent before selling them, in effect reaping a hidden commission. One colleague was even keeping a separate set of books with another brokerage firm so as to hide payments to that firm for bringing business to Merrill Lynch. The company was also holding bonds in its own account to conceal ownership by a large institutional client, a violation of securities laws. Quinn reported these problems to his boss, Joseph A. Moglia. Moglia felt Quinn was making a big fuss about things that happen all the time. He warned Quinn that if he went further and talked to the company's New York lawyers, he 'would never work on the street again'. Even though Quinn's sales increased in 1992 his bonus was reduced. In the spring of 1993 he was warned in writing that he was 'not a good team player'. He was told to keep quiet and remain 'loyal'. In December Merrill Lynch dismissed him as part of a seemingly unrelated downsizing. In response he then publicly blew the whistle on the company. In responding to Quinn's allegations Merrill Lynch said that it had listened to him and acted on some of his concerns.

At one level Raymond Quinn's story is a simple tale of the conflict between loyalty and voice, a heroic story about an independent moral individual. But the conflict between voice and loyalty, as Morgan suggested, is richly layered. Three themes in it are especially important: first, the mythic struggle between individual conscience and the amoral organization; second, collective groupthink; and third, the tension between legalistic values and problem-solving. All lead us to tell the new tales about organizational values, presented in Part II, about exchange values, corporate culture, and organizing ethics.

Many moralists would stress the personal choice facing Raymond Quinn and his personal integrity, contrasting it with the dehumanizing amorality of the large organization. Certainly, stifling open communication from honest managers like Quinn polarized the situation at Merrill Lynch. Such polarization is a fertile breeding ground for moral dilemmas. It is in such circumstances that business ethics is truly an oxymoron. But is the real problem that of the lonely moral individual versus the amoral giant organization? Or a clash, as Barbara Toffler notes,[5] between private personal values and corporate organizational values?

The 'Public' Manager and the Private Person

Many people would claim that [this] is how it should be: that individuals do and must separate their work (or public) lives, and the ethics of those lives, from their personal (or private) lives, and the ethics in that sphere.

Barbara Toffler, *Tough Choices*

The media like to frame such stories in terms of a heroic David battling a corporate Goliath; but in Quinn's case Goliath won. The interpretive frame rests on the conventional view that an organization's ethics are a product of the morality of its individual members. Many managers, to be sure, perceive morality as a private and personal matter. Business ethicists like Clarence Walton argue that managers of good character make organizations ethical.[6] This fits the common view that the organizations are merely the product of the efforts of their individual members. Accordingly, the personal projects of individual managers and stakeholders are the way the organization becomes ethical. While there is some truth in such views, they don't go far enough.

Raymond C. Quinn, in addition, was a moral individual dealing with an amoral organization. But here the story shifts. Quinn was not creating his own personal rules or insisting that Merrill Lynch follow them. Nor was he proclaiming a unique moral intuition or rebelling against the organization. Instead, he was properly concerned as a manager about dubious business practices that could cause Merrill Lynch serious problems with key stakeholders: the securities market authority and the investing public. Quinn was doing his corporate duty, not pursuing a personal, idiosyncratic, Quixotic agenda. Indeed, managers are not merely private individuals. Their duty is to perform their organizational roles properly and well. Quinn was acting in his proper official corporate role. He was doing what a manager is supposed to do—communicate sensitive information to his superiors. He was doing his best to persuade the company to handle a potential disturbance before it became a serious problem. The problem was that his manager, Moglia, did not want to listen to disturbing messages. If anyone was expressing personal values, it seemed to be Moglia; but he saw no moral problem. Only later, when Quinn was no longer a manager, did he freely make the personal choice to communicate his concerns to the general public.

But not all independent individuals are moral heroes. The frontier cowboy may be valued highly in US culture, but many cowboys were murderers. Stalin certainly set his own rules, with the result that millions died. Self-interested individuals may be termed rational by economists, but free-floating entrepreneurs cannot manage large corporations. Nick Leeson's own personal derivatives project warned us that purely self-interested agents can increase the risks for other stakeholders, including their own company. Many autocratic CEOs are independent-minded, but, Jackall showed us, they can cost their firms millions. Don Quixote was an individual following his own unique moral intuition, but instead of becoming a David successfully beating a Goliath, Don Quixote ended up tilting at windmills. Clearly, the solitary individual is not a privileged font of moral ideals.

People blow the whistle on their firm precisely because they cannot solve, or even report, serious problems inside its doors. It is their last resort, not their first choice. Only after one has failed to communicate a problem inside the organization should the option of taking it outside be considered, depending on how serious it is or how much of a risk to others inside or outside the firm it involves. Sometimes people find creative ways of opposing bad decisions or undermining a bad policy or program from within, e.g., through paperwork, delays, misdirection, etc.[7] Plain brown envelopes and 'deep throats' are preferred options for messengers reporting problems outside the organization to the media or to regulatory or governmental authorities. Given the career risk, anonymity is often necessary. The aim is not to make a name for oneself, or to pursue a personal vendetta or pet crusade, or even to blame anyone. The aim is to report the problem and get it solved.

This leads to the second concern. 'Whistle-blowing' is a misleading label for loyal feedback in the organization, for it tends to convert the notion of reporting problems into a legal dispute. Instead of being seen as voicing problems to help one's company, one is perceived as presenting oneself as a judge delivering judgement on a guilty offender who has violated the law. To interpret ethical problem reporting as whistle-blowing is in effect to *legalize* it and the rest of the ethical problem-solving process. Legalization is the process of diffusing legalistic procedures and norms throughout the organization and into its external relations.[8] The result is that problems are transformed into legal issues. Accusatory blame takes the place of problem-solving intelligence. Assigning guilt matters more than identifying causes. Messengers become the accusers, so their messages are not welcomed. Procedural nitpicking and adversarial combativeness exacerbate conflict and inhibit feedback about problems. To an extent that whistle-blowing converts ethical problem-solving into a legalistic, adversarial court case, it polarizes ethical communication in the organization, discourages feedback, and inhibits intelligent problem-solving.

Underlying this legalization of organizational voice and feedback is a confusion about the law and morality. Most North American firms stipulate in their conduct codes that they will obey the law, but businesses often resist doing the socially or morally right thing unless the law requires it. After the 1991 US Sentencing Commission guidelines proposed more lenient sentences for firms that had effective programs to prevent violations of the law, there was a rapid growth in corporate ethics codes.[9]

Nor do legal values coincide with ethical ones. Indeed, many citizens have voiced moral concerns about the laws regulating employment equity, health and safety, environmental protection, securities markets, corporate governance, and, of course, taxation. Fear of legal sanction is the beginning of business ethics, but it is not enough. Bruncor's *Code of Business Ethics* makes the point that ethics goes beyond the law: 'Laws and rules cannot guarantee ethical conduct; only people of integrity can. Our company . . . should be judged by the highest standards of ethical conduct.'

As we saw in the Prologue, ethical choice and conduct are not merely a matter of following laws or rules. The core ethic, rather, is a set of general values and performance maxims, of guidelines to help people deliberate their options and make informed choices. It is up to organizations and individuals to bring those values to bear creatively on problems as they arise in actual situations. There is no pre-set system of laws and rules to program the right choice. Ethical choice and performance require the full range of human problem-solving intelligence, on the part of both individuals and groups.

This brings us to the third concern, the morally stifling collectivist ethos of 'groupthink'. Corporate demands for unquestioning loyalty and collective conformity force the Hobson's choice on members of either voicing support or keeping silent. Such uncritical conformism exemplifies a serious organizational pathology, which Irving Janis identified and labelled 'groupthink'.[10] Groupthink involves intense in-group pressures that weaken people's reality-testing powers and independent capacity for critical judgement. Such groups see themselves as invulnerable. They believe in their own collective moral righteousness. They ignore or rationalize warnings and negative feedback, and pressure internal critics to conform. They view the world in polarized Us versus Them terms. Outsiders, whether competitors, labour, governments, consumers, or even other business units in the firm, are treated as enemies.

Many organizations stifle critical voices and demand conformism on the part of their members. The autocratic executive attacks messengers reporting problems. Bad news flows down, not up. One result of corporate autocracy and conformity is that individuals become alienated from the company. Employees, including managers, put the company to the test, find it fails, and park their loyalties elsewhere. Many become cynical and take care of *Numero Uno* first. The company comes a distant second, or third. If they can't exit to better employment, they find devious routes under and around corporate authority. Evasion, sabotage, spying, deceit, and other forms of chicanery may grow. So do wrongful dismissal suits.

Not all groups or social relations or organizational values are healthy. Indeed, groupthink violates the core values of open and honest communication, informed choice, and minimizing risks to stakeholders and one's own company. It reflects a real pathology in organizational values. But this polarization of organizational and personal values is much too reminiscent of the old tale about the dichotomy between business and morality. Groupthink is not fruitful ground for the economic growth or the moral development of the organization.

Nor is it helpful to frame the problem as a struggle between the individual and the organization. This is simplistic, and it tends to polarize the issues. Newer and better tales are needed. We already have read one, in Chapter 2. The Blakeley appliance company task force, for example, intelligently focused on its problem and thrived on feedback from employees, the union, suppliers, and other stakeholders. It was a healthy problem-solving group. As a result everyone benefited.

Let us add one important fact: Raymond Quinn was not rewarded by his organization for doing his duty and voicing his moral concern. He should have been. So the quality of our relations is what organizational ethics must see to. The corollary follows, however surprising: *organizational values can be as ethical as personal values*. The lesson is that ethical behaviour should be rewarded, not punished. This implies that the individual and the organization both need a common set of shared ethical values. This is the subject of Part II.

II New Tales: Organizing Ethical Values

Part II presents three new tales, all based on the assumption that each organization embodies some values. Firstly, economic *exchange values* are implicitly ethical organizing values; secondly, *social integration* through corporate culture reflects the core ethic to the extent that it minimizes risks and improves feedback; and finally, large companies can and should take *moral responsibility* for their performance and systematically manage their ethical values.

Exchange Values as Organizers

Inasmuch as every organization has its own set of values, one should ask to what extent those values are ethical. In the case of business organizations, the answer may surprise many people. Because a business organization is economic and commerce operates in terms of mutual benefit or exchange, they are implicitly ethical. Exchange values, Kenneth E. Boulding contends, are better socio-economic organizers than legalistic threat values.[11] Boulding postulates three 'social organizers': threat, exchange, and integration values. Each emerges within a different group of social institutions and has its own organizing principle, as shown in Table 3.1.

Table 3.1 **Values as Social Organizers**		
Organizing Value ↓	Base Institution	Principle
Threat	The State: legal, military, political	We Win / You Lose
Exchange	The Economy: production, markets	We Win / You Win
Social Integration	The Culture: family, tribe, nation	What We Want / You Want

All three values are formulated in terms of the kind of relationships they engender. All three, that is, involve a transfer of welfare, whether good or bad. Thus, Boulding comments, 'An exchange system is based on a transfer of goods, a threat system on the transfer of bads. . . . You do something nice to me or I will do something nasty to you.' Boulding contrasts win/lose threat values with win/win exchange values. Anywhere one side puts the other side at risk, especially unacceptably high risk of economic loss or danger to health or safety, threat values are the organizing principle in their relations— but threat is better at separating people than at connecting them. Whole institutions, such as armies, the law, and the State, are based on threat values, for these institutions use threat to defend people against crimes and invasion. So threat has its moral uses.

But threat values breed insecurity and fear. This separates and divides people. In the autocratic corporation, executives constantly need to watch their backs. Threats by executives, moreover, breed unproductive management and employee responses, from passive resistance, sabotage, and guerrilla tactics to whistle-blowing. When managers don't trust their subordinates and employees, they must police them. This increases the transaction costs of everyday managerial work. Threat values legalize business relations and problems. Bureaucratic organizations that stress legalistic compliance with rules and proper procedure also exemplify the legalistic side of threat as an organizing value.[12] Consequently, threat, Boulding says, 'is a poor means of getting rich.' From Bosnia to the slums of Los Angeles, communities dominated by threat values are economically depressed. They are neither peaceful nor productive. Economics and threats don't mix. Furthermore, threat values, like the dour Calvinist notion of duty, enforce morality on the pain of punishment. That leads naturally to the old dichotomy between morality and business.

In contrast, win/win exchange values are the opposite of win/lose threat values. Exchange values lead people to say, 'You do something nice to me and I will do something nice to you.' Exchange involves the promise of gain, not the threat of pain. So people are usually better off as a result of exchanges. Exchange encourages the transfer of goods in commerce, productive social relations, and communications. Exchange leads one to consider the welfare of others in relationships. Thus it facilitates life in groups and organizations. Exchange rests on communicating market information and voluntary choice in buying what is on offer. Such exchanges involve mutual benefit. Exchange brings people together, not unlike an ethics based on care and connection, as Carol Gilligan suggested, rather than on the separate self.

Exchange values underlie economic practices such as trade, production, and markets, and permeate economic institutions and organizations. Exchange is a way of ensuring the welfare for all parties to a deal, contract, or relationship. In exchange one acts on the basis of one's interests, true, but expressly as linked to the welfare of the others in the exchange relationship. It reflects the core ethical value of welfare. Since exchange means reciprocal welfare it is an implicitly ethical value. To the extent economics rests on exchange values, it, too, is implicitly ethical, and the organizational values of a business are implicitly ethical as well. Ethics are therefore natural to business, indeed, more native to business than to the law, the State, or the army. Reciprocating benefits among stakeholders is morally preferable to threatening them with loss of property or life. Exchange values, then, show that ethics and economics are not enemies but partners.

Ethics, exchange values suggest, arise within business, not outside of it. Ethics are not an import. Jerry Kohlberg understood this when he proclaimed that collaboration between financiers and management was better both for the Kohlberg Kravis and Roberts investment firm and for its clients. He was saying that exchange is a better way of organizing financier/client relations than risk. The Blakeley task force also operated on the basis of exchange values, namely, of stakeholder inclusion in determining its membership, of exchanging information widely, and of everyone winning by solving the problem.

The interplay of economic, social, and ethical motives may surprise those who want purity in moral motivation, but this is too abstract an ideal. In reality, human motives or intentions are mixed, especially in complex situations and where many people are involved. And that is commonplace in business, as Kohlberg and Boulding each realizes. Business values are commonly mixed, like human motives generally, and the company's interests are interlinked with those of its stakeholders. Despite the theory that everyone in business is there solely for the money, people in business are often intrinsically motivated by the work they do and by projects they identify with.

Ethical motives are commonly linked, for example, with other economic or technical motives. Human motivation is far too complex, rich, and ambiguous to be reduced to one single value such as money, power, sex, or fame. The business/morality dichotomy assumes pure economic and moral motives. Perhaps that purity explains why they are often seen to be incompatible. 'Good' or pure intentions untouched by practical realities all too often pave the way to the wrong place. We should instead expect and hope to find ethical motives interacting with business motives. This is a good thing, for if the mix involves positive interaction, reciprocity between economic benefits and moral goods, then ethical values will become more embedded in business practices and relationships. And that is surely the point of business ethics. Thus the Blakeley plant may not only want to reduce costs but also want to solve technical equipment and operation problems and to treat its employees well.

Exchange values, in sum, are more powerful social organizers than threat values, for they connect people. Reciprocity keeps them connected, for people like to maintain and enhance mutually rewarding relations. Exchange values hold the community of interests in the business together. Like management, problem-solving, and stakeholder relations, exchange reflects social as well as economic values, but exchange values are not the same as cultural values.

Ethical Cultures

Despite its admitted power, exchange is not a strong enough social organizer, Boulding holds, to explain the cohesive force in organizations. So Boulding sees the need for social integration values to bind people together in organizations. Integration, Boulding writes, is based on the principle, 'what you want, I want.' Integration reinforces 'rich interpersonal relationships' involving 'identity, love, benevolence, legitimacy', and loyalty. Social integration is the main function of cultural institutions like the family, the church, the nation. They bind people together across space and reproduce shared culture and values over the generations. This is well understood in traditional or relatively homogeneous cultures, for example, among Aboriginal peoples and in Quebec. Understanding the importance of culture and integration is essential to success in international business, as we will see later in Chapters 8 and 9.

Every organization has its own value system or culture, its ways and its values. Few groups of people are kept together purely on the basis of economic values. Exchange values help constitute businesses as communities of economic interests, but integration values underpin the cohesive forces of corporate culture. An organization's culture, Barbara Toffler observes, is 'the way one does things around here'.[13] A culture is a set of usually unwritten but powerful rules, rituals, and values that quietly socialize people into the group's ways. Integration reflects the reality that an organization is a complex network of interlinked responsibilities, interests, roles, and relationships. Organizations involve reciprocal benefits and mutual obligations. Integration values help organizations define and attain their common good. The more ethical the culture, then, the easier it is for people to do the right thing when performing their role in their organization.

Cultural values bind people together in business. Business partnerships often rest on trust. A long-standing successful collaboration between a financier or supplier and a company can lead to close friendships. People who work together similarly become friends and their families get together. Integration underlines the importance of the interpersonal side of managerial work and of speaking of companies as communities. Different organizations, Deal and Kennedy have shown, have different cultures and different values.[14] Every company has its own rituals and routines. You walk in the door and know you're at work, you're at Nova, Northern Telecom, Falconbridge, Spar Aerospace, the Bank of Montreal, Padulo advertising, Procter & Gamble, or Bulloch's tailor shop.

The Social Culture of Tailoring

John and James Bulloch, deeply religious Protestants, set up their men's tailor shop in downtown Toronto 50 years ago. For decades they operated a shop where customers could get made-to-measure clothing at a good price—cash, not credit. Bulloch's was a paternalistic, family-run company. While the Bullochs' northern Irish brogue dominated the first floor, the seamstresses and tailors on the second floor were all Italians. They were paid union wages and could get extended family leaves when needed, and still find their jobs waiting for them when they returned.

The relationship of ethics to organizational cultures is not simple. One finds *process cultures* in overly bureaucratic organizations, such as old-line banks and insurance companies, government ministries, and universities, where procedure and rules seem always to have precedence over human concerns and values. Too much integration, however, can mean groupthink. The integrative values in a strong corporate culture can become excessive when, as Mark Pastin has warned, 'A strong culture puts basic beliefs, attitudes, and ways of doing things beyond question.'[15] Overly strong cultures may impose a morally troublesome degree of conformity that inhibits negative feedback and problem-reporting, restricts communication, and discourages informed choice. As a result problems risk growing into crises. The pressure for conformity in such organizations suggests overly strong cultural integration values, where social integration can go too far and breed too much conformity. This may happen in some Japanese corporations. The 'Theory Z' organization, William Ouchi claims, inculcates intimacy, mutual trust, balance, and tradition and a 'holistic concern for people'; but it may also enforce social homogeneity, inhibit feedback, and encourage groupthink. On the other hand, too little integration means every man for himself, anarchic individualism, disintegration of organizational purpose, and disconnection in its community of interests. Neither alternative, too much or too little integration, is morally attractive.

The discussion of the conflict between loyalty and voice demonstrated a tension between personal and organizational values, but neither personal nor organizational values are themselves ethical. What is needed instead is the ethical integration of organizational and personal values. The first step to that balanced integration is found in exchange values. The second step is discerning the link between integration values and organizational culture. Deal and Kennedy classify corporate cultures in terms of the ethically significant norms of risk and feedback. This yields four species of corporate culture, as shown in Table 3.2.

Table 3.2: **Risk, Feedback, and Culture**		
	Low Feedback	High Feedback
High Risk	C1 Bet-the-company	C2 Autocratic/tough guy
Low Risk	C3 Bureaucratic process & procedure	C4 Responsive and responsible

In highlighting the importance of combining high feedback with low risk, the culture matrix is ethically significant. From the first, the core ethic's 'do no harm' maxim stressed the need to minimize risks; and following the risk matrix, one should reduce risks to acceptable or, preferably, optimal levels. The stakeholder map gives internal stakeholders more claim to inclusion in decisions, in direct relation to their risk exposure. In addition, problem-solving requires problem-reporting, and problem-reporting requires open communication inside the company. Communication, the third core value, is reinforced by the maxim to enable informed choices, which, as we have seen, requires organizations to encourage managers and employees to voice critical concerns inside the organization.

So Deal and Kennedy's idea of classifying cultures in terms of risk and feedback is an ethically powerful insight. Let us take each cell in turn. We saw a *low-feedback, high-risk culture* at Barings, and to a lesser extent in Ross Johnson's initial step in putting R.J.R. Nabisco in play on the Wall Street auction block, where individuals clearly seemed willing to 'bet the company'. Perhaps better examples of high-risk, low-feedback cultures are Johns-Manville, which covered up high-risk asbestos health concerns to the point of bankruptcy, A.H. Robin, which ignored medical feedback on the toxic effects of the deadly Dalkon Shield contraceptive device, and more recently, the tobacco industry (see Chapter 5).[16] Jackall's study of the autocratic corporation offered us two examples of the *autocratic/tough-guy culture*, although many might dispute the high feedback description. Other examples of tough-guy organizations with high feedback might be the extensive downsizing at AT&T and Scott under the clearly tough leadership of their CEOs, Robert Allen and Al Dunlap.

A bureaucratic obsession with rules and procedure epitomizes the *process culture*. In such organizations one encounters a legalistic stress on literal compliance with rules and procedures and a nitpicking accounting fervour: penny-wise and pound-foolish. The stress is on process over outcomes, in contrast to the performance orientation of the core ethic. While there is feedback, it is restricted to proper hierarchical channels. A stress on procedures typifies conservative financial institutions, such as traditional banks and insurance companies, for strict controls on records and money flows are essential to their integrity.

Finally, some companies exemplify the *high-feedback, low-risk culture* of the responsive, responsible organization. His earlier experience at General Electric led David Packard to see that bureaucratic committees and paperwork are no substitute for face-to-face communication between managers and employees.[17] So when he and Bill Hewlett founded Hewlett-Packard the door to senior management was always open. All employees, including senior managers, were on first-name terms. Executives walked around the office talking to employees and soliciting their views. Their informal 'management by walking around' style, or MBWA, helped establish trust between management and employees and kept the lines of communication and feedback open. By walking around, executives were not only informed about new ideas, they also heard people's concerns. The result was to help reduce the risks of problems turning into crises. Bill Hewlett put the company's view of employees well:

I feel that men and women want to do a good job, a creative job, and that if they are provided with the proper environment they will do so. It is the tradition of treating every individual with consideration and respect and recognizing personal achievements. This sounds almost trite, but Dave and I honestly believe in this philosophy. . . . There is a feeling that everyone is part of a team, and that team is HP.

In its own way, the story of Prudential Insurance of America involves high feedback and low risk, too.[18] Mark Jorgensen, head of the real estate division, reported to higher management that 26 of 141 properties appraised between 1988 and 1993 were overvalued by more than 10 per cent; this made Prudential's real estate funds appear to perform better than they were. But Jorgensen got nowhere, so he resigned and was replaced. After reports by outside lawyers and auditors concurred with Jorgensen, Prudential came to agree with Jorgensen. The company offered him his job back (but he declined on personal grounds). Prudential's CEO sent a memo to employees praising Mark Jorgensen for his courage in 'standing up for what he believed in' and exhorted employees who come across questionable conduct to follow his example and report it.

All four cultural types are of course exaggerated and oversimplified. They are highly idealized and general. Each has its strengths as well as its weaknesses. A degree of bureaucratic process, for instance, is essential to achieving the proper level of organizational control, confidentiality, and prudence in a bank. On the other hand, an entrepreneurial culture will take risks and encourage feedback, like the tough-guy culture.

Where a culture supports the values and performance norms of the core ethic, individuals should voluntarily choose to conform to them rather than oppose them. The fundamental point is simple. From the ethical standpoint a low-risk/high-feedback responsive culture would seem to be the preferred culture. What emerges from the whole risk/feedback culture matrix is the utter importance of open communication in business. Communication is the oxygen of problem-solving. If problems are to be solved, they must be reported, and people need to be encouraged to report them. This means a culture that encourages feedback, both negative and positive. High feedback, in addition, means early problem reports and a better chance to reduce risks before they reach unacceptable levels.

The above reflections on exchange, integration values, and culture lead to the conclusion that ethical organizations are learning organizations. Today there is much talk of innovative, learning organizations, usually in high-tech firms like Nortel, Spar Aerospace, Hewlett-Packard, and 3M.[19] Such businesses develop by adapting to changing markets and responding to social problems and concerns. A learning organization emphasizes communication and feedback in the service of minimizing risk. It favours ethical problem-solving and vigilant decision-making. It puts the fourth performance maxim, 'act, learn, improve', into practice. The ethical organization, however, should not only be responsive to change, it should also be organized to take responsibility for solving its problems and managing its values. To this end it will also need to codify its ethical values.

Organizing Responsibility

Having established that exchange values and corporate cultures are implicitly ethical, we can now ask how organizations act as responsible moral agents and make moral decisions. Internally, managers must account for their actions to their superiors for their work and for solving the organization's problems. Executives must account for their performance to the board and to the shareholders. Externally, furthermore, corporate officers are being held responsible for their company's actions. Negatively, managers like Peter Noriss, Barings' former CEO, and Michael Milken of Drexel Burnham, and the owners and senior officers of A.H. Robin, tobacco companies, Exxon, and many other firms are being held responsible for corporate misconduct, whether financial fraud, endangering consumer health, or polluting the environment. As the idea of business ethics gains greater social acceptance, organizations more and more are taking responsibility for their actions and for their values.

But how can a corporate entity take moral responsibility for its actions? One answer, in the peculiar thinking of the law, is to treat a corporation as a person.[20] This technical magic wand enables firms to enter into contracts, be sued, and answer for their deeds and misdeeds. In fact, however, corporations are not real persons. Rather, they are more or less well-organized groups of people. It is as relatively integrated and cohesive organizations that companies are held accountable by shareholders, unions, the media, consumers, academics, and politicians, who all praise or blame businesses for their products, profits, and socio-economic and environmental impacts. Demands for social accountability lie at the origin of business ethics itself. Accountability means having to answer to stakeholders, shareholders, management, employees, customers, and governments. It means that organizations take responsibility for their actions and for the values and processes that led them to act the way they did.

Certainly the size and complexity of the large modern corporation cause difficulties in organizing responsibility and accountability. Multinational corporations like Exxon, Standard Oil, and General Motors have assets in the billions and employ tens of thousands of people in many nations. The size of large firms reflects population growth and the rise of even larger, more diverse societies. Modern democracies all measure in the millions, and they are far more accountable than corporations. So size is no barrier to accountability and responsibility. Rather, Peter Drucker claims, the challenges of large societies 'are tasks which only large scale organizations can tackle. The job of this generation is not to abolish large scale organization. It is to make it perform—for individuals, community, and society alike.'

The real issue, then, is how a company is internally organized and managed. This, for many, leads into the debates about corporate decentralization, delayering, and downsizing. Each is relative. In an IBM or GM, decentralized divisions are much bigger than firms with a thousand employees. Decentralization can lead to confused, complex authority, reporting, and communications lines. Where excessive organizational layers are created to signal status and prestige, communication and responsibility may become more difficult. Size, in other words, is not an insuperable barrier to responsibility or accountability, and downsizing, as the next chapter will indicate, can go too far.

What matters is how well the company's decision-making, problem-solving, and communications are organized. In order for management and employees to take responsibility for their corporate roles, they should have the requisite authority, resources, and information needed to discharge their duties.[21] If a group or team like the Blakeley task force takes responsibility for a project, then it needs the requisite authority and resources and should receive the appropriate rewards for a job well done. When responsibilities are shared, who is responsible for which tasks and decisions should be as clear as possible. Just as responsibility needs to be organized, so the company's values also need to be systematically formulated or codified.

Codifying Ethics

Given that organizations have values and that exchange values and corporate cultures are implicitly ethical, then businesses can and should formally state their values. In a large modern corporation this usually involves explicit, written ethics codes, ethics officers, and in-house ethics programs. The aim is to ensure that values are realized in practice. While codes and programs do not an ethical business make, they do help send the message. In fact, ethics codes are a growing management tool in many Canadian firms. Data on 472 Canadian companies in the *Corporate Ethics Monitor* show that about 50 per cent have ethics codes, most for about eight years, and 47 per cent of these have updated their codes in the last two years. Employees have to 'sign off' on such codes in 23 per cent of firms surveyed, while only 19 per cent have internal ethics training. In the 1997 KPMG *Business Ethics Survey Report*, 66 per cent of the 251 corporations responding had ethics codes.[22]

There are several kinds of ethics codes, as research by Max Clarkson and Michael Deck shows.[23] Clarkson and Deck classify codes along a 'control' continuum, from externally imposed rules and requirements to internal, voluntary choice. Following their lead, we can classify codes into three types: value statements, compliance codes, and performance codes. Each serves different purposes. *Value statements*, like mission statements, express the organization's general values and self-understanding and identify its main stakeholders. *Compliance codes* set out regulatory and legal requirements, internal and external. *Performance codes* (or conduct codes) articulate specific commitments to ethical practices in various operational areas, such as employee relations, marketing, environmental issues, international affairs, and public affairs, as well as associated stakeholder obligations, not unlike a general, ethical operational protocol.

The three types of ethics code follow a continuum from verbally espousing values, to externally/legally required compliance, to internally self-enjoined conduct. The subjects touched on in codes take in every aspect of business, from human resources to marketing, environmental, financial, and accounting practices, integrity of records, conflict of interest, and dubious payments.

1. *Value statements.* A simple, uncluttered value statement should do one thing well:

state the company's core values. Such statements also help to legitimize discussion of ethical values in everyday business contexts throughout the organization. To be credible a corporate value statement should be simple and straightforward. It should express a small set of core values. It should make sense as a set. Eighty-three per cent of the companies responding to the 1997 survey had mission or value statements. Manulife, for example, sets out five main values: 'professionalism, real value to customers, integrity, financial management', and 'employer of choice'. Levi Strauss simply says that it provides 'branded casual apparel' and is fair to its employees. Gandalf's statement is equally simple and concrete: 'Gandalf is a company devoted to its customers in providing the best solutions in network infrastructure products and services.'

Vague motherhood statements, in contrast, should be viewed sceptically as moral wallpaper. Lofty corporate visions often do not reflect the real operational values in the organization. It is the 'internal game' or 'ground rules', Eileen Shapiro warns, that decode the real culture.[24] Some corporate statements speak of quality, but the reality may be a determination to get the product out regardless of defect rates. In another, vague talk of customer service really meant 'close the deal and get the order'. In *Fad-Surfing in the Boardroom*, Shapiro expresses concern about overly rhetorical value statements:

> *Mission Statement* 1: A short, specific statement of purpose, intended to serve as a loose musical score that motivates everyone to play the same tune without strict supervision. . . . 3: In some companies, a talisman, hung in public spaces, to ward off evil spirits.

In the research for this book, firms were asked to state and rank their main organizational strengths, values, and the three most important problems they faced.[25] The main conclusion from the 44 firms responding to the survey is that they ranked employee relations first overall, with customer relations a close second. Social relations, technical concerns, and managerial values came third. In the 1997 *Business Ethics Survey* employee and workplace issues came first, with handling company assets (including integrity of records) second and customer relations third.

2. *Compliance codes.* These typically affirm the company's duty to obey the law, comply with regulations, and follow its own internal procedures. Unfortunately, in many organizations morality stops there. It is primarily a matter of complying with the law and the rules. None the less, compliance codes are necessary and important. They facilitate corporate accountability. They are the first step beyond the rhetorical value statements towards performance. But more is needed if businesses are to avoid legalizing ethics. Indeed, many corporate ethics codes, like the Quaker Oats code quoted below, require more than compliance with the law. They call on employees to report problematic situations to management. Adherence to the company's ethics code is a condition of employment at Quaker Oats, as at many other firms.

3. *Performance codes.* These matter the most in ensuring that companies walk their

talk and that ethics permeate the organization. They should be specific enough to guide conduct in most operational areas. Most of the 20 codes received in the survey for this book have implementation mechanisms, such as employee sign-offs, compliance requirements, training programs, advice mechanisms, problem-reporting channels, and support systems. Performance codes help employees to commit to the company's values and put them into practice at work.

Implementing the Ethics Code at Quaker Oats

Quaker Employees: As part of the Quaker team you are required to report any dishonest or illegal activities as well as probable violations of . . . this code. . . . It is grounds for dismissal for any Quaker manager to initiate or encourage reprisal against any person who in good faith reports known or suspected code violations.

Quaker Oats, *Code of Ethics*

Many compliance and performance codes encourage employees to seek advice if they are uncertain about a situation or problem. The usual sources of advice are supervisors, senior corporate officers in human resources, financial and legal officers, auditing, senior counsel, the corporate secretary, and, sometimes, specific ethics personnel. At Bell Canada, Nortel, and Quaker Oats, phone numbers are given for employees to use to make reports or seek advice. Provigo, the Quebec-based wholesale and retail food distributor, gives its code to principal customers and suppliers, who are not only encouraged to read it but to follow it and to inform the company of any violations.

Of the 251 companies responding to the 1997 survey, 40 per cent had a senior manager responsible for ethics, usually a senior executive.[26] Tim Williams, ethics vice-president at Northern Telecom, a multinational corporation operating in 90 nations, sees his job as somewhat like that of an ombudsman who resolves differences among employees with ethical concerns. Managing ethics calls for a tolerance for ambiguity, for instance, in dealing with the matter of gifts in many cultures. Shelley Brown of Prudential Canada sees her work as promoting ethical behaviour through meetings, developing conduct standards, and helping answer specific concerns.

Organizations that are serious about ethical performance train their managers and employees appropriately. To ensure that ethics affect performance, ethical values not only should be codified but also should be integrated into employee incentives, job descriptions, and performance review. Performance depends on learning and training, yet only 21 per cent of the 251 respondents to the KPMG survey carry out any form of ethics training. Similarly, only 19 per cent of the 472 companies surveyed in the *Corporate Ethics Monitor* pursued such training. In addition, this training should be backed up by incentives and performance evaluation. Bell, Nortel, Syncrude, Xerox, and some banks do employee ethics training using cases. Improvement, not perfection, is the aim of ethics codes. And such codes should be bolstered by on-the-job support and incentives for performance improvement.

Summary

Chapter 3 first considered the conflict of loyalty and voice in the autocratic corporation. Instead of feedback and voice, conformity and groupthink reign in such organizations. But *feedback and voice* are essential to reporting and solving problems. The new tales are, firstly, that *exchange values* are preferable to *threat values* as a basis for ethical organizational values. Exchange, especially when understood as reciprocity, shows that economic organizations are implicitly ethical. Secondly, *social integration* helps to design an ethical corporate culture and build on exchange, but integration can become so strong as to engender groupthink, stifle voice, and prevent feedback. Thirdly, the need for voice shows the importance of communication and risk-minimizing values. The result was an ethical classification of corporate cultures. A *low-risk, high-feedback* culture seemed best able to absorb the values and maxims of the core ethic. Finally, corporations need to organize responsibility for their values and ensure their accountability for their actions. To this end they also need to codify their values in three types of ethics codes: *value statements, compliance codes,* and *performance codes.* One evident conclusion emerges from the study of ethical organizational cultures: a business is a community of interlinked interests, a complex network of reciprocal welfares and mutual responsibilities. Following through on this insight, the next two chapters will focus on two key business stakeholders—employees and customers.

Part Two

Journeying Further

The aim of Part Two is to apply relevant aspects of the core ethic to remaining key business functions: employment, markets, and technology, and then to examine the core ethic as it relates to such external fields as the natural environment, social and international values, and planning for the future. Each chapter brings relevant elements of the core values and ethical performance maxims to bear on business questions, whether internal or external to the organization.

Chapter 4

❖

Working Values

Boss: Knock, knock. Employee: Who's there? Boss: Not you any more.
Scott Adams, *The Dilbert Principle*

The pursuit of equity and equal economic opportunity demand a fundamental restructuring of the economy. Everyone who wants to work should have a chance to work.
Lester Thurow, *Zero Sum Society*[1]

Mutinous Waters

Sandro ran a good ship. Most of the officers and sailors had worked for him for years. He paid them all well, and the food was good. When they docked at London or Antwerp and offloaded Aldo's goods everyone got some leave and relaxed. Aldo was always telling people the story of the Tuscan wool workers' strike a few decades earlier. In 1378 they had rebelled for the third time in 30 years—against the low pay and high production quotas imposed on them.[2] Sandro worked his men hard, certainly; but he treated them decently, too, unlike many other merchants and captains over the years. Several centuries later, for example, the sailors on the British ship, the Bounty, rebelled and mutinied against their mistreatment at the hands of its autocratic captain, William Bligh.

The main aim in Chapter 4 is to use the core ethic to clarify the quality of management relations with its major stakeholder, the employees (often including middle management, too). Part I begins with old tales of management/labour hostility, employee insecurity, and a tragic story of deadly work. Underlying all these stories are threat-based employee relations. In 'reactive downsizing', employees, including managers, are seen as nothing but a cost. Staff is shed merely to enable short-term profits and share-price rises or to increase already bloated executive compensation. Nor is merit always the key to reward, when only white males are believed to be competent workers.

Part II explains that new and better tales about equity and inclusiveness are needed. Many businesses respect the primary core value, respect for life itself. In such firms, management works with employees to reduce workplace health and safety hazards to minimal levels, and employees are encouraged to report health and safety problems. Instead of reactive downsizing, firms explore more productive ways of pruning waste and equitably sharing the gains with employees. Equity also leads management to treat all employees fairly in terms of their competence and skills, regardless of race, ethnicity, or gender. Competence matters even more in today's high-tech economy. Knowledge workers can and should be partners in managing technological change and governing the company. Part I, however, begins with the tragic tale of Westray mine.

I Old Tales: Work Risks

Deadly Work

On 9 May 1992 two massive explosions rocked the southwest coal seam of the eight-month-old Westray coalmine in Pictou County, Nova Scotia.[3] Twenty-six miners lay dead.

Clifford Frame, the owner of the Westray mine and CEO of Curragh Resources, had good relations with high-ranking Conservative Party politicians in Nova Scotia and Ottawa. Westray coal from Tory Pictou County would compete with that from Liberal Cape Breton. Although federal bureaucrats did not support the project, Prime Minister Brian Mulroney's government in Ottawa approved an $85 million loan guarantee for Westray. Altogether Frame amassed about $100 million in government subsidies, or $103 for every $100 in mine development costs. From the first he protested that he faced high financial risks.

It was well known from the beginning that there also were high risks of explosion from coal dust and methane gas. In a 9 November 1988 letter Frame warned federal and provincial officials of the potential hazards in developing the coal seam at Westray. He wrote:

> As Westray moves underground in the development of this mine, we are pre-pared to cope with the following problems: unforeseen geological faults, excess of water, poor roof and floor conditions, excess gas, mortality on new equipment, unskilled and inexperienced personnel, underground fires, and others.

Despite Frame's concerns, Westray hired mine managers who did not have the requisite skills. Gerry Phillips, the mine's general manager, for example, appeared to have mis-represented himself as an experienced mine executive with a mining engineering degree; but he had not held a supervisory position in a mine since 1980. A senior engineer responsible for planning the mine had never before worked in an underground coalmine when he took the job. One underground surveyor had failed to qualify for his provincial certificate.

Their mining plan was to produce coal from the highly unstable southwest section of the mine. The 300-foot-deep southwest seam had one of the most dangerous concentrations of methane gas in the world. There were frequent rock falls. In the year before the explosion, Nova Scotia Department of Labour inspectors reported several cave-ins and cases of excess coal dust—one just 10 days prior to the explosion. There had also been a report of waves of methane gas in the southwest area. Roof collapses frequently sent tons of coal down, and the coal dust was over 30 centimetres deep in some areas.

Witnesses at the public inquiry investigating the disaster testified that both Gerry Phillips and Roger Parry (the mine's underground manager) berated supervisors and mineworkers who reported problems in the mine. Parry, Phillips, and Frame, the owner, all refused to speak to the public inquiry, and Frame refused to release his company's internal report on Westray. Colin Benner was the only Westray manager who agreed to testify. He was in charge of the mine for the month prior to the explosion. Benner told the inquiry he could not explain why the explosion occurred, given the legal protections of worker safety in the province and the up-to-date equipment in the mine, and that he had planned to implement a better management and employee safety responsibility system in the mine.

Dan Dooley, a veteran miner, stated at the inquiry that Parry was very upset on hearing that one miner had anonymously reported the unsafe conditions to the Department of Labour. Miners attested that they were under so much pressure to produce that they could not implement well-known safety methods. Production came first for Roger Parry, Dooley said. He reported that Parry said to him, 'Production is number one, not safety. Production, production, production. Stone-dusting was to be done between shifts. Never stop production to stone-dust.'

An expert in mine ventilation, Andrew Liney, told the public inquiry that it would have taken about a week to eliminate the dangerous gases in the mine, via simple improvements to increase the fresh air flow and sealing off a high gas area. This would also have increased productivity; but far less adequate plywood and plastic sheet barriers were used. Liney characterized Phillips's view that there was no methane gas problem in the mine as either cynical or deluded. There were, moreover, many violations of Department of Labour regulations. Liney expressed doubts about competence of the provincial mine inspectors, and their commitment to their job. His 'gut, instinctive reaction' to the situation at Westray was that 'It was an absolutely unbelievable disgrace. But to have achieved quite so many misdemeanours and breaches of regulations . . . and practices contrary to good ventilation practice in such a short period of time in such a small mine has got to be seen as almost unique.'

The day before the explosion, mine mechanic Wayne Cheverie testified that he saw a mine supervisor recalibrating a monitor that shut off a machine when the methane level was too high. The result was that the machine continued to run despite a high risk of explosion. When Cheverie threatened to report the tampering to provincial inspectors and the local media, the supervisor warned him he would be fired if he made a formal complaint.

Mining is skilled work, often requiring extensive training, but Westray miners were sent underground to work in difficult conditions using complex equipment within days of being hired, with little if any training. Many of the miners understood the hazards of coalmining and knew the methods for preventing explosions: neutralizing the coal dust with stone dust and ventilating the methane gas. But, some testified, reporting safety problems usually meant getting a reprimand or a suspension. Complaining to the Nova Scotia Department of Labour could mean losing your job, and Pictou County has a 20 per cent unemployment rate. Like Wayne Cheverie, they needed the work to support their families.

Albert McLean, a Department of Labour inspector, denied finding serious safety violations in the mine. On his visits, he testified, he found the mine basically safe.

McLean said he telephoned a day ahead of his visit, and was accompanied by management as he toured the mine. Perhaps this explains why most miners didn't report problems to him. But some did; five months before the explosion Carl Guptil, a miner, had complained about dangerous methane gas and coal dust conditions to mine inspectors Albert McLean, John Smith, and Fred Doucette. McLean said he was unfamiliar with the new mechanized, highly productive mining technology used at Westray. That equipment raised a great deal of coal dust. On his last visit McLean did not report high methane gas levels, but some miners testified they had complained to him about the gas that day.

Miner Clive Bardauskas alleged that a few months before the explosion McLean told him that the Westray mine was the worst he had ever seen.[4] McLean said he had ordered Westray to dilute the coal dust 11 days before the explosion, but nothing was done to ensure compliance.[5] McLean, the miner testified, also told him that he reported problems about the unstable roof and the use of non-flame-proof farm tractors, but his superiors took no action. He saw other potentially unsafe practices, but management told him they had exemptions from provincial regulations. Wayne Cheverie told the inquiry that McLean told him he, McLean, did not have the power to shut down the mine, and that he blamed miners and supervisors for tampering with monitors and the ventilation system, thereby triggering the blast. Donald Cameron, the Premier of Nova Scotia at the time, blamed the miners for the explosion. Roger Parry and Gerry Phillips have been charged with criminal negligence causing death and manslaughter.

X Factors

Several witnesses at the public inquiry into the Westray mine disaster testified that the risks of an explosion were dangerously high and that employees were not encouraged to voice critical concerns or report problems about highly risky work practices. A high-risk, low-feedback tough-guy culture pervaded the operation. Legalizing an internal business problem, Chapter 3 suggested, is not always the best way to solve it; but when the problem involves serious risks to life or property—unsafe work practices or conditions, dangerous products, fraud—recourse to the law is usually obligatory. In the past, executives and owners were rarely made criminally liable for such practices, but being an executive or director is no longer a protection against criminal charges, especially when employee or consumer deaths needlessly occur. This was the case with the National Film Recovery Systems firm in Chicago.

Homicide at National Film Recovery Systems

In June 1985 Steven O'Neill, Gerald Pett, and Charles Kirschbaum, the senior executives of National Film Recovery Systems, were found guilty by a Chicago court of the murder of Stefan Golab, and were sentenced to 25 years in prison. Golab, one of their workers, died in 1983 from exposure to poisonous cyanide fumes at their plant. Management had not warned their employees, many of them illegal immigrants, of the serious health risks from exposure to cyanide, and they ignored many cases of worker illness. Nor did they make a known, inexpensive antidote to cyanide poisoning available to the workers. They had even ordered workers to scrape the poison warning off cyanide drums.[6]

Culpable homicide in the workplace can lead to a charge of murder and to spending 25 years in jail, as the executives running National Film Recovery Systems found out. Culpability is the legal equivalent of moral accountability. If executives can claim responsibility for the healthy economic performance of their firm, then they must also accept responsibility for operating a workplace that exposes workers to unacceptably high health and safety risks and for refusing to listen to employee reports of health and safety problems. Profit, production, and sales pressures are no excuses for harming or killing employees.

In both cases cited above the hard, adversarial assumptions of the Theory X view of management/labour relations seem to be at work.[7] Theory X assumes that workers are lazy, ignorant, and even criminal, so they must be constantly supervised and watched. They must therefore be 'coerced, controlled, directed, threatened with punishment'. In consequence, management would see employees who voice concerns about health and safety risks or who refuse what they perceive to be unsafe work as self-serving. Too much concern for health and safety, after all, may lower productivity.

In contrast, minimizing health and safety risks is a primary, direct moral responsibility of management. And employees, too, have a role to play in reducing workplace health and safety risks to an optimally low level. Health and safety are direct, shared responsibilities of management and employees, for they are internal stakeholders whose decisions can affect the level of risk.[8] Implementing this seemingly soft, collaborative view of shared health and safety management, the National Rubber Company in Toronto discovered, can result in surprisingly 'hard' pay-offs, such as reduced costs and improved productivity.

Safety and Productivity at National Rubber

Facing a 38 per cent decline in sales, the National Rubber Company of Toronto also was experiencing a high rate of lost-time injuries. The Workers' Compensation Board fined it $500,000 for safety violations. National Rubber employed about 500 people to make such rubber auto parts as mud flaps. The new CEO, Ted Pattenden, felt that all injuries could be prevented and that improving safety might save $1 million in costs. Subsequently, the company scored 68 per cent in a Workers' Compensation Board safety audit in 1993, up from 17 per cent in 1991, and $6 million in losses were turned into a $4 million profit. Product quality and employee morale both improved. When Linnet Getfield twisted her arm separating sticky rubber sheets, technical staff solved the problem by reducing the stickiness of the rubber, making it easier to handle the sheets. The new mind-set encouraged workers to solve other problems, such as quality control; as Getfield observed, 'You don't send out garbage.'[9]

While most companies recognize health and safety to be fundamental moral obligations, many still allow Theory X assumptions to affect other areas of management/employee relations. X factors, for instance, are apparent in the recent trend of companies to engage in 'reactive downsizing'.

Reactive Downsizing

Telltale signs of 'reactive downsizing' are aggressive cost-cutting and extensive lay-offs. It is usually rationalized by the common claim that management has little choice but to downsize because of extensive economic and technological change. Nor does it always work as expected. It may cause more problems than it solves. It may not only involve inequity in distributing costs and risks among the firm's internal stakeholders, making employees and administrative managers bear the brunt of corporate cutbacks; it may also impose more costs on the company than gains.

Management is reacting to widely observed technological and socio-economic changes. They underlie the 'jobless recovery' of the 1990s. Since 1979, Jeremy Rifkin claims, 43 million jobs have been eliminated in the US economy, while only 27 million were created.[10] Canadian and European unemployment rates have hovered around 10 per cent or more for several years. Over the last decade, major firms like IBM, GM, Boeing, Sears Roebuck, and AT&T have undertaken massive workforce reductions, often around 20 per cent. CN Rail, for example, has cut its workforce by two-thirds over the last 20 years. In the last few years Stelco cut 52.6 per cent, Petro Canada, 45.8 per cent, and Imperial Oil, 33 per cent.[11]

Work itself is changing. Not only blue-collar industrial jobs are being lost, but also white-collar jobs: secretaries, cashiers, middle managers, and professionals.[12] The US Dunlop Commission on the Future of Worker-Management Relations discerned a structural economic shift at work since 1960, from full-time to part-time and from high-skilled high-paying manufacturing work to unskilled low-paying service work. Wages have been stagnant, worktime is lengthening, and work is being de-skilled. One of the (intended?) effects of downsizing may be to drive wages down or at least to keep them stagnant.[13] Insecurity is rampant in most 'advanced' economies. Employees and middle managers are often at higher risk than shareholders and executives. The result, the *New York Times* comments, 'is the most acute job insecurity since the depression. What companies do to make themselves secure is precisely what makes their workers feel insecure.'[14]

One factor in the recent downsizing trend is deep and widespread technological change, yielding a much greater productivity in white-collar, managerial work as well

as in industrial labour; but there are signs that the productivity gains are not being equitably shared with employees. This may be due in part to the Theory X assumption that
technology is productive, but labour is not (a theme we will explore in Chapter 6). One
aspect of the technological rationale is that many managers interpret decision-making
and problem-solving primarily in quantitative technical terms. As a result, they focus on
the financial and accounting numbers, such as profits, returns, and share prices, and
tend to treat employees like numbers, too, that is, as dehumanized productivity factors.[15]

Under the Theory X model the first resort of cost-cutting executives is to lay off
employees, including middle managers. Labour is viewed primarily as a cost; so productivity gains mean cutting labour costs. Even though employees and managers are
directly affected stakeholders, they are usually informed late and poorly, if at all, about
job cuts, and they are excluded from participating in the decisions that significantly
impact their interests.

The inequity in distributing the risks of the jobless recovery and the benefits of
improved productivity are apparent when one contrasts relatively stagnant employee
wage levels with fast-increasing executive compensation: salary, bonuses, and stock
options. Such compensation is reaching new highs and often growing faster than corporate profits (from an average of less than US$300,000 in 1965 and $1 million in
1985, executive compensation has now reached $5 million).[16] In 1995 and 1996 com-
pensation for Canada's top 50 CEOs increased by over 100 per cent on the average,
while revenues were up only 25 per cent and 21 per cent respectively and profits
increased 22 per cent and 34 per cent.

Reactive downsizing distributes benefits and risks inequitably among key stakeholders: shareholders, executives, middle managers, and employees. It reinforces the
primacy of shareholder over employee interests. Indeed, downsizing is often rationalized in terms of what is best for the shareholders. Investors' demands for quarterly profit and share increases clearly put the welfare of other business stakeholders at risk, and
these others are *internal* stakeholders.[17]

Executives seem to benefit from downsizing much more than their employees. In
1995, for example, Al Dunlap, CEO of Scott Paper, merged Scott Paper with Kimberly-
Clark. In the post-merger restructuring he let 11,000 employees go (35 per cent of the
workforce), including many administrative managers.[18] In response to Dunlap's cost-
cutting the market value of the company stock increased by $6.5 billion, and after the
downsizing he received $100 million in executive compensation, including stock prof-
its. Or take Robert Allen, AT&T's chairman. In 1995 he cut 20,000 jobs; but he also lost
$7.5 billion in an attempted hostile take-over of NCR in 1991. The employees got the
message: 'The wits at AT&T quip that the chairman would soon fire everyone but himself, and AT&T would stand for [CEO Robert] Allen and Two Temps.' Allen, like Dunlap,
profited handsomely, making $5 million over and above his $3.3 million salary when
the stock went up in response to the downsizing.

Since most executives usually have large positions in the company stock they stand
to benefit from any share-price increases in response to downsizing (but there are con-

cerns about possible dilution due to high executive stock ownership).[19] Stock markets, moreover, tend to react to lay-offs positively. On 8 March 1996 the New York stock market plummeted 171 points (3 per cent) in response to the news that employment figures had improved dramatically. Wall Street repeated the performance one month later. Underlying this inequity in executive and employee compensation (including administrative managers) is the Theory X assumption that the firm's primary obligation is to its owners, not its employees. It was succinctly stated by Robert Bertram, director of the Ontario Teachers Pension Plan: 'Corporations don't exist to create jobs. The No. 1 priority is creating shareholder wealth.' Such views have led many to question whether modern corporate capitalism develops at the expense of its (former) employees.

'Vision Quest' at Chase Manhattan Bank

In 1993 Chase Manhattan Bank went through a cultural change process that stressed 'customer focus, respect for each other, teamwork, quality, and professionalism'. Then Chase merged with the Chemical Bank. As a result of the merger Chase cut its workforce 28 per cent by 1995, while its assets grew by 38 per cent. Managers referred to laid-off employees as 'saves', i.e., savings to the company. One manager bragged of the fact that he had laid off hundreds without a lawsuit. Those still working feel insecure and dispensable, not to mention cynical, suspicious, overworked, and stressed out. Many take an industrial view of the job, punching in at nine and out at five: 'It's pay me, don't play with me.' Others have learned to spot where the safest jobs are and (re)train to get them. There are even signs of survivor guilt among those remaining. As one employee put it. 'I ran into B today. He wasn't offered a job and is devastated. . . . Any sense of joy I felt I had at being on the "Schindler's list" of employees who've got jobs with our new parent corporation has been wiped out by experiences like this.'[20]

Doubts about the benefits of such aggressive, reactive downsizing are growing. It is often driven, Eileen Shapiro warns, by management fads such as corporate restructuring, total quality management, and re-engineering.[21] Slavishly accepting such ideas can lead management into damaging the core productive competencies of the organization. Such ideas have led many managers to overdo cost-cutting and lay-offs. Over 300 large US firms have tried re-engineering. They dropped over 300 employees on average; but less than half of the companies gained market share from the exercise.

In fact, reactive downsizing has its costs. Severe, frequent, or global cutbacks, even in an environment of revenue or share-price decline, sometimes do not yield improved business performance. One 1992 study showed that only 37 per cent of firms that reduced costs succeeded in increasing profits, 17 per cent enhanced their competitiveness, and 40 per cent increased productivity.[22] Employee morale declined in 83 per cent of the firms. The Chase Manhattan experience was not uncommon. The old saw is true—cutting costs does not increase sales, as Peters and Waterman warned over a decade ago: 'The numerative analytical component [in conventional management rationality] has an in-built conservative bias. Cost reduction becomes priority number one and revenue enhancement takes a back seat.'[23]

One problem is the assumption that cutting labour costs is the highway to productivity gains.[24] This leads management to see massive lay-offs as the solution to their productivity problems. And lay-offs can involve costly severance payouts and lost employee knowledge. Remaining staff, as a result, can be overworked and stressed out, and lowered morale may hurt productivity. The result of excessive lay-offs and cost-cutting, *The Economist* warns, is 'the anorexic corporation'. An anorexic company is so constricted and overstressed that it lacks the capacity to respond to upturns. Even a call for voluntary retirements may lead to the loss of valuable employees, as a Connecticut insurance company recently discovered.

Unexpected Volunteers at Connecticut Mutual Life
At Connecticut Mutual Life Insurance company executives, seeing lagging sales and profits (not losses, note), asked for voluntary resignations to help cut costs. They expected only 475 employees to opt for the generous offer. Instead, 1,650 did. Since management had not previously announced which jobs would survive, they later had to engage in a rearguard action to persuade half of the volunteers to stay because their skills were needed. Ultimately 890 left, including 220 whom management did not want to lose. Uncertainty about the future was one of the main reasons for the massive rush to leave, not the generous buy-out. As Shirley Brown, a middle manager who took the offer, said, 'A lot of people are fed up with the way they have been treated. They have been screwing around with everybody's job for years.'[25]

The Connecticut Mutual Life story shows the need for careful management when cost-cutting and downsizing are being discussed. When workforce reductions are necessary, they should be carefully and sensitively managed. What is needed is not harsh, reactive downsizing, but careful pruning and equitable sharing of productivity gains.

II New Tales about Equity and Inclusion

Pruning and Sharing

Downsizing, Patricia Norman explains, means reducing costs in order to improve the business performance of the company. It requires an intelligent, ethical problem-solving approach. Cost-cutting should not be treated as a panacea for all business performance problems. Where it is indicated, it should be used with care. Responsible cost-cutting is like careful pruning—one prunes a healthy, overgrown tree; one does not uproot it. Pruning should be directed at any unproductive costs, employees, and divisions, high debt, poor investments, excess capacity, or inefficient plants. Cuts should be measured—a scalpel is preferable to a shotgun. Pruning should help improve overall business performance and contribute to corporate renewal.[26] Even healthy firms at times may need to lose excess weight; but cutting off a limb and starving the brain are something else entirely. When lay-offs are unavoidable, employees should be supported and helped to find new jobs, as was done at Stroh's Brewery.

Supportive Lay-offs at Stroh's

In 1985 Stroh's had to close its Detroit brewery and eliminate 1,159 jobs. Peter Stroh, the president, wanted the company to do all it could to help them. Management announced the closure four months in advance. A liberal severance package was developed with union support, including an extensive outplacement program and transition support. An intensive job development campaign involving Detroit area employers generated 1,400 job offers. Peter Stroh personally wrote and called companies to help former employees, and 70 per cent of the workers used the program. The rest chose to retire. As a consequence all salaried employees and 98 per cent of hourly workers found jobs. The program cost Stroh's US$1.5 million, plus $600,000 in state government support (about $2,000 for each worker), far below the much higher costs of public assistance for the unemployed.[27]

Where cuts are needed all the options should be considered: cutting overtime; reducing/rearranging the workweek; reducing benefits and wages; days off without pay; redeploying and retraining employees. These should be discussed with affected employees, who, as much as possible, should be informed and given choices from a set of options. Throughout the pruning process the employees' welfare and that of the organization should be aligned so that the process is fair. Cuts in compensation and worktime should be distributed equitably, starting in the executive suite and moving down, not the other way around. Instead of, say, laying off 10 per cent of the employees, companies should consider reducing overall worktime or expenditures by 10 per cent, as Hewlett-Packard did.

Hewlett-Packard's Nine-Day Fortnight

In the 1970s a decline in orders led Hewlett-Packard executives to consider a 10 per cent cut in output and payroll; but they wanted to avoid lay-offs. After discussing the problem with employees the company decided to distribute the cuts evenly across the company. In their 'nine-day fortnight' strategy everyone, executives and employees alike, took every second Friday off, with a 10 per cent cut in pay. There were no lay-offs.[28]

Just as Hewlett-Packard's nine-day fortnight exemplified equitable risk-sharing when pruning, so equity should also lead to sharing the benefits of technological change with employees.

New technologies, especially in electronic telecommunications, have enabled the automation of much administrative work and the elimination of many management positions. Increased productivity is, of course, a solution to business problems of achieving profitability and growth. But the solution brings with it a new challenge, that of sharing productivity gains with employees. The time has come to implement that solution, for employees are allies of management. All belong to the same community of interests. If the enterprise commits to them over the long haul, workers will likely respond in kind.

Given the extensive change facing business today, the old Theory X ways should be discarded. As the costs and problems of reactive downsizing show, these old ways represent an inadequate response to change. Instead of reactive downsizing, proactive management of technological change is needed, contends Sylvia Chrominska, executive vice-president of human resources for Scotiabank.[29] Management, she feels, must manage change over the long term and not merely react to short-term market trends. Technological change means changes in employees' work and in how their work is managed. The very notion of a bank branch is rapidly changing, as are financial services and institutions. VanCity Credit Union, for instance, is developing a new, completely electronic 'virtual bank' system.[30]

Good management, Chrominska believes, cannot afford simply to substitute new technologies for good employees. The bank must prepare to redeploy and retrain its employees. A strategic approach is needed, for, she adds, 'Planning is the key. . . . A well-managed company manages the size and needs of its workforce well. . . . A company needs to determine what human, technological and financial resources are needed to meet the needs of all its stakeholders—customers, employees, shareholders, and suppliers.' In Chrominska's view, companies that avoid downsizing tend to plan better and are commited to employment. They not only avoid short-term fixes, they tend also to develop their business strategies around their core strengths, communicate well, and support skills training.

If business is to mitigate the harsh effects of the jobless recovery, then management needs to respond creatively to technological change.[31] Some of the responses are not that new. Some were tried over 60 years ago, in 1932 during the Great Depression. The US government and the union movement called on business to shorten the workweek. Large firms like Sears Roebuck, Standard Oil, and Kellogg's voluntarily complied. Kellogg's moved to a 30-hour week and also increased hourly wages by 12.5 per cent, to offset the loss of two hours each day. W.K. Kellogg said a few years later:

> This isn't just a theory with us. We have proved it with . . . five years' experience. We have found that with the shorter working day, the efficiency and morale of our employees is so increased, the accident and insurance rates are so improved and the unit cost of production so lowered that we can afford to pay as much for six hours as we formerly paid for eight.

Today the move to a four-day workweek has already begun. Bell Canada has reduced its workweek to 36 hours from 38 after discussions with its union.[32] This move prevented the lay-off of 13,500 installers and technicians. In 1993 Volkswagen in Germany reduced its workweek from 37 hours over five days to 29 hours over four days, and workers took a 10 per cent pay cut. The company needed to cut costs, but it also chose to share the productivity gains it realized from technological change and automation. The response was greater efficiency, improved morale, some new hirings, and increased returns. Such approaches not only share productivity gains from technological change equitably inside the firm, they also help keep people employed. The time has come to combine efficiency and equity, as Lester Thurow has long maintained.

> ### Equity and Productivity
> Decisions about economic equity are the fundamental starting point for any market economy. . . . The time has come, however, to admit that the pursuit of . . . equal economic opportunity demands a fundamental restructuring of the economy. Everyone who wants to work should have a chance to work.
>
> Lester Thurow, *The Zero Sum Solution*[33]

Equity at Work

Equity and fairness should not only govern cost-cutting and productivity decisions, they are also required in hiring and evaluating employees. Equity implies Theory Y, which reverses the human relations assumptions of Theory X. It is natural, Theory Y holds, for human beings to employ their energies in work and play. People tend to accept responsibility and support an organization's objectives to the extent that they are recognized and rewarded for their efforts. Intelligence and imagination in addition are widely distributed among the population. Theory Y suggests that the capacity for 'creativity and ingenuity is widely . . . distributed in the population.' It is not restricted to White males. The core principle of employment equity, then, is simple: it is to recognize a person's competence and excellence, regardless of irrelevant social characteristics, such as ethnicity, race, religion, age, gender, or sexual orientation. The aim is to combine Kant's respect for persons with good management sense—hiring and keeping the best people, for their good and for that of the company. Prejudice and discrimination, in other words, don't pay.

The evidence, however, shows that women, ethnic and racial minorities, and the disabled are overrepresented in lower levels of the organizational hierarchy and in lower-paying, less skilled jobs, and are underrepresented at the management and executive levels.[34] Women, for instance, represent only about 2 per cent of the directors on boards of Canadian firms, 11 per cent of executives, and about 20 per cent of administrative or middle management, while they compose about 37 per cent of the workforce. Unions are more equitable, inasmuch as women make up 25 per cent of union executive positions. What is true for women generally is even truer for the other target groups.

But companies are committing themselves to employment equity: 40 per cent of the 472 companies surveyed by the *Corporate Ethics Monitor* in the last six years have employment equity programs. Equity provisions in corporate conduct codes usually stress the need to link equity with the merit and ability of the individual. The aim of employment equity and human rights programs, then, is to treat people fairly, recognize their competence, and respect their dignity as persons. It is not to override merit and disregard competence. To define equity hiring targets abstractly, in terms of the percentage of women, ethnics, or other target groups in the general population, is to court disaster. Unavoidably, merit and performance will be ignored. And to the extent merit is ignored, charges of reverse discrimination become credible.

On the other hand, equity and merit are partners, not opponents. To the extent that companies care for equity in employee relations they will walk their talk and develop equity programs. This means setting the achievable targets over time. To demand that a chemical refinery set a target of 50 per cent women in hiring chemical engineers is neither realistic nor desirable, for it would entail radically lowering competence requirements. Unfortunately, at present female chemical engineers are not available in larger numbers (although their ranks are growing). So equity targets should be set within an achievable range, as defined by the proportion of each group with the requisite skills in the appropriate regional labour pool. On this understanding equity is possible. The Levi Strauss company, for instance, has long hired and treated Blacks equally with Whites in its plants in the southern US.[35] Indeed, women, ethnic and racial minorities, and homosexuals are represented throughout the company in numbers much higher than in the average North American firm. Ethnic minorities have gone from 18 to 36 per cent of Levi Strauss management, and women from 32 to 54 per cent of management.

A full human rights approach must also cover problems of racial and sexual harassment. Harassment policies should be clearly defined, involve fair procedures, and use trained, impartial personnel in the adjudication process. Such policies should avoid any taint of political correctness. Responding to harassment allegations in timely and fair fashion clearly requires a delicate combination of human relations and legal skills: sensitivity to the complainant and fairness to the accused, respect for the evidence, and a commitment to confidentiality. Those handling complaints should be scrupulously fair, impartial, and trained in evaluating evidence. In addition, clear definitions of harassment are needed. Vague, ambiguous complaints about unwelcome behaviour or language, verbal abuse, or a hostile work environment may involve highly variable perceptions. Allegations of sexually or racially improper language or conduct may arise from misunderstandings, personality conflicts, short tempers, impatience, performance problems, or hidden agendas, as well as from sexist or racist prejudice. Informal but confidential discussion or mediation is often the best way of dealing with impropriety problems and with unsubstantiated allegations.

On the other hand, when faced with serious, independently confirmed charges of ongoing verbal or behavioural abuse or prejudice, a more formal quasi-judicial response is indicated. An impartial investigation and hearing may be needed. Thus, a charge of sexual extortion (i.e., trading hiring, raises, or promotions in exchange for sexual favours) should require due process. There should be an impartial tribunal that operates with the presumption of innocence, the right to question one's accuser, and the need for independent confirmatory evidence. Human rights staff should therefore be trained in investigatory procedures, the handling of evidence, mediation, impartiality, and confidentiality. They should not be appointed simply because they come from a gender, ethnic, or racial advocacy group.

Response to complaints should be timely, but the process should not go on forever. There must be closure. Publication of any harassment charge by any party to the action should be grounds for reprimand and even dismissal. The mishandling and premature revelation of harassment charges have led to lawsuits for defamation of character.[36] Importantly, as Provigo's code of ethics notes, people found innocent of any such charges should be treated as innocent. People's reputations, after all, are at serious risk. Where serious abuse is found to have occurred, a heavy sanction should be imposed. If the problem is even more serious—that is, a matter of sexual or physical assault or of hate propaganda, for example—then one is dealing with a possible criminal matter, and management should consult with security officers or the police.

Finally, favouritism is the other side of harassment. As Bell's ethics code states, 'showing undue preference for someone (i.e., favouritism) is just as unethical as discrimination.' Instances of sexual/racial harassment and favouritism should be treated as employee relations problems. Both management and employees should collaborate in identifying and solving such problems and in preventing their recurrence. The main underlying concern is equity. All employees, including executives, should be treated fairly and offered equal respect as persons, so that in their work they can develop their competence and skills to the highest degree.

Intelligent Work

The core value of communication and the 'problem-solving' and 'act, learn, improve' maxims all lead one to assume that work requires a variety of practical, socio-economic intelligences. Equity requires companies to recognize and reward competence. The core ethic, then, offers a value system for adapting to the growing high-tech knowledge economy. The belief that work involves intelligence is an idea whose time has come. Knowledge workers reflect the importance of technological innovation in the modern economy. Ours is an age in which knowledge has itself become a key productive force. Work is becoming ever more knowledge-intensive; and knowledge work has spread beyond a small coterie of experts and managers into the workforce itself. The growth sectors of Canada's economy, Nuala Beck contends, are telecommunications, healthcare and medical technology, and scientific instrumentation.[37] In each, work demands a high degree of knowledge, of professional, scientific, or managerial expertise.

Robert Reich has come to a similar conclusion. He distinguishes three types of work:

❖ routine productive labour in the old industrial system

- ❖   low-skill, low-paid routine services
- ❖   high-skill, high-paid symbolic analysis.[38]

This last involves the key skill of identifying and solving problems at work and the brokerage-like social skill of productively linking problem identifiers and solvers. These skills involve a variety of intelligences, from the interpersonal communication skills of helping customers identify and solve their problems and the linguistic/logical intelligence of symbolic analysis to the practical, administrative, and social intelligence of brokerage and exchange.

Knowledge workers are a productive asset much more than a cost. Companies should therefore invest more in developing employee know-how and intelligence. This is implicit in the Theory Y assumption that people want to improve their skills. So management should develop employee knowledge to its productive optimum. This approach also reflects a centuries-old ethic of excellence, of developing human skills to their optimum performance levels, implicit in Aristotle's ethics.[39] Knowledge workers can, and therefore should, have more control of their work and related decisions about work. The knowledge economy, in other words, calls for a more equitable and participative corporate community.

In commenting on the shift to a knowledge-based 'post-capitalist' economy, Peter Drucker offers a picture of a decentralized knowledge-based organization characterized by problem-solving and teamwork.[40] There are three different kinds of team, Drucker suggests. Firstly, there is the rigid structure of the baseball team or classical orchestra or bureaucratic organization. Each player has his fixed role and script. Each is externally, and centrally, co-ordinated with the others. Next is the decentralized and structured, but highly adaptable, task force team. These are found in hospital emergency ward triage teams and in Canadian-style hockey teams. All members can adapt their role to fast-changing situations and even temporarily shift into other players' roles as the situation demands. Nurses and physicians confronted with numerous critically injured patients have no time to quarrel about hierarchy, regulations, or paperwork. Team members shift with the task at hand, and the team is task-focused.

Toyota's Cambridge, Ontario, plant, which opened in 1986, appears to be one of the most innovative and efficient in Canada.[41] A 'guiding principle' in Toyota's value system is to 'foster both individuality and teamwork'. Executives do not have special offices set apart from everyone else. All employees, managers included, wear the same outfit. Employees are chosen in part for their communication, social, and teamwork skills—in recognition of the broad socio-economic range of human intelligence required of them. Work teams are encouraged to identify and solve problems and to improve their performance.

Finally, Drucker adds, even more flexibility is found in the jazz combo. Here the players signal each other and control performance as a group. The Blakeley plant task force had to invent its script as it went along, like a jazz combo, and was flexible and task-focused, like a triage team. As companies try to respond to rapidly changing technologies and markets, they, too, may need to develop equally flexible teams. Such highly adaptive teams require equally flexible workers, who must therefore be educated and intelligent. Indeed, Drucker concludes, in a knowledge economy:

> *The educated person now matters.* He or she . . . needs to be able to bring his or her knowledge to bear on the present, not to mention molding the future. . . . intellectuals see the organization as a tool . . . to practice their specialized knowledge. Managers see knowledge as a means to the end of organizational performance. Both are right.

Opportunities for Participation

The old, X-based adversarial approach to management/employee relations not only risks employee health and safety and leads to reactive downsizing, it also excludes employees from sharing in the benefits of organizational productivity and growth. Yet today's knowledge economy puts different demands on firms to preserve and enhance their core competences by maintaining the requisite levels of highly skilled employees. This requires management to be fair in recognizing each person's abilities, regardless of gender, ethnicity, etc., and to develop and enhance the skills and intelligence of their employees. Those skills need to be broad and flexible so that employees can be redeployed to meet changing demands resulting from changing markets and new technologies.

More Knowledge Workers, More Employee Participation

The most successful large corporations . . . offer job security, and internal development of people. . . . They provide endless opportunities for employee participation. They regard their people as members, not mere employees. . . . Knowing the critical importance of the corporation's long-term well-being, they [are committed] to the business they are in instead of pursuing strictly financial objectives with only the stockholders in mind.

Kenichi Ohmae, *The Mind of the Strategist* [42]

The rise of a highly productive, knowledge-based economy requires greater employee development and participation in organizational decision-making, as Kenichi Ohmae argued in 1982. To the response that such a strategic approach does not apply in today's lean and mean economy, one must reply first that 'mean' means adversarial. Making enemies of your employees is neither ethical nor intelligent. Lean, however, means careful pruning, and sharing the productivity gains from pruning throughout the organization. Productivity is compatible with sustaining the organizational community of interests. The fewer layers the organization has, the more possible it is for its employees to share in information and decision-making at all levels. Finally, the more intelligent and knowledgeable employees are, the more they can contribute, and indeed the more their contribution may be needed.

One already finds various forms of employee participation in decision-making in various firms. Canadian Tire, for example, has an employee/management committee with 14 elected employee representatives and four senior management representatives, who meet monthly to discuss a wide variety of issues that affect employees and the company.[43] Lincoln Electric of Canada, a subsidiary of an Ohio company, has a similar employee/management advisory council, composed of eight elected employee representatives, one for each division, and the company president. Both companies also have employee profit-sharing plans. About 9 per cent of the 472 firms surveyed by the *Corporate Ethics Monitor* had profit-sharing plans for all employees, while 32 per cent had executive stock plans.[44] In the US pension funds and employee stock ownership plans together give workers ownership of US$150 billion of US company stock, as well as an indirect say in company decisions. One finds employee stock ownership in about 12 per cent of the 1,000 largest US firms. But more is required.

Employee ownership can and should go beyond stock ownership. Various ethical values support the increased inclusion of employees at all levels of company decision-making, up to and including the board. These values include:

- ❖ reciprocal welfare and exchange
- ❖ equitable sharing of risks and benefits
- ❖ informed consent
- ❖ healthy stakeholder relations.

Such an approach is part of an already developing transition to the more inclusive corporate property system mentioned in Chapter 1. In Germany, for instance, employees are involved with management at the highest councils of companies in both board and executive policy-making.[45] Worker representatives sit on company supervisory boards, as well as on management/worker councils throughout the organization, and discuss problems affecting employee welfare, such as production issues, workplace design, and shift work.

A common criticism of allowing employees on the company board is that this creates a conflict of interest when the board deals with employee relations, wages, and benefits. But many directors are open to criticism on the grounds of interest conflicts, such as lack of arm's length dealing with the company, and board rules already provide for disclosing such conflicts and excluding oneself from the relevant votes. (CEOs, for example, do not vote on their own performance evaluation or compensation proposals.) In addition, the ethics codes in many companies already have provisions warning employees against conflicts of interest in dealings with customers, suppliers, and competitors. So companies already have the tools for handling conflicts of interest.

Unfortunately, North American corporations typically do not consider more participatory reforms until the business faces imminent demise. Only as a last resort do most firms even consider the possibility of an employee buy-out. The result is that the development of more inclusive corporate governance systems is done in haste, under pressure, and often linked to extraordinary concessions and risks for all involved. The 3,500 workers of CP Express and Transport, for example, were divided about buying out the company because it also involved a three-year wage freeze and loss of dental and hospital benefits, and the company faced increasingly tough international competition.[46] None the less, 56 per cent approved the buy-out, for the alternative was more lay-offs. The buy-out was the less untenable option.

In 1992, on the other hand, Dofasco, the steelworkers' union, and the New Democratic government of Ontario negotiated a $500 million employee buy-out to save Algoma Steel of Sault Ste Marie from impending bankruptcy.[47] This represents the largest experiment in employee ownership in North America. It was extensively deliberated beforehand and reflected a co-operative partnership among Dofasco, the previous owner, management, the steelworkers' union, and the provincial government. Algoma employees had to accept a 14.5 per cent wage reduction, no bonuses, and one week less of paid vacation for two years. Some resented the concessions and others were angry that the union had earlier put them through a four-month strike as well. In addition, 1,600 of the 5,100 jobs (31 per cent) would be cut over the next five years. As Jack Ostroski, president of the steelworkers' local at Algoma Steel, commented, 'There's no blueprint. A lot of this is ad hoc, and the first two years are critical. . . . We've shaken up Bay Street, and now we'll be under a microscope for a while.'

The employees at Algoma Steel now have a 60 per cent controlling ownership of the company and they elect five directors. The employees have the power to approve a board decision to sell the company, to invest outside the steel industry or the local community, or to issue shares that would dilute their holdings below 50 per cent. The union had to accept the need for professional managers, who themselves had to learn to respect workers' knowledge and skills. There is a joint labour-management corporate steering committee, consisting of four union reps, the CEO, three senior executives, and a representative of non-union employees. Their mandate is to discuss workplace issues, retraining, restructuring, and worker participation. Joint management/worker task forces were created on cost reductions, workplace redesign, and technology.

Although the new company began with a debt of $800 million, the Algoma experiment seems to be working. Over $400 million has been invested in technological modernization, making Algoma a low-cost, continuous-improvement, high-quality, market-oriented steel producer. It has become the most profitable steel company in North America. In 1994 sales increased by 23 per cent, net income was up to $127 million, bank debt was down to $67 million (from $103 million in 1993), and capital investment doubled. A new high-quality steel strip mill is being developed. Steel shipments are up 5.6 per cent.

Algoma was the third such buy-out under the Ontario NDP. The others were De Havilland aircraft in Toronto—now part of Boeing—and the Spruce Falls mill in Kapuskasing (which has just been taken over by Tembec, with employee approval). All in all, new, more inclusive forms of employment and work are developing. They not only transcend the old ways in which business was organized, they also highlight the limits of traditional unionism, as Leo Girard, the Ontario director of the United Steel Workers union, has acknowledged:

> My dad believed workers had made the wrong trade-off when industrial unions were created in the 20s and 30s. We needed to have influence on the methods of production, but we traded off our entitlement to a share of the control of the workplace for management . . . tolerating unions. . . . It's not enough to say you don't trust management. . . . How can we make the economy stronger and improve the lives of workers? That's the challenge.

Summary

Chapter 4 showed that (1) fundamental ethical principles of care for life should govern management/employee relations. (2) Instead of aggressively downsizing the workforce in unthinking reaction to inevitable technological change, and then increasing executive compensation, management should prune waste carefully, keep productive employees, and share the productivity gains with them. Fairness should govern the distribution of risks and rewards in the workplace. (3) With the rise of a knowledge economy, firms need to develop their employees' skills and problem-solving intelligence to the fullest, regardless of gender, ethnicity, etc. (4) Employees and administrative managers should be invited to participate appropriately at all levels of organizational decision-making and governance. In all these ways of using ethical problem-solving, businesses can improve the quality of employee relations and enhance the internal community of interests on which their productivity rests. The next chapter expands that community to include that most important business stakeholder, the customer. The following chapter will expand on the theme of technological change.

Chapter 5

Marketing Values

The consumer isn't a moron; she's your wife.
David Ogilvy, *Confessions of an Advertising Man*

What the customer thinks he is buying and what he considers 'value' is decisive—it determines what a business is, what it produces and whether it will prosper. . . . It is to supply the consumer that society entrusts wealth-producing resources to the business enterprise.
Peter Drucker, *The Practice of Management*[1]

Shipping Trade

Sandro hoped that the European traders would pay well for the finished cloths, spices, and metals Aldo was sending them, and that he could find good quality wool for Aldo to sell to the fussy Tuscans. He hoped to get to London early in the season, before Aldo's competitors got the best of what was on offer. Aldo had given Sandro a 'letter of advice' stipulating the terms of trade. It stated the amount and value of the goods being shipped, and also instructed Sandro on the price and other terms of sale, as appropriate to each port. Since the market for spices, cloths, and the other goods often fluctuated in response to demand and to rumours of supply problems, such as ships lost to piracy and storms, prices often varied. So Sandro had to be skilled in selling Aldo's goods to the merchants in the ports, and in buying new supplies to ship back. If they were successful he, Aldo, and Cosmo would reap some profit. Then the compagnia *could move on to newer enterprises in the trade fairs in northern Europe.*

The aim of Chapter 5 is to disclose ethics at work in market relations. It begins with the old story, described in Part I: produce cheap, sell dear, manipulate consumer impulse, advertise misleadingly, and maximize your profits. Milk the consumer for all he is worth. Design dumb for housewives. It gets worse, as the story of the tobacco industry suggests: hook the consumers to a product that puts their health at risk. Once more that fundamental ethical value, life itself, is at issue.

Nor does classical economics tell us a moral tale. In free markets, it says, people make rational, free choices based on their self-interest and complete information. Consumers are not stupid, but buyers should beware of vendor tricks. Commercial practices are often not that respectable. Markets involve puffery, haggling, and making deals. Salespeople certainly are not moral heroes. Advertising is more like rhetoric than straightforward information. Indeed, there are so many ads, many feel, that mass marketing has commercialized society and distorted fundamental social values.

On the other hand, in Part II core values are seen to reside in the heart of the market relationship, whether a modern urbanite is buying a TV or an Asian Bedouin is buying a horse. There is a tacit ethic in the marketplace involving reciprocity, communication, and exchange. Creating and keeping customers is the purpose of business. Entrepreneurs need to offer their customers good value and not subject them to health and safety risks or misinform them. Exchanges involve reciprocity, a mutually (not necessarily equally) beneficial deal for buyer and seller alike. As markets grow larger, however, producers need distributors, suppliers, retailers, and advertising agencies to reach consumers, just as Aldo needed Sandro's help to ship and sell his goods in distant markets. So ethical values must influence product distribution, marketing and promotion, and the delicate relationship between advertising agencies and their business clients.

I The Old Tale: Buyer Beware

Smoking and Mirrors

In 1964 the office of the US Surgeon General announced that smoking causes lung cancer.[2] In 1966 cigarette packages and advertising in the US were required to carry messages warning that smoking involves serious health risks. In the early 1980s the Surgeon General reported that about 350,000 Americans per year died from cigarette-related cancers and lung and heart diseases. In 1988 he declared that cigarette smoking is addictive by the same standards that apply to illicit drugs. It was the top public health issue in the US. In February 1994 the US Food and Drug Administration (FDA) announced that it was considering regulating cigarettes as a hazardous drug. In August 1996 President Clinton supported the FDA proposal.

Large tobacco companies like Phillip Morris and R.J. Reynolds (the tobacco side of R.J.R. Nabisco) gain significant profits from selling cigarettes. As Warren Buffet, the financier, explained, cigarettes are a good investment: 'It costs a penny to make. Sell it for a dollar. It's addictive. And there's fantastic brand loyalty.' At a 1962 conference Addison Yeaman, a lawyer for Brown and Williamson, stated that 'We are in the business of selling nicotine, an addictive drug effective in the release of stress mechanisms.' Ross Johnson of RJR said it well: 'Of course it's addictive. That's why you smoke the stuff.' In their spring 1994 testimony before a US House of Representatives subcommittee, industry executives denied that they manipulate nicotine levels to ensure that smokers feel the relaxing effect of nicotine, despite FDA research showing that this is done. They also continued to deny that cigarettes cause cancer or heart disease, claiming that only a statistical correlation has been proven. A.W. Tisch, CEO of Lorillard Tobacco Co., said to the subcommittee, 'We have looked at the data and the data that we have been able to see has all been statistical data that has not convinced me that smoking causes death.'

True, a statistical correlation is not a causal explanation, but as early as 1952 epidemiological studies by Dr Richard Doll had identified a known carcinogen, benzopyrene, in cigarettes. In 1953 Dr Ernst Wynder's team at the Sloan-Kettering Cancer Center in Manhattan demonstrated a causal relation between the tar in tobacco smoke and cancer. In 1958 the British American Tobacco Company funded research showing that benzopyrene was released in tobacco combustion. German research identified a whole set of even more carcinogenic compounds named nitrosamines. At the 1962 industry conference Dr S.J. Green, research vice-president at British American, argued that 'We should adopt the attitude that the causal link between smoking and lung cancer was proven, because then . . . we could not be any worse off.' By the early 1970s industry labs had identified the health hazards in detail, confirming the earlier findings that smoking was addictive and caused heart and lung diseases.

Since the 1960s tobacco industry concerns about the health risks of smoking inspired research projects into safer, 'health-oriented' cigarettes with less tobacco smoke and minimal biological effects. One sought to isolate the dangerous elements in cigarette smoke and separate them from the rest, e.g., via filters and chemical additives. Another project studied how to deliver a satisfying nicotine dose while reducing the harmful chemicals in smoke, and other studies isolated the hazardous chemicals in cigarette smoke. But their attempts to develop a safe cigarette failed; there were taste problems. The lower the nicotine levels, the less the enjoyment or relaxation effect.

In 1974 British American's lab was closed. Industry executives were concerned that making safer brands would implicitly acknowledge the health risk in smoking. This might make it difficult to justify the sale of the other brands and weaken their legal position. In 1980 Dr Green resigned from British American and went public with his concerns about the health risks of smoking. His widow says he was disillusioned when the company said his research, being the intellectual property of the company, could not be published. In a BBC interview Green charged the industry with abdicating its moral responsibility: 'The position of the tobacco industry is dominated by legal considerations. It has retreated behind impossible, perhaps ridiculous, demands for what in PR terms is called scientific proof—usually the first reaction of the guilty.'

In fact, almost as soon as the industry was aware of the health risks and the addictiveness of smoking, the issue was legalized. The lawyers took a very different view from that of the scientists. For over 30 years tobacco industry lawyers opposed attempts to make the industry legally liable for the addiction and health effects of their products (in contrast to conventional practice in both the automobile and pharmaceutical companies). In 1985 Brown and Williamson lawyers decided that sensitive research documents on health risks should be removed from the company files and sent to England. The papers included legal department comments on research projects showing industry awareness that smoking is addictive and dangerous to one's health, as well as research into attitudes of young females to smoking. The legal advice was that industry research should be kept confidential to protect the companies from litigation. After 400 lawsuits the industry's legalistic strategy is clear. It is to deny any causal links, to delay, to exhaust the plaintiff, and never to settle or to break ranks. The average suit takes 10 years and costs over US$10 million. It is not evident how such a legal strategy can be reconciled with the ethical obligation to reduce a product's health risks and inform consumers of such risks.

Following its public relations campaign strategy, the industry has argued since 1954 that there is no proof that cigarette smoking causes cancer. In 1971 Brown and Williamson's publicity campaign had the Orwellian label, 'Project Truth'. Author Philip

Hilts terms industry P R 'the disinformation machine'. Its aim has been to sow doubt in the minds of the public. One of the stated objectives of the 'Project Truth' P R campaign was 'To expose the incredible, unprecedented and nefarious attack against the cigarette [as] the greatest libel and slander ever perpetrated against any product in the history of free enterprise.' Another was to ask how this 'libel' could be reconciled with the right to free speech.

Since the early 1970s cigarette advertising has been banned from North American radio and T V and most magazines, and smoking is banned or restricted in many restaurants, workplaces, and public buildings. The industry, Hilts reports, has long targeted its ads at adolescents to gain new smokers, and with effect. Cigarette marketing campaigns have been criticized for misleadingly associating smoking with young healthy people, as in Philip Morris's 'Marlboro Man' campaign, or with a sophisticated lifestyle, as with R J R's Dunhill brand.

But now the battleground is shifting. The first major legal defeat for the industry came when Antonio Cipollone won his 1984 lawsuit over the death of his wife, Rose, from smoking. Cipollone's lawyers had unearthed internal industry documents showing that the tobacco companies were aware of the health risks of smoking, but had none the less misled the public with ads presenting its products as safe. To date 22 US states have launched a $4 billion lawsuit against the major tobacco companies and trade associations and the Hill and Knowlton advertising agency. They are seeking damages to reimburse them for the health care costs of treating smokers' diseases. The tobacco industry, in the view of the attorney-general of Texas, 'has violated every standard of ethical business practice'. The US Justice Department is considering perjury charges against tobacco company executives for testifying to the congressional subcommittee that nicotine is not addictive.

In September 1995 the Supreme Court of Canada ruled the ban on tobacco advertising unconstitutional. Five of the nine Supreme Court judges agreed with the industry view that banning all tobacco advertising was an excessive means to the end of public health and a violation of the right of free speech of corporate 'persons'. The industry also repeated the old claim that there was no causal connection between tobacco advertising and increases in smoking. Less intrusive means, the Supreme Court majority felt, should be found to achieve the public policy ends. In effect, this decision put greater store in treating corporations as persons with the right of free speech than in reducing the health risk to real people resulting from the commercial promotion of smoking. The consequences are enormous, Alan C. Hutchinson of the Osgoode Hall Law School contends: 'Outside of legislative control, discipline is left to the corporations' consciences, the dubious discipline of the marketplace and hamstrung elected leglislators.'

On the other hand, the Chief Justice, speaking for the minority, saw the advertising ban as justified. Companies, he argued, would not spend $75 million a year if they believed that tobacco advertising did not work. He noted that advertising dangerous products merited only a low level of constitutional protection, on a par with hate-mongering and pornography, and that the profit motive is irrelevant to free speech. The minority opinion held that informing Canadians of tobacco's addictiveness and its proven health hazards was a higher public policy objective, and noted that much advertising is directed to youth. In late 1996 the government of Canada reintroduced legislation to regulate tobacco more strictly and to restrict advertising. In the US the tobacco industry was seeking a compromise with the government that would include new FDA rules aimed at preventing teen smoking, allow the sale of tobacco products to continue, and involve some degree of protection from lawsuits.

In March 1996 the first major crack appeared in the legal armour of the tobacco industry. Liggett Group Inc., a small US cigarette company accounting for 3.6 per cent of the market, broke ranks with the industry and agreed to settle its share of the large class action lawsuit brought against the tobacco industry. Liggett will pay 5 per cent of pre-tax profits to a maximum of US$50 million per year for the next 25 years and will hand over revealing internal files. Its decision reduces its legal fees and the risk of bankruptcy, and makes the company a more attractive acquisition.

Product Liability

The tobacco story raises core ethical concerns, notably serious health risks in using a product and informed choice about those risks. It shows what can happen when the market turns into a threat system. It also suggests the old amoral view of business as somehow apart from morality. Products are termed goods, which implies that using them should be safe. Producers therefore have a primary responsibility of 'due care'. They are morally responsible, and legally liable, for the health, safety, and environmental risks of their products and for informing consumers about those risks. Threat, as Boulding held, discourages trade. So producers should reduce such risks to minimal, acceptable levels. *Caveat vendor* is as valid as *caveat emptor*.

Market relations are assumed to involve an exchange of benefits between buyer and seller, not a benefit for the vendor and a major health risk for the consumer. Sellers and producers are both assumed to have reduced product risks to minimal, acceptable levels and are responsible for communicating them to buyers. Consumers also need clear, standardized information about product materials, uses, and risks. Hence the need for warnings about the health risks and addictiveness of smoking on cigarette packages. Nor should dangerous products be promoted in misleadingly attractive fashion. Hence the need for advertising bans on tobacco products. Consumers should be able to assume that the ordinary, responsible use of products that producers and vendors offer on the market does not impose unacceptable risks on them, but that is precisely the risk from the normal use of cigarettes. Thus, it might be argued, they should take reasonable precautions to foresee and reduce such risks. That would mean not smoking—not purchasing or using the product at all.

Another unspoken assumption is that consumers are also responsible for the normal use of a product, so moral responsibility to minimize risks in the marketplace is shared between producers and consumers. 'Liability' is the legal term for moral respon-

sibility. Under US law a business is 'strictly' or absolutely liable to foresee even consumer abuse of its products. This is also a major reason for the high costs of civil litigation. In large modern markets in many nations, with millions of consumers of diverse
cultures, it is not always possible for a company to foresee all the potential misuses of
a product, or even all its uses.

Consumers are responsible, too, for using the product as designed. Risks, like
gains, are a shared responsibility. You shouldn't pour Drano into juice glasses.
Automobile firms, as Ralph Nader has shown, are responsible for making cars as safe as
possible within the accepted costs, price, and marketability, and assuming adequately
informed consumer choice; but automakers are not responsible for the wild, dangerous
antics of cowboy drivers. Nor are personal computer manufacturers responsible for the
criminal activity of hackers. Many companies, like Procter & Gamble, take product safety seriously. P&G responded to reports of health problems with its new super-absorbent
tampon in timely fashion. Ethics and economics are interconnected.

Relying on Procter & Gamble

In 1980 the US Centers for Disease Control in Atlanta reported that many women
using super-absorbent tampons were experiencing a previously unknown, potentially fatal 'toxic shock syndrome' of high fever, rash, diarrhoea, and drops in blood
pressure. Procter & Gamble's Rely tampon constituted 71 per cent of the tampons
involved. The company immediately withdrew the Rely tampon from the market and
advertised widely to warn women of the risks. Procter & Gamble worked with
research and health agencies to catch additional cases, and for several years supported further research.[3]

Amoral Markets

In market exchanges both parties benefit. The core value of reciprocal welfare is respected. But classical nineteenth-century economics had a very different, amoral, view of
markets.[4] Firstly, everyone is assumed to be a 'rational egoist', singlemindedly concerned with maximizing his/her own self-interest; secondly, rational choices involve
perfect, and costless, information; and thirdly, any social costs are not borne by the firm,
for they are external to the market. Let's take each assumption in turn.

Certainly one must question the belief that everyone is a rational egoist, singlemindedly focused on maximizing self-interest, or that all economic behaviour is in this
sense 'rational'. While much human behaviour is purely self-interested (and some is
altruistic), an equally sound hypothesis would assume that most social behaviour
involves linking the interests of several actors, that what is good for parents is good for
children, that what is good for sellers is also good for buyers. Reciprocity, far more than
self-interest, makes the world go round. Entrepreneurs project and figure out what
products or services consumers might want and then provide these for them, at a price.

Consumers purchase the products or services because they need or want them, and in so doing help the entrepreneur to make some money and perhaps even a profit. Then both come back to the marketplace and do it again, and again.

Pure self-interest does not explain these transactions, for self-interest leads to win/lose threat relations in which one party maximizes gains at the expense of the other. Rather, market exchanges work because each party reaps an adequate, satisfactory benefit, not because each maximizes his or her own gains. Markets, as Boulding said, involve win/win exchange values. The welfare of the seller is reciprocally interlinked with that of the buyer. That is why markets are so successful as social binders. Each exchange is a temporary, short-term mini-community of interest. Mutual benefit explains why people keep repeating the experience.

Secondly, classical economics makes the extraordinary rationalist assumptions that buyers and sellers have 'perfect knowledge' of the market, that each knows what all the other players are doing and all the relevant prices and goods being exchanged at the time. Perhaps this was possible in Adam Smith's small, provincial eighteenth-century Scotland. It certainly is not in today's mass markets. The core ethic, in contrast, brings us down to earth again, in stressing the value of communication and informed choice. Both imply that effort and intelligence are needed for buyers and sellers to obtain and communicate appropriate market information and then make informed market choices. If perfect knowledge were the case, there would be little need to discuss ethical problem-solving, informed choice, uncertainty, learning, groupthink, or the problems of information communication and access. The assumption of the core ethic is that limited information is the human norm.

One must therefore question the classical view that information is somehow instantaneously and costlessly communicated through markets. This view does not explain why so many companies invest so much time and money in trying to obtain, maintain, and communicate information. Indeed, gaining access to and control of sensitive business information is an important dimension of market competition.[5] Black intelligence, or corporate espionage, is a growth business, and security a growing business risk. Firms spy on their competitors, steal their trade secrets, modify their patents, and hire a competitor's executives. Take, for example, the story of José Lopez, a former senior General Motors executive, hired by Volkswagen in March 1993 as a managing director; GM was very concerned that Lopez gave VW proprietary GM information about new product plans, innovative factory design, and parts purchasing procedures. GM initiated legal proceedings against VW and Lopez (who has now left VW). While there are recent signs of a negotiated settlement between the companies, the principle is clear. Since proprietary corporate information is an extremely valuable commodity, ethically and economically, some firms require employees to agree not to join competing firms for a specific period of time after quitting and not to entice others to join them at a competing firm.

The third problem with classical economics is the social costs of businesses run on amoral, 'rational egoist' principles. Self-interested agents will internalize their gains and externalize the costs of their activities. As a result, the public will find itself paying for the socio-economic and environmental impacts of 'rational' business people. To avoid such embarrassments classical economics abandoned all pretence of science and talked about an 'invisible hand' that magically produces the commonweal out of self-interest.

Modern societies and the core ethic have taken a different view of the matter. Society will seek to have those costs borne by the organizations that caused them. This has happened. It is what led to the rise of the social and welfare state since the turn of the century. Through various social mechanisms, self-interested individuals, businesses, and all citizens share the costs of essential services like education, health care, unemployment, bankruptcy, urbanization, policing, and so on. Capitalist economies have prospered in the bosom and with the support of the welfare state in which its markets operate; and business is a social as well as economic activity. It is better, therefore, to view markets in terms of reciprocity and exchange, for they are social, and implicitly ethical, relations. This socio-economic understanding of markets is much more productive, socially and scientifically. It discloses an implicit ethic in market relations, as well as an affinity for economics deep in the heart of ethics.

II New Tales: Market Ethics

We have seen that products are meant to be beneficial, not dangerous, and that economics should recognize the importance of reciprocity in markets. Now to explore the complex ethics of marketing itself. Marketing is central to a company's success, for it facilitates sales and yields revenues. Part II picks up the theme of an implicit ethic in market exchanges, starting with the notion of 'good value' in products and services, moving to the marketing network of suppliers, distributors, and ad agencies, then concluding with advertising.

Good Value

An old market tale is to produce cheap and sell dear. In a phrase, *caveat emptor*. A better tale, one implicit in the market exchange ethic, is that of *good value*, a competitive combination of price, quality, and service.[6] Quality and service can be as important to the customer as price. It is the value of the whole package that satisfies customers and makes entrepreneurs successful. Entrepreneurship involves insight into what consumers want and a willingness to take productive risks with one's capital to offer it to them. It requires an ability to create a new wealth by understanding markets and offering good value to consumers. In small or technical markets value may be easy to determine, but in large, open, mass markets involving millions of people, market values rarely stand still for long. Often they cannot be ascertained with pinpoint precision. Nor is good information always available when needed.

Entrepreneurs create customers by seeing the market from the customer's perspective. Each must project and consider the other's interests, however minimally, whether a modern city store is selling a VCR or a Mennonite farmer is buying a horse. Good businesses want to give customers value. In mass markets value varies with perception as well as supply and demand. Typically, both seller and buyer benefit from the exchange; both sides must feel they have a good deal. The extent to which they are satisfied reflects a convergence of their interests, not just the satisfaction of separate self-interests. Selling is intrinsically social, a form of exchange.

There are, of course, tensions between producer and consumer interests, the two poles of the market relationship. Where the price is too low and quality or service too high, a business cannot reap adequate returns; where the price is too high and quality or service too low, the consumer is not satisfied. In the first case lowballing the price or underestimating the quality or service level is the problem. In the second, self-interested profit-maximizing clashes with quality and customer service. Some entrepreneurs, to be sure, seek to manipulate consumer wants and make a lot of money, fast. But they violate the exchange ethic of the market, and they put future sales at risk. Also, as Gordon Sharwood claims, this creates openings for the competition.

A Consumer Society Wants Ethics

The movement from a production-oriented society to a consumer-driven society means that ethics are enforced on producers increasingly by the customer just refusing to buy again. . . . if you don't treat customers right they don't come back again and it is harder and harder to make money off a one-time hit in today's society.

Gordon Sharwood, CEO, Sharwood Company[7]

To succeed over time, businesses need to provide good value to customers. The term 'customer' is itself ethically significant, for good value in the sense of customer satisfaction reinforces the custom of buying good products and services. As companies grow, Peters and Waterman maintain, they should remain 'close to the customer'.[8] They should do what they know best and 'stick to their knitting'. Good value, good products, and good services are common elements in business ethics codes. Nortel sees customer satisfaction as a way of gaining market leadership, while for Provigo this, along with good service, is 'the cornerstone of the company'. To the extent that customers are happy, the exchange relationship may continue over time. When customers feel loyal to firms and come back for more, both parties gain some economic security, a key hedge against risk in today's unpredictable marketplace. Entrepreneurship means care for quality, experimenting with a new product, and then learning from one's mistakes to improve it. This concern for excellence reflects the 'act, learn, improve' ethical maxim.

Equity in customer relations contributes to good value, too. Trade has long involved a tolerance of socially diverse customers. Sellers who treat people unfairly because of their gender, race, ethnic group, or other difference will lose their business. They do not make those customers happy, as the story of good value in women's shoes shows.

Good Shoe Values

For decades women who wanted comfortable, supportive dress shoes could not find them. The beauty myth led most shoe companies to offer women only fashionable, narrow, pointed high heels; but they cause bunions, calluses, corns, and pinched nerves. The average North American woman's foot is a size 8; but the best selling shoe size was a 7-1/2. Over 90 per cent of orthopaedic surgery on feet is done on females. Women in business often have to spend over $200 to get dress shoes with low heels. Today the shoe industry has finally caught up with the customer and now offers shoes for women that both support the feet and look good.[9]

Unfortunately, equity is not always part of trade. Racism, too, has been a problem, leading many businesses to refuse to serve Blacks in the US and South Africa. But differences of class, sex, religion, culture, race, or age are immaterial to making a sale. Indeed, by enhancing the ethic of tolerance implicit in all trade, retail firms and banks across North America have learned to adapt to diverse consumer preferences in ethnically rich urban neighbourhoods. They also employ socially diverse staff who understand their customers.[10] Consumers can bring ethics into the marketplace, too. EthicScan Canada publishes *The Ethical Shoppers Guide* to help consumers make ethically informed purchases. It uses a wide set of ethical indicators, such as employee relations, environmental performance, community involvement, and international relations. The *Guide* profiles 1,200 products sold by 83 companies in Canadian supermarkets.[11] In large mass markets, most enterprises cannot themselves promote, distribute, and sell their goods directly to consumers. Instead, they must enter and use marketing networks.

Ethical Marketing Networks

Ethical values should govern not only the buyer/seller relationship but also the quality of relations between different businesses in a marketing network—for example, a network of suppliers, distributors, retailers, and advertising agencies. Marketing refers to activities designed to distribute and promote products and enhance sales.[12] The marketing network extends the community of interests of the company beyond its internal stakeholders: owners, management, and employees. Success in the marketplace often hinges on how well producers, suppliers, distributors, retailers, and ad agencies all work together. In mass markets producers rarely sell directly to buyers, so the quality of these relationships is critical.

A producer's *relationship with suppliers and distributors* is focused on marketing and sales, in contrast to the purely financial concerns of an investors' partnership. Good suppliers can make a firm successful by reliably supplying quality goods on time, according to specs, and at a good price. Good supplier/purchaser relations are often close and can last for years. When times are tough, suppliers may offer their partners credit. Trust is essential to good supplier relations, too, Nortel's code adds, for the company depends on its suppliers to respect any confidential information shared with them as part of their business relationship. Tenders put out for supplies should be at arm's length, and all suppliers should be given an opportunity to bid on the contract without any favouritism, side deals, or kickbacks. Normally, suppliers should remain free to sell to the purchaser's competitors. Unless a close partnership is developed, the relationship is arm's length and contractual.

Problems can arise about gifts and questionable payments in such relationships. While small items like business lunches, pens, and the like are usually acceptable gifts, especially in a long-standing healthy business relationship, many company's conduct codes prohibit large gifts or special payments to suppliers, distributors, and retailers, kickbacks for shelf space, or other special 'considerations'. Nor should distributors exert undue influence over a reseller's choice to handle a product.

Advertising and marketing are the last stop in the marketing chain prior to actually selling a product to a consumer. Given the size, scale, and diversity of the modern marketplace, most businesses need the help of marketing and advertising professionals to communicate with their consumers or understand their preferences. Since many firms do not have this kind of expertise in-house, they may contract with independent advertising and marketing agencies for their services. Designing effective advertising for large markets tends to involve considerable expertise in marketing, rhetoric, ad design, and communications media. That is why businesses need advertising agencies to help market, advertise, and sell their products. Many ads are the product of the creative work of an advertising agency for a business client. Clients range from business and governments to charity and interest groups. Full service agencies, such as McKim Media and Padulo Integrated in Canada, and Saatchi and Saatchi and Ogilvy Mather internationally, provide a wide range of services to their clients:

* ❖ market research
* ❖ marketing campaigns
* ❖ design
* ❖ public relations
* ❖ media consultation
* ❖ advertising.[13]

Many agencies specialize in specific services, product lines, media, or markets. In the UK agencies are independent professionals who control marketing and advertising campaigns, but in North America the relationship is contractual and clients have more say over advertising. The agency has to satisfy the client's needs, and the client should respect the agency's competence.

Agency/client relations can be delicate and embroiled with clashing egos. Clients pressure agencies to produce results.[14] Creative people in agencies may be taken up in the cleverness of their work, or so arrogant about their own expertise they may neglect the client's need to improve sales. On the other hand, clients who think they are marketing geniuses, or who nitpick each detail of an ad campaign, can undercut the work even of a good agency. Agencies cannot afford to let a client pressure them into a bad campaign, for it can hurt their reputation and affect their business. This matters, for advertising is a highly competitive world.

Differing Agency/Client Perceptions

Agency A in a Canadian city had an $8 million account for promotional campaigns for a multi-levelled mall. Its client was C, a well-known retailer that had the 'anchor' store and owned the mall. A's campaign was so successful that D, a competitor of C, approached A about a $20 million retail campaign contract. While A's CEO saw no conflicts, he consulted C, who perceived a conflict. C wanted to continue working with A, but A was free to take D's offer. And did.

One major ethical concern in agency/client relationships is conflict of interest, as the above story shows. Clients often seek competitive bids from agencies, while agencies are always soliciting new clients. When clients seek competitive bids and estimates, the estimates for preparing a proposal or a campaign should be well founded and not subject to arbitrary increases. Sensitive business information needs to be respected by both parties. Such reports are the property of the client, and for the client's use only. Competition between agencies should not extend to plagiarizing someone else's ideas. However, creative people are constantly collecting competitors' ads and mining them for ideas. So cross-fertilization and sharing of ideas is inevitable.

Advertising Values

The main aim of advertising is to communicate product information to consumers in order to influence consumer perceptions of the goods on offer and to engender sales.[15] Ads try to persuade consumers to increase consumption of existing products or to try new products. They are also used to locate prospects, reinforce brand loyalty, and stimulate demand. Companies usually need to engage advertising agencies in the appropriate market network to promote their products or services. It is important to note that advertising is a business cost, just as agency/client relations are contractual business relations. Advertising itself, then, does not directly increase profits.[16] Nor do ads themselves close sales, but it is sales that bring in returns. If ads are successful but too costly, they may not yield profits. So success depends on the cost and effectiveness of one's advertising.

While much commercial advertising may be tasteless, the time has passed when anyone can say it is unnecessary and keep a straight face. On the other hand, advertising involves a variety of ethical values:

❖ honesty in communication
❖ the tension between effective advertising and consumer choice
❖ the commercialization of social relations

❖   equity in marketing to diverse cultures
❖   social advocacy advertising.

Advertising is a form of commercial communications; but, one must ask, can ads provide consumers with adequate information about products? And should they? In response, trustworthy communication and informed choice are fundamental ethical and market values. Advertising is like a seller's opening position in negotiating a sale with potential consumers. It assumes certain classic negotiation values. No one, for instance, is expected to be totally open about his/her own negotiating strategy or to communicate all sensitive information, and everyone knows it, or at least should know it.[17] On the other hand, everyone is expected to negotiate fairly and in good faith. Where negotiation is still customary in closing a sale, the aim for both parties is to position themselves within a common agreement range where both will be satisfied with the final deal. That is what trading classically was all about. This includes advertisements; for advertising, with all its imprecision and ambiguity, can be seen as an opening move in this classic trading game. Since prices today are usually not negotiable, advertising focuses on other matters: product values, consumer perceptions, and image. For advertising to remain a trustworthy form of communication, however, it needs also to inform the consumer adequately. Good ads send clear, trustworthy messages about the products on offer. In this way they help reinforce the mutual benefit, exchange ethic of the market. Advertisements, in effect, should communicate good value.

Good value in turn requires informed consumers. In its *Business Conduct Code* Moore Corporation, a global leader in business forms, labels, and direct marketing, stresses the need to communicate honestly with customers and not to misrepresent products, services, or prices, even when stressing their benefits. Similarly, Xerox's *Business Conduct Guidelines* call on salespersons to explain fully to the customer the product capabilities, contract terms, and additional operating costs.

Don't Insult the Customer's Intelligence

You insult [the customer's] intelligence if you assume that a mere slogan and a few vapid adjectives will persuade her to buy anything. She wants all the information you can give her. . . . Good products can be sold by honest advertising. If you don't think the product is good, you have no business to be advertising it. If you tell lies, or weasel, you do your client a disservice.

David Ogilvy, *Confessions of an Advertising Man*

Good ads, therefore, should contain significant material information about the products or services on offer, depending on the genre and media used. They involve what Rick Padulo, CEO of Padulo Integrated, a Toronto full-service ad agency, terms 'clarity of offer'. In fact, much advertising is informative, such as classified newspaper ads and retail flyers. Mail order, classified, catalogue, and retail advertising must contain enough information to sell the product. In such cases what ads communicate may be as important as how they say it.

Advertising that is deliberately deceptive, distorts product information, or misleads consumers crosses the line of both moral and market acceptability.[18] Dishonest ads reinforce public cynicism about advertising. If consumers find that products or services do not live up to the original offer, they become even more sceptical of advertising. Moreover, advertisers and agencies are liable for fraudulent or misleading claims in the ads they produce.

Consumers like bargains, i.e., discounts on regular prices. But misleading sales ads are a common concern.[19] Ads stating '40% off regular prices' are misleading if the regular price is inflated or never demanded. Endorsements should come from people who actually use the products. Research surveys cited must be substantiated, and product or service limitations should be disclosed. Another problem is putting a few loss-leader goods on sale as bait to attract consumers into stores, and then switching them to higher-priced goods once the few low-priced sale goods are gone. Also, some stores have seemingly endless liquidation sales. On the other hand, retailers note that controlling the volume of goods sold in a sale is sometimes difficult, but they can control the length of time of a sale. Most retailers, such as major department stores, combine high regular prices with low prices on sales and promotions, but others (e.g., discount houses and Wal-Mart) prefer an everyday low-price strategy.

To deal with such problems the Canadian Advertising Foundation has formulated its own guidelines for honest advertising for its member firms. It covers accuracy, clarity, disguised techniques, price claims, 'bait and switch' tactics, guarantees, comparative advertising, scientific claims, testimonials, health and safety, and advertising to children. The code's main principle is clear: 'Advertisements must not contain inaccurate or deceptive claims. Advertisements must not omit relevant information. . . . All pertinent details of an advertised offer must be clearly stated.'[20]

Direct marketing by mail, phone, and other media is one way in which businesses can directly contact the consumer. Such mailings, however, annoy many consumers. I have received some self-proclaimed 'free' offers asking me to send money for handling, mailing, and the like. The most memorable was one about my guardian angel.

Angelic Marketing

Out of the blue, in the spring of 1996 The Angel Inspiration Center wrote to tell me about their 12-month 'free trial' of 'a very special report for you called "Vincent Di Norcia's Guardian Angel".' In her supporting letter, Elizabeth Marvelles, the project monitor, writes, 'I have discovered how you can make immediate contact with your Guardian Angel. . . . You are not buying your Special Report on how to contact your Guardian Angel. You are only trying it out.' However, in order not to buy my report I am asked to send my angel $48 ($39.95, plus shipping, handling, and taxes). Perhaps the meaning of 'free trial' changes as one approaches angelic levels of being? Having done some theology in my day, I forced myself to decline the offer in favour of less costly and more trusted routes to the divinity.[21]

The Angel Inspiration Center is not, it seems, a member of the Canadian Direct Marketing Association. The Association has a code of ethics for direct marketers, which deals with most of the concerns consumers have about direct marketing, notably accuracy of claims and allowing consumers the option of refusing unsolicited mailings (merely by contacting the Association and asking to be delisted from its members' promotions).

Certainly, a degree of exaggeration or puffery is common in marketing and advertising.[22] Puffery usually involves vague general claims like 'the right car for the right person'. Consumers generally understand that such claims are not meant to be literally true. The context is persuasive communication, not technical or scientific communication. Selling has always involved the arts of commercial design and persuasive rhetoric. Rhetoric is as old as humanity and is a normal, expected element in advertising. It is, after all, both natural and intelligent to put one's best image forward.

Advertising is a commercial form of rhetoric, designed to persuade people to accept one's message. Rhetoric, as classical philosophers held, is morally legitimate. The commercial use of persuasive rhetoric in the service of commerce is at least as morally respectable as political and legal rhetoric. The exchange values of the marketplace are largely preferable to the threat values implicit in much legal and political rhetoric. As rhetoric, however, advertising stresses its persuasive purpose over its information content. Persuading others to choose your products or to agree with your views is legitimate, as long as you have a good case and you present it honestly and fairly. This is what classical rhetoric taught. It differed from advertising mostly in its field of application. Aristotle and Cicero assumed that rhetoric was to be used in the public arenas of politics and the law courts.[23] A lawyer's role was to present his client's best case to the court and get his client off; political rhetoric served to persuade citizens and legislators and other interested parties of one's political views or policy preferences.

Similarly, an advertiser's job is to persuade consumers to buy particular products and services. Persuasive ads are meant to be effective, to sell the goods on offer. But can ads be such effective persuaders as to undermine consumer freedom?[24] Until the early 1970s, for example, the tobacco industry pitched a lifestyle and peer group image cigarette advertising campaign to adolescents between 11 and 17 years old.[25] The campaign successfully persuaded many of them to take up the smoking habit. But young adults 17 years of age and over resisted the ad campaign. So the effectiveness of advertising may be related to the impressionability of the consumer. John Kenneth Galbraith has argued that advertising is so pervasive in our society that it renders consumers dependent on the manipulations of advertisers and marketers. On this reading advertising is effective, and consumers are neither informed nor free. Marshall McLuhan agrees: 'Effective advertising gains its ends partly by distracting the attention of the reader from its presuppositions and by its quiet fusion with other levels of experience.'[26]

Certainly mass markets are diverse and complex information environments. Today there is an unending barrage of commercial messages in all manner of places, even painted on buildings. In developing a campaign, clients and agencies discuss client needs and creative ideas. Advertising messages are so numerous and products are so technically complex that William Leiss speaks of 'high intensity markets'. Consumers, as Leiss observes, are 'faced with the problem of continually reinterpreting their needs in the context of a rapidly changing array of goods and services.' Indeed, many in the industry speak of 'media clutter'. Given that clutter, advertising campaigns are designed to draw the consumer's attention to the product or service and differentiate it from the competition. A main aim of any mass marketing campaign, then, is to develop a 'unique selling proposition' that penetrates the chaotic mass media information environment and gets the consumer's attention.[27] Then, hopefully, it might sell the products and services on offer.

True, the unending barrage of bewildering information makes informed consumer choice difficult. None the less, to say that advertising controls consumer choice and that consumers cannot develop an intelligent response to the information barrage is exaggerated. Talk of perfect knowledge or total consumer sovereignty or total dependence is too abstract. Contemporary consumers are all too familiar with the constant stream of ads, and they are sceptical. They switch media, disregard ads, and zap the commercials all the time. Evidence of their scepticism shows that consumers are wading through the clutter and making relatively informed and intelligent choices.

On the other hand, advertising has commercialized modern mass culture. Modern commercial information environments raise concerns about their capability of reinforcing consumer desire to shop for unnecessary products and about distorting social values.[28] Markets in themselves set no limits on growth, affluence, wants, or needs. They reinforce insatiable consumption and a 'possessive individualism' in which people's identity is tied up with their property. Mass markets, money, and advertising together create a market society in which human problems are defined and solved in purely economic terms. One consequence, Karl Polanyi observed, is 'the running of society as an adjunct to the market. Instead of economy being embedded in social relations, social relations are embedded in the economic system.'

However, some critics of advertising sometimes erroneously think that ads should communicate complete information about the products being advertised—a variant of the perfect knowledge assumption of classical economics. A related error is to assume that information can be presented artlessly, without attention to the design of the message, the medium, or the information environment in which it occurs. On the contrary, all forms of communication, not just advertising, involve design values and some degree of persuasiveness. Effectively communicating any message involves editing, quality design, and style. Messages should be designed to fit the genre and the medium used to transmit them. Rhetoric stresses the way one communicates: style, design, genre, and tailoring the message. All have an impact on the effectiveness of any communication. The relative weight of design and style values to material information varies with one's purpose in sending a message and with one's target audience. Scientific communications, for instance, involve different style, media, editing, and design choices than do literary, interpersonal, bureaucratic, or commercial communications. So the idea that selling should involve purely cognitive information without any rhetoric or design is mistaken.

Advertising, being commercial communication by design, naturally gives great weight to stylistic and media design values, as well as to product information. Good design supports the 'clarity' of what is on offer, without dishonesty, and attracts the attention of the consumer. The complexity and clutter of today's mass media advertising environment, moreover, demand simple, arresting, well-designed ads, often without the detailed information that many rationalistic critics deem morally obligatory. In addition, message design, style, and rhetoric change with the times and the markets.[29] Baby boomers had a sense of entitlement, but today's so-called Generation X feels disenfranchised, apprehensive, and sceptical. They are more focused on useful products than on hype or image. Thus straightforward, no-frills ads that stress product value work better with them.

Many ads raise questions of taste and social values. Ads, David Ogilvy said, should be 'well-mannered' but not 'boring'.[30] Advertising should avoid gender and cultural stereotyping as part of the sales pitch. Advertisers and agencies are increasingly sensitive about gender, racial, and ethnic issues. The gender stereotype in many ads offers the beauty myth of young, attractive, powerless women, in contrast with strong men always in control.

Some advertising, however, does use dubious gender and racial images to promote goods.[31] And advertising to impressionable children and adolescents is a morally sensitive area, as the tobacco industry has discovered. Certainly, attitudes to nudity vary greatly. Context matters a great deal. What is acceptable in *Cosmopolitan* may not be appropriate on prime-time TV. Many people found the sexually suggestive poses of adolescent youths in recent ads for Calvin Klein jeans and perfumes offensive, but US sales of Klein's jeans doubled in apparent response to the ads. Several US retailers pressured Klein to pull the ad campaign, and the company did. Calvin Klein himself said he did not see the ads as pornographic. Rather, they were 'about modern young people who have an independent spirit and do the things they want to and can't be told or sold. None of that came through.'

Despite some aggressively competitive ads, no comparative commercial ad even comes close to the harsh negative tone of recent US political advertising. During the November 1994 US congressional election campaign, negative political advertising was criticized for being fraudulent, racist, and sometimes for using McCarthyite smear campaigns.[32]

Political Ads: Don't Call It Advertising

This is filth. If a reputable corporation produced advertising with the same exaggerated claims for their products and then failed to deliver . . . their executives would be fined or led to jail in handcuffs.

Ketchum Advertising Agency, San Francisco, November 1994

Finally, advertising often promotes social values. Social issue campaigns have spawned some creative ads, from Saatchi and Saatchi's famous pregnant man ad in support of birth control to the Harvard School of Public Health's 'Squash it' campaign to persuade youth to walk away from fights and violence.[33] Here ads serve ethical and social rather than commercial purposes. Entertaining, informative advertising is often more effective than abstract arguments, preachy, moralizing rhetoric, proselytizing, and threats of sanctions. This confirms the view that advertising is a legitimate form of mass or large-scale commercial and social rhetoric, and that exchange values are morally preferable to threats. Good design and good values make for good communications.

Benetton's Social Advertising

Different Benetton ads showed Nazis and Black power advocates saluting during the Olympic medal award ceremony, a nun and priest kissing, an AIDS victim dying with his family present, and a White angelic girl kissing a Black boy with devil's horns. 'We choose not to advertise the product', Luciano Benetton explains, 'but to make these statements. We are looking for new ways to communicate that are not traditional because we think people are no longer interested in old ways of communications.'

Oliviero Toscani, Benetton's photographer, sees himself as presenting hard-hitting images of life, death, sex, religion, and race. He sees himself as a photographer: 'I take pictures. I don't sell clothes. I regard myself as a journalist. I upset people because I mix genres—suffering and commerce, journalism and advertising, reportage and fashion. But that's how the world is! Why is it right to produce and wrong to sell? What is all this moral censorship, this hypocrisy?'[34]

Benetton is especially noted for using controversial social advertising to market its clothing. Context is important. People watch violence on the media without complaining, but do not expect to see social messages in advertising. Some feel that the company's ads exploit social issues to sell product. On the other hand, one might also say that it is ethically comforting that social values are successful in selling goods.

Summary

Beginning with old tales about unsafe products, 'buyer beware', and amoral economics, Chapter 5 went on to discuss the market ethic itself. The story about the tobacco industry reinforced the core value of life and the moral obligation of companies to minimize any health risks in their products. Secondly, classical economics was seen as amoral and abstract. Instead, markets involve an ethic of good value in products and services. Exchange values imply reciprocity between sellers and buyers. Thirdly, ethical values improve the quality of relations among businesses in the marketing network that links producers with suppliers, distributors, and advertising agencies. Fourthly, advertising itself should be honest, equitable communication, the effectiveness of which is compatible with informed consumer choice. The values of advertising should reinforce equity and fairness in the marketplace. Indeed, advertising is often used to advocate and promote social values. The tobacco industry story, which opened the chapter, showed the importance of technical, scientific research values in today's marketplace. This raises the question of ethical values in developing new technologies, the subject of the next chapter.

Chapter 6

Technical Values

Technology is not preordained. There are choices to be made.
Ursula Franklin, *The Real World of Technology*

All courses of action involve risks.
Niccolo Machiavelli, *The Prince*[1]

Shipping Risks

Sandro was always concerned about storms and survival during the long voyages from Italy to England, for his ship was small, under 1,000 tons. Maritime technology had not changed much in thousands of years. Sandro had only his ship between himself and the terrible, awesome force of the ocean's stormy seas and powerful winds. Sandro's friends told many tales of being blown off course by sudden tempests. Shipwreck was a very real risk. On the other hand, the trading routes were well known and navigation was an established art. About a century later it would be immeasurably enhanced by the development of the small maritime telescope. With the steam age, ships finally became independent of the wind. Now there is electronic navigation. Many ships are huge, with some oil tankers displacing over 200,000 tons. Despite all their new electronic gear, most oil tankers still have old-style, high-risk, easily penetrated single hulls.

This chapter begins with two old tales about (mis)managing new technologies. First is the sorry tale of some of the difficulties women experienced with breast implants and the related conflict between the law and science as problem-solving methods. The second is the much neglected tale of the ability of large firms to use their market powers to suppress competing new technologies. Both tales refute the deterministic myth that managing technology is impossible. Both show, instead, that businesses can exercise a significant degree of control over innovation. On that basis, Part II explains, new tales can be told about following ethical values in designing and developing new technologies. A private property ethic is recommended for handling intellectual property and data security problems with information stock technologies. Also, a common property system is shown to be appropriate to handling communication flow and network problems of privacy. Both are needed to ensure the level of information integrity and sharing required in today's technological society, information age, and knowledge economy. Finally, the chapter closes by presenting an ethical approach to technological innovation, which stresses a redesign ethic based on continuous improvement in minimizing risks.

I Old Tales: Mismanaging Technologies

Industrial-Strength Implants

One fast-growing area of technological innovation is medical devices, such as heart valves, pacemakers, drug dose controllers, and breast implants.[2] Anything inserted into the human body is potentially a serious health risk. Although new pharmaceuticals undergo extensive laboratory testing and clinical trials to reduce health risks and meet regulatory requirements, medical devices for a long time escaped rigorous testing. In 1963 silicone gel breast implants were introduced by Dow-Corning. While some women sought them to mitigate the terrible trauma of a mastectomy induced by breast cancer, most were implanted by plastic surgeons for cosmetic reasons. In the early 1980s, ads for Même breast implants made by Bristol-Myers Squibb for cosmetic purposes appeared in the Montreal newspapers. Plastic surgeons were telling women that the implants were safe, but even then medical research indicated that 10 per cent to 40 per cent of women suffered from scar tissue hardening around the implant.

By 1983 Canadian Department of Health regulations required manufacturers to submit safety and efficacy data on any new device to be implanted in the human body. In June 1988 the US Food and Drug Administration (FDA) in Washington followed Canadian policy and required pre-market review of silicone gel breast implants. In July 1988 FDA inspectors visited a California breast implant factory, only to find that it had no protections for sterility and kept no records of the raw materials used. The manager of the plant that made the polyurethane for the Même implant expressed surprise that a substance used in oil filters and carburetors was being used in breast implants.

Dr Jacques Papillon of Hotel Dieu Hospital in Ottawa was becoming concerned that companies were introducing a new medical technology without doing adequate prior testing and research. And plastic surgeons were inserting them without adequately assessing the risks. At the same time a similar consensus was forming in the research and standards group of the Department of Health. On 6 January 1989 they wrote that each year about 400 Ontario women had Même brand, polyurethane (PU)-based breast implants removed. Problems with the Même implants, they stated,

> may occur as early as during the implantation or as late as five years later. The complications include severe persistent infection and incorporation of PU into surrounding tissue with severe difficulty in removing infected remains. The rough surface of the PU-coated implant makes insertion more difficult and demands a larger incision. . . . The risks and severity of the complications seem to outweigh the possible advantages.

They recommended a national registry for all breast implants and a mandatory patient information program. But Department of Health management, concerned about commercial risks to the industry, did not act on the recommendations.

Dr Pierre Blais, one of the group, was still not satisfied. In September 1988 he had published research showing that polyurethanes were known to deteriorate in the body and could release hazardous chemicals like 2-4TD. He asked why implant design was based on commercial polyurethane foam, the safety, efficacy, and quality of which were not reliably known. It was not stable, tended to get entangled with breast tissue, and was difficult to remove. On 20 February 1989 Blais wrote a memo arguing that silicone-based breast implants 'are unfit for human implantation and are potentially hazardous' to patients. He later went public with his concerns. As a result Blais was fired for insubordination.

By 1990 concerns about the safety and reliability of the Dow-Corning silicone gel breast implants were reaching crisis proportions. The Dow-Corning implant represented less than 1 per cent of revenues of the company, jointly owned by Dow Chemical and Corning Glass. Its 33 plants made 8,700 products, such as auto parts, bakeware, adhesives, and medical tubing, and 5,000 industrial silicone products. It enjoyed over US$2 billion in sales in 1994. In 1984 Dow-Corning lost a lawsuit in which it had been accused of concealing problems about the implants. In 1989 a Washington public health activist group persuaded a judge to order the FDA to release data on breast implant studies. The judge criticized Dow-Corning for using secrecy protections from previous lawsuits to prevent him from hearing expert witness testimony.

In April 1991 Bristol-Myers Squibb suspended sales of the Même breast implants. There had been an internal debate in Dow-Corning about the breast implants, partly in response to complaints from plastic surgeons about women refusing to use them. In January 1992 the FDA discovered that Dow-Corning, in response to litigation, had sealed memos reporting staff concerns about the safety of its implants for 20 years. A 1983 memo noted the lack of valid long-term data showing the safety of the gel. Budgetary cost-cutting prevented the FDA from testing the breast implants itself, despite the numerous cases of gel hardening, implant breakdown, tissue invasion, and the leakage of hazardous chemicals like 2-4TD. As one woman reporter remarked, would such laxity have been allowed if the problem concerned male testicular implants?

John Swanson had shaped Dow-Corning's award-winning corporate ethics program, which focused on the values of integrity and openness. In December 1990 Swanson was given responsibility for managing the breast implant issue. He soon received a memo from the company's medical director, who was concerned that the company was trying to destroy internal reports about complications. In his mind this violated both the corporate code and professional ethics. In 1990 a litigation attorney acting for Robert Rylee, vice-president for Dow-Corning's health business, had asked a company researcher to destroy all copies of a memo reporting that 30.3 per cent of women with implants experienced problems and that 13 per cent had them replaced within five years. Such information, Rylee believed, would compromise the company's legal position. In June 1991 Swanson was shocked by a *Business Week* story citing evidence that Dow-Corning had known about animal research linking implants to cancer and other illnesses for at least 10 years. He felt that Dow-Corning should abandon its defensive attitude and suspend production and sale of the implants. But company executives said they thought the implants were safe, and the board was concerned about weakening the company's legal position in possible litigation. The breast implant issue had been irretrievably 'legalized'.

Pressure on the company only increased. In late December 1991 a California woman won a US$7.3 million judgement against Dow-Corning. In January 1992 the FDA called for a voluntary moratorium on breast implants, and the company stopped production. In 1993 Dow-Corning suffered a $300 million loss. The company faced a class action suit representing 410,000 women and the prospect of 200 trials. Such a tidal wave of mass tort litigation often forced defendants to settle out of court regardless of the strength of their case.

Colleen Swanson, John's wife and a trained dental assistant, herself had a breast implant for cosmetic reasons. Before going ahead with the implant she had been assured by her plastic surgeon and company scientists that they were safe. She knew that silicone was biologically inert. Soon after insertion, however, she began to suffer severe migraines. Within two years she experienced numbness and stiffness in her arms and chest, rashes, fatigue, and back and joint pain. Then her breasts hardened and there was a constant burning in her chest, arms, and hips. She was certain the implants were the cause, and in June 1991 she had them removed. The surgeon told her that the left implant had been ruptured for some time and the other was leaking silicone. In August 1992, after being rebuffed by Dow-Corning's legal department, Colleen Swanson sued the company. In May 1993 John Swanson left Dow-Corning. For him the critical moral issue was the company's failure to respond to early warnings about implant problems.

However, the scientific evidence backing plaintiff claims was inconclusive. Their lawyers argued that they did not have to prove causation, merely show 'a link' between the implant and the subsequent ailments. Dow-Corning's scientific case seemed stronger. Subsequent epidemiological and immunological research showed that no definite disease could be linked to the implants. A June 1994 *New England Journal of Medicine* study found that none of 749 women with implants had excess medical problems. In late 1996 the company and the courts were talking of having independent, impartial experts assess the scientific evidence.

In December 1995 the Canadian Supreme Court ruled that Dow-Corning was derelict in not warning a BC woman about breast implant risks. By 1979, the court found, the company had already received 78 complaints, but it said nothing to the medical community until 1985. Manufacturers, the court felt, are responsible for warning consumers and the medical community of potential defects in their products. Warnings should be given as problems are reported, rather than delayed until the company is certain about the causes. To make an informed choice, women must rely on manufacturers and professional medical advice. The duty to warn, the Court added, 'varies with the level of danger entailed by the ordinary use of the product. In the case of medical products, the standard of care to be met by manufacturers in ensuring that consumers are properly warned is necessarily high.'

Mismanaging Innovation

The breast implant tale demonstrates, once more, that companies need to respond to problem reports, however ambiguous, about worrying risks in new products. Developing new technologies or applying old technologies to new uses, e.g., as medical devices, should be guided by ethical as well as economic values. As the breast implant story shows, several values are commonly operative in technology development:

❖   commercial
❖   legal
❖   technical
❖   the core value of life, or health.

This in turn gainsays the *technocratic fallacy*, or the view that technical values rule over all others. Technical values, as the theory of multiple intelligences showed, only reflect a narrow slice of the wide range of human problem-solving intelligences (see Chapter 2). And the breast implant case shows that commercial and legal values can override technical values.

Moreover, in the conventional management of medical technologies like pharmaceuticals, therapeutic values and concerns about health risks often override both commercial and technical values. The result sometimes is the withdrawal of new technologies due to their unacceptably high health risks. All too often, however, new technologies are commissioned for the market with insufficient testing, and companies ignore data about harmful side effects. As a result risky new products are not withdrawn until many people have suffered, needlessly. Thalidomide, a sedative developed in Germany over 40 years ago, for example, was allowed on the market without adequate testing. It caused about 8,000 severe birth defects in Europe and Canada before it was finally withdrawn. In the US a similar calamity was largely prevented because a vigilant federal government medical health officer persisted in refusing to approve thalidomide.[3] The breast implant and thalidomide stories both show us how new medical devices and drugs can get lost in the cracks when their development is not guided by sound medical and technical norms.

A related concern is the so-called technological imperative, according to which organizations must follow the most rationally efficient and best way indicated by technological innovation. If it's technologically possible, it must be done. On the contrary, there is no technologically predetermined path to the Utopia of rational efficiency, as Ursula Franklin noted when she stated that 'There are choices to be made.' The reality of commercial technological development outside the medical field is a continual tension between commercial and technical values.

Sometimes, Richard Dunford claims, the economic result is that new technologies lose, and are suppressed, usually for competitive commercial reasons.[4] Oil companies, for instance, have sought to suppress competing solar energy systems, and automobile companies have resisted pollution control technology. Manipulating patents is the most popular means of suppressing a technology. By consolidating patents, AT&T was able to delay the introduction of a handset phone combined with a dial for 20 years. Patent pools, or sharing patents to block entry to a market by new firms, have been used by firms in the same industry to prevent newcomers from entering their market. Patent pools were used by some oil companies to control the crude oil-producing process, and by AT&T, RCA, General Electric, and Westinghouse to control the development of radio. But mutual litigation and even anti-trust charges tended to fester among the pool partners. Another tactic is a patent blitzkrieg, or taking out many patents to block a competitor. On inventing nylon, Du Pont blitzkrieged patents for a range of molecules with similar properties.

Other technology suppression techniques are: trade secrets (which keep new processes from becoming known), limited licensing (which helps one restrict new technologies in a specific market), and even acquiring the competing firm so as to stop commercial development of an innovation. By buying up companies as well as patents, for example, GE stopped the innovation of fluorescent lighting on its introduction and was able to saturate the incandescent light bulb market. This strategy died when Sylvania was finally able to get fluorescents on the market.

In the business world, obviously, economic values tend to reign supreme. Such concerns as cost constraints, profit targets, and competitive pressures frequently override technical values, such as quality, efficiency, innovation, and good design. Large oil companies, for example, have long resisted developing environmentally safer double-hull tankers on cost grounds (see next chapter). Technical and economic efficiency norms commonly clash in commercial engineering practice. Clashes between professional engineers and their managers over technology development dot the history of engineering.[5] And the acceptance of new nuclear reactor designs is more a political choice than a matter of efficiency or safety. Technical values, thus, do not always prevail over economic ones when companies develop new technologies. Technological innovation is not predetermined, so technological change is not inevitable. If there are choices in managing innovation, there are ethics, too, even in information systems.

II New Tales:
Knowledge Economy Ethics

Moral Ambivalence in the Information Age

A new age is upon us and no one can halt its progress. . . . There is a vast promise but also new perils . . . [of] severe social stratification, unprecedented invasion of privacy, structural unemployment, and massive social dislocation. . . . *The future will depend on what we as businesses and as a society do.*

Don Tapscott, *The Digital Economy*[6]

Don Tapscott shows a deserved ambivalence about technological 'progress' in this new 'Age of Networked Intelligence'. Wisely, he warns us that the socio-economic impacts of technological change are not automatic. They depend on 'what we do', on our choices and values. Businesses, therefore, should follow ethical as well as technical and commercial values when developing new technologies. Indeed, as the coming sections will explain, the core ethic can be central to technological innovation and the knowledge economy on which it reflects.

Our high-tech knowledge economy rests on a growing 'technostructure' of knowledge workers and professionals, for whom the 'problem-solving', 'act, learn, improve', 'informed choice', and 'do no harm' maxims are all significant guideposts. The new telecommunications technologies imply the core values of communication and reciprocal welfare and property in developing an ethic for managing information stocks and communication flows. The core ethic, as we shall see in the last section, can help management steer technological innovation away from socio-economic, health, and environmental hazards and enhance the benefits of change.

Technostructure Ethics

As Kenneth Boulding wrote nearly 30 years ago, 'Economic development is primarily a learning process . . . and the capital goods in which it is embodied are merely material structures that reflect knowledge.' Boulding argued that all production comes from knowledge, meaning scientific research, technical know-how, and, as we shall shortly see, the storage and communication of information.[7] About the same time John Kenneth Galbraith identified the rise of a new productive group in business, the technostructure. It is composed of scientists, engineers, professionals, computer programmers, managers, consultants, financial experts, creative people, and writers in the media, marketing, and advertising. Robert Reich terms them 'symbolic analysts', for they work with ideas. They transform information and knowledge into economically productive forces.

Professionals, especially engineers, hold a strategic position in the modern knowledge economy.[8] A profession is an occupation that uses specialized knowledge in the service of others in exchange for some benefit. But a major problem with the technostructure and professionalism is the tendency of technical values to override ethical and social values—another form of the technocratic fallacy.

Every profession, however, has its own ethics code, often backed up by law. Such codes set out the professional's obligations to the public, clients, employers, and the profession itself, as Table 6.1 indicates.

Such codes show that all professions are guided by social as well as technical and economic values. In consequence, professionals often have to balance competing demands: obligations to their clients, their employers, the public, and the profession. Conflicts of technical and commercial values, for example, are common.

The clash of engineering, scientific, or technical problem-solving values with commercial gain-maximizing (or legal liability-reducing) values is an old story. Not infrequently, loyalty to one's employer conflicts with one's responsibility to the public welfare. But the duty to client, direct stakeholder, and public welfare is paramount, especially when serious health, safety, or environmental risks are in question. Physicians should rank care for their patients' health as their highest priority, and most do. But

Table 6.1 **The Ontario Professional Engineers Act (s. 91)**	
1	It is the duty of a practitioner to the public, to his employer, to his clients, to other members of his profession, and to himself to act at all times with—
1.i	Fairness and loyalty to his associates, employers, subordinates or employees
1.ii	Fidelity to public welfare
1.iii	Devotion to high ideals of personal honour and professional integrity

when some professionals forget their responsibilities to care for their clients' and stakeholders' welfare, tragedies happen—from the Westray mine to breast implants, to Chernobyl. Unfortunately, professional engineers who report critical problems may be overruled by management, as shown in the stories of tragic system failures, like the NASA Challenger rocket disaster, Union Carbide's tragic Bhopal plant leak, and a poorly designed cargo door that once was used on the DC-10.[9] Also, the professional duty of accountants to report problems they discover on auditing a company's books overrides their contractual relation with its management. One may question how tobacco industry lawyers interpreted their professional obligations when they placed their client's confidentiality higher than revealing critical material information about health risks to consumers.[10]

So the technostructure is not above ethical values. Indeed, professional independence contributes to the public welfare not only by minimizing risks but also by professionals using their technical knowledge to serve clients and the public to the best of their ability. This is the core ethical principle guiding all professional services and technical know-how. It is expressed by the professional view that one should always use the best available knowledge and seek to achieve the highest possible performance standards in serving one's clients and the public. Professionalism from this point of view combines the technical knowledge ethic with a care for social welfare values. The ethical value of the growing technostructure lies in making knowledge useful. The mission of professionals and knowledge workers is to bring the best available knowledge and high sociotechnical expertise to bear on solving the problems of their clients, and through this, to contribute to the general social welfare.

This knowledge ethic, unfortunately, is not always respected when management deals with employees. Theory X assumptions lead old-line management to treat employees as ignorant, without skills, knowledge, or intelligence, and as nothing but costs to the firm. On this reading productivity lies in the technology, not in the worker.

The sole purpose of innovation, it follows, is to improve productivity by reducing the cost of labour and number of workers. Commercial values override technical to the extent that, as Jackall reported, such firms commonly prefer to keep cheap, old systems going rather than investing in better, more innovative technologies. The one technical value they favour is increased output; or, to quote the words of one Westray miner: production, production, production. Theory X assumptions lie behind the trend to replace workers with computers and robots. But robots can't run factories. New systems fail, in even newer and more critical ways.[11] Computerization changes both organization and work. Larry Hirschorn makes this point chillingly, by noting the user-unfriendly ergonomics of the operating room design of the nuclear reactor at Three Mile Island. So merely replacing workers with robots, or, as Sylvia Chrominska warned, tellers with ATMs, does not automatically increase productivity.

Theory X leads businesses to misunderstand the role of technology in the workplace and breeds the mismanagement of change. Technological change needs to be managed well, for it involves complex social and ethical as well as technical and commercial values. In addition, introducing new technologies into the workplace can create opportunities for a wide range of choices about the way work can be organized.[12]

Thirty years ago, for instance, Eric Trist studied productivity in British coalmines, where Theory X management views reigned supreme. He proposed that the companies should both update their technologies and develop more co-operative labour/management relations. On improving both the social and technical systems together, output at those firms increased by 25 per cent, absenteeism and accident rates were halved, and operational costs were lowered. Technology follows nature's laws, Trist concluded, but humans work in socially constructed, purposeful groups. In dealing with professional or line employees, encouraging them to use their know-how, skills, and intelligence creatively and independently can pay off handsomely, as the tale of the maverick engineer at Hewlett-Packard suggests.

Hewlett-Packard's Maverick

At Hewlett-Packard engineers are encouraged to share ideas and leave their experimental designs and prototypes out in the open where everyone can see them and discuss them. They may take electrical and mechanical components home for their personal use and tinker with them as they like. So HP engineers are encouraged to be independent. But a maverick engineer who favoured development of a new kind of display monitor was vetoed by management all the way up to Dave Packard himself. None the less, he persisted in working on it at the plant, despite management objections. Eventually over 17,000 were sold, bringing US$35 million to the company. Packard gave him a division to run and awarded him a medal for 'extraordinary contempt and defiance beyond the normal call of engineering duty'.[13]

Supplementing the technostructure's professional knowledge ethic today is the rise of electronic information and telecommunications systems. Increasingly, we live in a wired world. Computers represent a historically unprecedented communications medium. They offer immense electronic memory, blindingly fast processing, precise calculation, and sophisticated control systems. The first clue to ethically managing communications systems comes from Kenneth Boulding, who suggested that knowledge is a highly productive commodity. It takes two forms, he added, namely as stocks and as flows.[14] Information-processing involves both storing and communicating information. The very speed and volume of electronic processing systems raise ethical problems, but information stocks and communication flows raise different ethical problems and call for different solutions.

Information Stock Ethics

Electronic technologies have vastly increased media storage capacity. Whole encyclopedias are reduced to small plastic disks. The word 'memory' now refers to any information storage system, not just the human or animal brain. Data are stored in various storage systems, whether paper or electronic media, as well as in personal and organizational memory.[15] Media store many different kinds of data: personal facts, corporate data, messages, medical files, poetry, creative graphics, ideas, scientific research, music, and whatever 'data' humans want to save or develop. They are all termed 'information'. The variety of information stocks reflects the variety of human needs and, of course, knowledge.

A company's information stock includes corporate records, databases, financial data, organizational processes, employee skills, knowledge and learning, research and development (R&D), patents, and trade secrets. The section in Bell Canada's ethics code on intellectual property, for instance, gives as examples company 'patents, copyrights, trademarks, work methods and practices, computer software, operating systems, written materials, e-mail, voice mail and inventions'.[16] Xerox's code provision on intellectual property mentions engineering and manufacturing know-how.

Information is produced through intelligent work. People and firms expend significant time, effort, and money in producing, acquiring, using, and/or managing information important to their lives and work. So information is not a free good.Accordingly, information is valuable and needs to be managed. Information stocks are therefore best treated as private intellectual property. This allows the owners and producers of the stock the right to set the terms on which others may access and use their information assets. It makes their consent essential to such access and use.

Intellectual property rights are important because information increasingly has economic value. The more value proprietary information as a productive asset has, the more the risk of data loss or damage needs to be minimized and access to it needs to be controlled. Organizational knowledge and data are company resources. Productively used for research, commercial, or other practical purposes, information yields enhanced cognitive returns. It becomes knowledge. To the extent that such knowledge is costly or scarce, it has value as a commodity in an appropriate market. Preserving the company's stock of information and knowledge for its use and development can be critical to a business's survival and growth.

Unauthorized access or damage to an information stock therefore violates ethical property norms, and much computer crime does occur inside businesses. Using another's intellectual property without consent is a form of theft. Forced access into another's database is an invasion of privacy. Hackers who use their computer skills to raid databases aren't technically creative. They are electronic liars and thieves. To destroy a business's, government ministry's, researcher's, or hospital's information stock is the moral equivalent of burning down a library. Worse, hackers who damage medical files risk homicide.

Since information stocks are open to various risks of theft, damage, or unauthorized access and use, companies can, should, and do regulate access to their information stocks. This information represents the firm's intellectual property. There are several classic ways of protecting intellectual property: by media security, organizational confidentiality, trade secrets, copyrights, and patents. Technical protection of proprietary information stocks involves various forms of media security, such as memory, backup, and recovery systems, passwords, and encryption.

Organizational confidentiality takes diverse forms. Many firms set rules to regulate the handling and release of sensitive and proprietary information about pricing, costs, sales, R&D, customer lists and data, markets, inventory, strategy, plans, personnel files, and other forms of intellectual property. We have already seen the importance of not losing key knowledgeable employees, whether through mismanaged downsizing or commercial espionage, and of market intelligence. Financial and communications firms, like banks and insurance and phone companies, go to great lengths to protect customer privacy.

To manage confidential corporate information Hewlett-Packard's ethics code grades it into four classes of descending sensitivity: private management information, which 'may not even be copied', confidential internal information, material for internal use only, e.g., for training, and proprietary information, such as technical data disclosed to suppliers and business partners as part of contractual relations.[17] Release of sensitive information to customers requires them to agree in writing to its restricted use. Everything else is not private and can be shared and communicated outside the firm.

Trade secrets, in contrast, are business secrets. They are not protected by patents, for that would require their publication. Coca-Cola, for instance, jealously guards the formula for its syrup. Trademarks, in addition, give a firm a monopoly over distinctive product names or symbols, such as Sunkist, Kleenex, Xerox, etc. Each is a unique proper name.

Copyright is the classic way of protecting property rights in information and symbolic goods, such as art works. It is especially appropriate for information producers, creators, inventors, etc. The principle of paying royalties to creative artists whenever one buys copying media like blank tape is currently being considered in Parliament. It simply recognizes the intellectual property ethic.[18] Today most firms require their employees to honour software copyrights and licence agreements when installing, using, or copying software. Encryption and charges for decoding can be used to protect copyrighted material. Electronic violation of copyright is a growing concern. Hackers and rogue offshore companies copy commercial software programs and CDs and sell them on black markets. This is theft of intellectual property, little different from plagiarizing research.

Computer programs are a complex form of intellectual property. In 1994 Microsoft was allowed to trademark the word 'Windows' for its computer operating system, even though 'windows' is a common noun or generic concept.[19] MS 'Windows', in contrast, is the proper name of a specific software program. It is a particular stock of instructional information intended for sale in markets. As such, it needs copyright protection. New programming methods, languages, and so on are technical innovations that can and should be open to copyright or patent protection.

Through patents, we have seen, firms establish their ownership of new knowledge and innovative technology, but they must also publish that information and license outsider use. Companies like Bell and Hewlett-Packard and many universities share the returns of innovation with inventor-employees. Patents represent a temporary knowledge monopoly. A famous recent commercial knowledge monopoly involved SABRE, American Airlines' computerized reservation system.

The SABRE freeware gave American Airlines what Harold Innis called a 'monopoly of knowledge' as well as a product monopoly.[21] Innis saw the monopolization of valuable knowledge, often based on complex, user-unfriendly media or codes, as a basis for

> ### Knowledge Monopoly Risks
> SABRE is a sophisticated and powerful computerized reservation system that radically reduced the time that travel agents need to make flight reservations. It matched passenger volume with the available seats. SABRE was freely given out to many travel agents, but it was also a sales distribution system. Its display was biased in favour of showing American's flights, and it often delayed or misstated competitor information. Through its SABRE freeware American Airlines gained significant, near-monopoly economic power.[20]

economic and social power; but he also noted that all knowledge monopolies 'invite competition'. In similar fashion, monopolies of technological innovation are today seen as levers of economic growth for firms. Such monopolies, however, are both constrained and protected by patents and licences, and of course, as Innis suggested, they encourage competitors to bring improved and better-priced versions to market. Knowledge monopolies are socially buttressed by a private intellectual property right in the new idea or product. As the SABRE case suggests, knowledge monopolies are in tension not only with competitive markets but also with the need to communicate information. This suggests the need for a communications flow ethic to balance the exclusionary tendency of private intellectual property rights in information stocks.

Communication Flow Ethics

'Information is a verb, not a noun. Information has to move. . . . Information is perishable. Information is a relationship. Information is a life form.'[22] John Perry Barlow's words, though perhaps hyperbolic, capture the dynamism of contemporary communication flows. Already the instantanous communication of events on the other side of the globe is 'normal'. The constant flow of electronic messages raises different ethical problems than do stable information stocks. The gigantic mass of information flowing at the speed of light without loss in accuracy constitutes a phase shift in human communications. Unlike relatively stable information stocks, communication flow processes are highly dynamic. Instead of passive access to unchanging information stocks, communication flow processes are interactive, for users both exchange messages and modify their information content. Information, or meaning, changes as a function of the messages people send and receive from each other, and the quality of information can be dubious, as evidenced in many e-mail chat groups. So increased communication does not always mean better knowledge. Since information flowing through communication networks is in constant flux, there is no fixed, stable stock of intellectual property.

None the less, communication is essentially beneficial. It reflects a core ethical value. The speed-up and increase in message flows through electronic communications networks provide great benefits to modern scientific, technological societies and their knowledge economies, and reinforce the central place of communication values in democracy. Communication reflects reciprocity in the realm of information, resonating the free exchange of goods in open markets. Cheap, easily accessible, and near-instantaneous electronic communications networks serve the communications needs of hundreds of millions of people.

But high-volume, high-speed flows of messages in modern communications processes and networks raise some ethical problems, such as risks to users' privacy and to data security. There are tensions between the commercial privatization of information stocks and the open sharing of information required in communication processes and networks in education, learning, and scientific inquiry. So an appropriate communication flow ethic is needed. Communication flows should not be treated as private property but as the common intellectual property of all who access the flow of messages or an inquiry or learning process. A common intellectual property right in communication flow processes and networks would both protect messages and data and enhance user rights to participate in an inquiry or learning process and to send and receive messages. It would allow one to swim with the flow, dip in and take out what one wants, and also master heavy cross-currents of open debate and criticism that are essential to learning and research. Such a common property right would still enable control of the communication system and recognition and returns to information givers and knowledge producers. But first to the problem of privacy.

Bill Gates on Privacy in the Information Age

The days are nearly gone when you can count on the inefficiency of information technology to protect your privacy. Networks and other new tools will make it simple for information to be gathered, correlated and called up.[23]

Privacy, Bill Gates warns us, has become a serious social concern precisely to the extent that electronic communications have increased the speed and volume of communications. Information that consumers volunteer to a business travels widely, through various networks, and can be accessed, stored, and used by many different organizations, all unbeknownst to the consumer. Welcome to the information age. You can't leave home without it. A typical but highly simplified communication flow path is illustrated in Table 6.2.

Table 6.2: **Simplified Communication Flow Path**					
Information giver ➡	Node 1 / Gate-keeper 1 ➡	Node 2 / Gate-keeper 2 ➡	Node 3/ Gate-keeper 3 ➡	Node 4/ Gate-keeper 4 ➡	Information taker
Purchase in Store A (BC)	Company A Database (Alberta)	Phone Systems	Bank B Clearing-House (Ontario)	International Satellite Link	Credit Firm C Database (New York)

In reality, of course, flow paths are much more complicated.[24] Each purchase, e-mail message, or web-site link passes through countless gates and nodes, which are controlled by gatekeepers such as phone systems and clearing-house operators. And the flows are interlinked in complex networks. The table discloses the different direct stakeholder interests involved, and at risk, in communications networks. There are three: information givers, takers, and gatekeepers.

In this example, the consumer is the information giver. She/he supplies data, from personal and otherwise private information stock, to banks and stores, which credit companies take and organize into credit reports. Once the information is entered into the electronic flow at store A, it may only take a micro-second to reach bank B, which takes the information and stores it, but the flow path does not end there. B then sends it to C, a credit bureau. C takes the information and stores it, only to associate it with other similar data and then sell it, for example, as a credit report to D, a client. B and C both take and give information. The phone and satellite system operators are communication network gatekeepers. So A, B, and C represent three types of direct stakeholders involved in communication flows.

The second stakeholders are information takers, like banks and credit agencies. Banks sell consumer data to a credit bureau, which refashions them into credit reports and market research information for its clients. Most financial firms take sensitive personal and business information about loan applicants and entrepreneurs. Every time we use credit cards or ATMs we give data to information takers. We enter the international world of electronic databases. Almost no information about consumers' financial, buying, reading, viewing/entertainment habits remains truly private. While in Orwell's *1984* the totalitarian state was Big Brother, today he might run a credit bureau, as the Equifax story suggests.

Does Big Brother Run a Credit Bureau?

'You can't play "I've got a secret" with Equifax', the *Wall Street Journal* says. 'It already knows. And it's passed your secrets on to the bank, the credit card company, the auto dealer and insurance company.' Equifax is the largest provider of consumer information in the world. (The name means 'equity in gathering and presenting facts'.) It has data on 120 million individuals on file. Equifax rearranges the information it takes to create 'value added' products for its commercial clients; about one-third of its business is in providing credit information, and another third in insurance information. It also provides card and cheque payment services and various general information and database services. Its databases include data gathered from credit cards, bank accounts, investments, mortgages, income, work, driving records, legal actions, and government data.

There have been privacy problems. In 1991 Equifax and Lotus together developed Marketplace Households, a CD-ROM database on about 120 million people, for sale to direct marketers and businesses. Although it included some privacy protections, widespread concerns about accuracy and the commercial use of sensitive personal information led to the project's termination. In 1994 Equifax released Citibank consumer credit files to the bank as part of a promotion for its new, preapproved credit card. In response to public concerns, Equifax later agreed to reinvestigate any credit information disputed by a consumer within 30 days and to delete any information it cannot verify.[25]

Informed choice is essential to communication ethics. Information givers who volunteer data to some information taker should be informed about its possible uses and have some say over how it is used. The only data collected by information takers should be what is needed for their purposes. Matching and cross-linking of identifiable data should be subject to the givers' approval. They should also have the right to view their files and ensure their accuracy, at the takers' expense. Companies whose business is information should respect such consumer guidelines.[26]

Where, for example, such companies as credit firms and marketing agencies sell the information volunteered by consumers in the marketplace, or use it for market research, they should compensate consumers, or research subjects. It is in effect a commercial commodity. Communication in such circumstances is a market exchange. Perhaps consumers might be offered discounts in exchange for volunteering commercially useful information. This kind of reciprocity both respects givers' private intellectual property rights to their own personal information stocks, and recognizes the economic value of the data given to commercial information takers. Where information is supplied for professional purposes, professionals are usually paid for the service.

The third stakeholders are the information gatekeepers, who run the phone, Internet, and satellite systems. They control the nodes in the flow path, that is, the phones, satellites, or internet connections. Gatekeepers such as system programmers, network managers ('sysops'), technicians, and engineers are all information professionals. At the broad communications end, information givers merge into information producers, such as writers, journalists, editors, researchers, and even artists.

But the concern here is mostly with gatekeepers in electronic communications media. Information professionals comprise a large segment of the technostructure. Their task is to facilitate users' access to communications networks, maintain communication flows (traffic management), and ensure data quality and accuracy, message security, and efficient transmission. They also need to preserve the integrity of the network, by scanning and filtering traffic flows for inappropriate messages or unauthorized users, and prevent any risk to messages, users, or databases. Often, they consult with user groups and direct stakeholders on such policies.

Information professionals are the gatekeepers of the communication ethic in the information age. They not only need to develop the highest level of skill using the best available information technologies, they also need a professional code of conduct. In fact, the Association for Computing Machinery has already developed a code that commits information professionals to honour intellectual property rights, including copyrights and patents, and respect user privacy.[27] The ethics codes of many firms have similar provisions. Bell Canada's code, for instance, provides for proper computer system access and use, password protection, virus protection, and protection of message, data, and system security.

The more open communications networks are, the more easily they are abused and message security is threatened. Concerns about message and data security and unauthorized users and uses are very real problems in many networks. In a recent study of 1,300 North American firms by the accounting firm of Ernst & Young, 30 per cent of the organizations using the Internet reported attempted break-ins within the previous year.[28] About 25 per cent of security-related losses were due to deliberate system violations by both internal staff and external intruders. None the less, 75 per cent of the companies surveyed still allowed external access to their computing resources by customers and suppliers, 72 per cent did not have staff training programs, and nearly one-third had no data or message security policy.

Moreover, a small group of expert 'crackers' (or criminal hackers) disdains the customary values of trust and respect for information and knowledge on which communication networks rest. Crackers are not just kids playing games. Clifford Stoll, communication system manager at the Lawrence Lab system in Berkeley, California, and himself a scientist, helped police find Robert Morris, whose virus 'wormed' into the Internet in 1988.[29] It crashed thousands of systems for two days, causing millions of dollars in lost messages or data and downtime for countless offices, businesses, and research organizations. It also damaged several hospital databases. That talented programmers devote their time to breaking into computers, destroying information, and blocking communications networks is truly a corruption of the communication ethic that modern communications media so powerfully embody.

Crackers neither support nor advance electronic communications and computing. Instead, they use their technical skills to violate the core value of communication itself. The contradiction is stark. The mere threat of viruses in a communications network inhibits the flow of information. Security precautions constitute new gates. Not only do crackers transgress the communication ethic, they destroy information stocks when they invade networks. So hackers violate both private intellectual property rights in information stocks and common property rights in communication flows. They slow down the flow, and increase the transaction costs of communication. Crackers are not harmless adolescents just having some fun. Rather, Stoll feels, they 'violate the trust and openness on which all communication rests. Fears for security louse up the free flow of information. Science and social progress only take place in the open. The paranoia that hackers leave in their wake only stifles our work.'[30]

Stoll's comments are on the money. Open communication is fundamental to scientific research, technological progress, and democracy itself as well as to the development of a knowledge-based economy. Scientific inquiry, for example, requires openness and the free exchange of ideas, that is, communication, if it is to succeed in winnowing any kernels of scientific truth from the great chaff-heap of errors and false leads. Unless knowledge is communicated it cannot be tested, refined, or improved. Without communication we cannot learn. Since knowledge grows through being communicated and shared, communication processes and networks should be as open and free as possible.

The free, open flow of communications is essential to everyday life, free markets, electronic networks, scientific research, and the commercial development of innovations. The need for open communication in electronic networks, for example, led Don Tapscott to argue that 'Nobody owns the Net. Every participant owns it.' Tapscott suggests, correctly, that communication flow processes cannot be treated as private intellectual property, in contrast to information stocks.[31] The need to communicate morally overrides claims to commercialize knowledge and opposes any attempt to monopolize knowledge in one's private information stock. Communicating means sharing, not hoarding. When messages are diverted and hoarded into private or secret information stocks, data hibernate. They do not grow into knowledge, for the purpose of a stock is merely to conserve and preserve data, not to develop it.

Open communication, then, is the lifeblood of the information age, education, science, and the knowledge economy. The pronounced tendency of commercial interests to privatize scientific knowledge, however, threatens to hamper the very scientific enterprise on which it rests. There are already some instances of businesses that have sought to restrict scientific inquiry in order to secure or enhance their profit.[32] Already firms that contribute to funding research with commercial potential share in any commercial gains resulting from that research, even when it is done in publicly supported universities. British agricultural interests, for instance, supported the research that led to the recent cloning of the Scottish lamb named Dolly. There is a real danger that businesses might seek to influence the selection of professors and to redirect research more towards commercial problems than to pressing scientific or social questions.

Sometimes commercial concerns interfere in the research process itself. Knoll Pharmaceutical, whose thyroid hormone drug dominates its market, has sought to prevent the publication of the results of research it had funded because the study showed that competing products were just as efficient as Knoll's. Also, some biotech firms have pressured scientists to publish research results prematurely so as to affect positively a public stock offering. But premature publication violates the proven practice of peer review, which minimizes the risk of error in scientific inquiry. In addition, researchers have been pressured to exclude some co-researchers from any publications, for it is easier to obtain a patent with a smaller group of inventors. Such exclusion exemplifies a private intellectual property right, in contrast to the common intellectual property requirement that all who contribute to advancing an area of knowledge should share in the rewards.

Another reason why a common property approach is appropriate is that communication flow processes and networks are not free goods. They are limited in capacity, and in fact some have already approached their technical flow capacity limits, or bandwidth, and there have been slowdowns in the flow of message traffic. Universities, governments, firms, and other organizations already control members' Internet accounts, and most Net providers and many Web sites charge service costs. Nor is education or the scientific advancement of learning a free good. It often requires costly human and technical resources, and those who teach, learn, and produce knowledge all deserve economic support as well as social recognition for their efforts.

Here Tapscott's view that 'every participant' owns the Net is suggestive. It hints at what is needed for scientific inquiry and other communication flow processes: an open, inclusive, common intellectual property right, one that maximizes user or participant access and minimizes control and costs. Some degree of control is necessary to reduce risks to message and data security and to user privacy, to pay for operating costs, and to enable appropriate rewards for knowledge producers. None the less, managing a communication network is still managing a flow process. The aim should be to charge as little as possible, exercise control as inobtrusively as possible, and facilitate access and use as much as possible.

Only a common intellectual property right offers the required blend of maximal openness and minimal costs. It alone is appropriate for efficiently and inobtrusively managing communication flows in modern networks, whether social, commercial, or scientific. Such networks need to remain as open, free, cheap, and inclusive as possible, all the better to enable information to develop into ideas and knowledge. The quality and productivity of information depend in significant part on the inclusive openness, ease of use, and open access of the communication media through which it flows.

In conclusion, an appropriate communication ethic for a modern knowledge economy requires two different kinds of intellectual property rights:

❖ *a private intellectual property right* to manage, conserve, and protect information stocks and ensure that information givers, producers, and owners reap appropriate returns from others' use of and access to their information stocks;

❖   *a common intellectual property right* for the unending volume of messages flowing through communication networks, with the fewest possible restrictions on discussion, access, or use. Administrative costs should be low, as on the Internet and electronic media, or nil, as in everyday conversation.

Ownership and control of communication flows must therefore be as open, cheap, and inclusive as possible. For this, as learning and science show, is one of the best ways to enhance the cognitive quality of the information transmitted. This is further complemented by a private intellectual property right in information stocks. In fact, a balanced mix of common and private property rights, economic history has shown, is both efficient and durable.[33] Indeed, all advanced modern economies represent some mix of private and common/public property. Having explored the twin problems of a contemporary information and communications ethic, we can now move on to the related question of the innovation ethic that underlies the production of knowledge.

An Innovation Ethic

As we saw with the tobacco industry, silicone breast implants, and the suppression of technology, companies make choices about developing new technologies, from the time research is approved through every development stage to marketing the finished product. And those choices can and should be ethical. It is also clear that different values govern technology choice: commercial, technical, legal, therapeutic (in the case of medical technologies), and, of course, ethical values. Professionals, because of the privileged position society has conferred on them (or has allowed professionals to confer on themselves), are especially obliged to ensure that their knowledge not only brings commercial returns but also enhances customer or client welfare and that of the other indirect stakeholders, such as affected publics.

The newer a technology is, however, the less its effects are predictable and the more difficult it is to foresee its risks. Few people foresaw the extensive social effects of the mechanical printing press, the automobile, the plane, the contraceptive pill, or the computer, or the extraordinary speed-up of the flow of information from electronic telecommunications networks.[34] Typically, the benefits of radically new technologies are touted loudly and the risks ignored. Utopia is coming, soon. This was said for the steam engine, radios, the car, nuclear energy, and electronic media.

One clue to guiding ethical foresight in developing innovations is that technologies commonly develop through a life cycle, following a classic S-curve pattern.[35] The newer a technology, the less its effects are predictable or controllable. In the first, earliest phase of innovation, all one really knows is the technology itself. The system's message resides only in the 'medium', in its design, materials, possible uses, and—often unintended— abuses. Unfortunately, the more radical an innovation, the more difficult it is to read these messages. New technologies are often misinterpreted in terms of the old ones they replace. The automobile was originally termed a 'horseless carriage'. Gutenberg's press was at first seen as a new form of manuscript technology, whereas in reality he had redesigned print itself by standardizing and separating the letters, thereby enabling the mechanization of printing. The totally unforeseeable result of this mechanization of communications was the widespread, bloody social revolutions of the sixteenth century.[36] The same mistake happened with computers. The first ones were seen merely as sophisticated calculating machines, but they are not machines at all. They are electronic communications, information-processing, instructional control, and game-playing/home entertainment systems, and more.

Once invented, new technologies compete with the old to survive. The private automobile fought to replace public streetcars, TV to pre-empt radio and the book, and computers competed with typewriters and calculating machines. After a while technologies proliferate and increase, as is happening now with computers. Instead of radical innovation one sees adaptive variation in new systems. Indeed, radical innovation is the exception, not the rule.[37] Eventually the basic design is standardized and the system becomes simpler to use, like the model T, the personal computer, and the VCR (but the technical innards may remain complex). Many are imitations or near knock-offs. Acquiring and modifying existing or competing systems is commonplace. Novelty and brand differentiation replace innovation. The new technology has become a mass market product.

This shift from innovative technology to market commodity can cause problems for firms with an overly technical bias, such as Intel.[38] When Intel failed to respond quickly to rising user concerns about a small technical flaw in its pentium chip for IBM PCs, the eventual replacement of the chips cost Intel US$475 million. As users become less expert, the need to adapt the design to consumer knowledge levels and preferences increases. What Intel forgot was customers are direct stakeholders in the business. In many high-tech firms, such as 3M, Motorola, and Hewlett-Packard, consumers and sales staff work closely with engineers and managers to design products from the ground up. In this 'house of quality' approach to technological product development, the company interlinks technical quality, cost controls, price levels, and customer satisfaction.

At this point a wealth of experience, good and bad, has been acquired, and a large stock of sociotechnical knowledge about the technology, its uses, benefits, and risks has been developed. Everyone has moved high up the learning curve. Risk foresight and control are greatly facilitated. So there is little excuse for not foreseeing and minimizing the risks of mature technologies like cigarettes or breast implants, cars, or, increasingly, computers.

Eventually every technology shows its age. Decline sets in. The risks and costs outweigh the benefits, as with old technologies in mines, paper mills, factories, automobiles, etc. The technology reaches built-in limits of its design.[39] Problem reports are so common that the need for a new system is increasingly evident. Foresight approaches hindsight. Then the technology cycle recommences *da capo*. 'New' systems appear, some with a 'back to the future' character. Fast trains like the TGV, for instance, are eliminating air routes in France, and streetcar lines have been reintroduced in Los Angeles and San Diego.

One key lesson from the technology life cycle is that system *redesign* is the rule. The newer a design, the more it needs to be debugged and redesigned. The idea that there is only one true design for any system is quite false. As a system develops through its life cycle, its costs, risks, and technical problems become more evident. Ethical technology development, then, should stress high sensitivity to early warnings, constant vigilance in reporting, and intelligence in solving problems. In brief, it should be guided by vigilant and long-term risk-minimizing redesign principles, rather than short-term gain-maximizing values.

But one caution is in order. Judgements about risk levels are technically and socially complex.[40] They tend to vary with stakeholder bias. Inventors and producers tend to promote benefits and downplay risks; competitors, critics, consumers, and users often take the opposite tack. For this reason, recourse to the best available scientific and technical expertise as well as consultation with users and consumers are not merely recommended but necessary. But there is no zero risk; nor is there any single true or perfect number to measure most health, safety, environmental, or even economic risks. Ultimately, it is a matter of vigilance, learning, intelligence, and commitment to reducing risks to optimal levels.

The 'house of quality' model requires engineers and firms to get outside the organization and consult with users and direct stakeholders about the risks as well as the benefits of any innovation. This involves conducting tests and pilot projects, identifying problems, and correcting them. It can involve redesigning and improving products and systems to make them as robust and resilient as practical.[41] This may require patient investment capital and entail accepting a front-end load of higher development costs and sometimes delays, for example, to test and solve design problems and consult users and direct stakeholders. But it should eventually pay off in much improved designs and fewer bugs, recalls, and hazards once systems are commissioned or products are marketed. The end result is higher returns.

To weaken the natural bias for positive feedback, negative feedback or problem reporting must be systematically built into the way organizations function. To this end, any organization engaged in new technology development should create an autonomous *risk control unit*, staffed by appropriate professionals. A risk control unit should enjoy access to all needed information, be able to consult stakeholders as it wills, and have the authority to report worrying or unacceptable risks to the highest levels of the organization. In an emergency situation the unit should have a veto over commissioning high-risk technology or products, analagous to the right of workers to refuse unsafe work.

Without the commitment to redesign, consultation, and vigilance, the likelihood of costly rear-end loads of critical system failure increases. This can be catastrophic in human and economic terms, and can even bankrupt the firm, as happened in the case of A.H. Robin over the Dalkon Shield IUD device, Dow-Corning over the breast implants, and Johns-Manville over asbestos. And today a similar crisis faces the tobacco industry.

Summary

In conclusion, the stories of leaking and toxic breast implants and of technology suppression have shown the need for and the possibility of ethical technology development. This theme was further pursued in the argument for private intellectual property rights in information stocks. In contrast, communications flow through shared, open networks, and the free flow of communication evokes a common property ethic. A property system is needed in both cases because the production, storage, access to, and use of information are neither costless nor unlimited. Finally, ethical values can and should guide the development of innovative technologies, using the clue of the technology life cycle. This requires commitment to learning and to the risk-minimizing redesign ethic. So envisaged, ethical technology development holds great economic and social promise and will be especially important in solving environmental problems, as the next chapter will show.[42]

Chapter 7

Natural Values

Everything is connected with everything else.
                                    The First Law of Ecology

Not only is it ethical for a company to improve its environmental performance,
but it is sound business practice.
                                    Welford and Gouldson, *Business Strategy*
                                    and the Environment[1]

At Sea

Once under sail, water is your environment. A ship is but a speck in an endless sea. When Sandro's small ship sailed the Mediterranean and the Atlantic 600 years ago the crew threw their garbage into the ocean. Sometimes the fish and the birds gobbled up the food wastes, but most of it disappeared from view. The ocean surface changed only with the sun, the sky, and the wind. Today the sun still colours the seas, clouds still scud across the sky, the wind still moves the waves, and the ocean is still vast. But it no longer seems infinite. Flotsam, garbage, and oil patches are seen everywhere, and the fish stocks are declining. Water, water, everywhere, but there is less to drink.

In Chapter 7 for the first time we are venturing outside the company as a social organization—to explore how business can improve the quality of its relations with the natural environment. In this journey we are guided by the core ethical value of life—including all the species in surrounding ecosystems, not just humankind. For over a century industrial civilization thought its technologies and markets could treat nature with impunity. In consequence, as Part I explains, the rich waters of life were poisoned by chemicals and denuded of fish. The business world had forgotten the Greek myth of Prometheus, who thought he could control fire and conquer nature. As a result he was chained to a rock forever for the sin of overreaching pride. Business, Chapter 7 explains, must stop repeating the Promethean tale. In 1989, Exxon found out that its confident expectation that its oil tankers could travel the tricky waters of Prince William Sound without incident led to ecological tragedy. A slightly different but familiar tale is told about green markets. Environmentalists are so upset by the destructiveness of the modern industrial economy that they refuse any compromise with business, even with firms trying to develop green products. The same activists cannot accept the scientific research that shows that chlorine is not the main factor in the pollution caused by pulp and paper mills.

In contrast to such hard adversarial attitudes, Part II explores the possibility that ethical, economic, and ecological values all converge in environmentally proactive businesses. To clarify environmental performance in business, four measures of ecologically beneficent practices are introduced, and then complemented by indirect socio-economic and technical indicators. Together, both sets of measures suggest a model of good environmental performance in business based on the best available science and technology. This model integrates pollution reduction and ecosystem recovery with economic performance. As a result, the goal of environmental management is seen to be reciprocity between humans and nature. On this basis a systematic model of environmental management is presented, with reference to current practice in proactive firms. We begin, aptly, with an old tale about a new oil tanker.

I Old Tales about Tankers, Diapers, and Chlorine

Tin-Can Tankers

The waters of Prince William Sound are extraordinarily bountiful in sea life and birds.[2] But the waters are tricky to navigate and often spotted with ice chunks from the nearby Columbia glacier. Navigation problems with ice and reefs are familiar to the captains and crews of the huge ships sailing to and from the port of Valdez, Alaska, at the head of Prince William Sound. Valdez sits on a geological fault. In 1964 it was extensively damaged by a major earthquake. None the less, in 1974 this is where the government of Alaska, in co-operation with the oil industry, the source of 80 per cent of the state's revenues, decided to locate the Alyeska oil pipeline outlet. The pipeline supplies 24 per cent of US domestic crude. From the first, that decision was opposed by regional environmentalists and local fishermen.

On Wednesday, 23 March 1989, the night was clear and the winds calm. At 9:30 p.m. the *Exxon Valdez*, the largest US oil tanker, slipped out of the port of Valdez and entered the sound. She was carrying 1.26 million barrels of oil. The *Exxon Valdez* is a huge, 987-foot, 200,000-ton behemoth. It takes three to four miles to stop and a mile to turn around. While the ship had the latest electronic navigation systems and automated, labour-cutting technology, the Exxon oil company had chosen to keep the old, single-hull design, even though any rip in a single-hull tanker would allow the oil to pour right out.

Columbia glacier ice is common in Prince William Sound in the spring. Trying to avoid such ice, the *Exxon Valdez* got US Coast Guard approval to move out of the 100- to 500-foot deep and 10-mile wide shipping channel onto a well-charted area pockmarked with reefs four to 13 metres below the surface. A Coast Guard admiral, Paul Yost, later termed the move 'unbelievable'.

At 12:04 a.m. the next morning the *Exxon Valdez* ran aground on Bligh Reef, 25 miles out from the port of Valdez and three miles east of the shipping lane. Bligh Reef is clearly charted. The *Valdez* was doing eight knots an hour. The first strike on the reef occurred two and a half hours after leaving port. It was 12:28 a.m. when the final impact came two or three miles later. The first rock tore three holes in her starboard tanks; the second, eight. Through those holes 240,000 barrels of oil (over 10 million US gallons) poured into the waters of Prince William Sound.

For two days the weather was calm, but then high winds arose, reaching 70 miles an hour. The winds moved the *Exxon Valdez* oil slick 'like a superhighway', commented Frank Iarossi, president of Exxon Shipping. The slick quickly covered 500 square miles of Prince William Sound and nearby waters. The sound's closed-in geography boxed much of the oil in, polluting the extensive shoreline. The result, Richard Golob, an oil spill expert, said, was 'a clean-up nightmare'. The Alaskan oil industry had always maintained that its clean-up plan could contain a major spill within five hours, but its response was slow and confused. Exxon says it was ready to begin clean-up operations in a few hours but could not get official authorization from state or Coast Guard officials until 6:45 p.m. on Saturday, 26 March, 42 hours after the spill. Steve Cowper, Alaska's governor, declaimed that the clean-up was beyond 'all the equipment available in America' and declared Prince William Sound a disaster area. He also charged Exxon with buck-passing. On 29 March an aide to President George Bush laconically observed, 'Nobody is in charge here.'

The clean-up eventually cost Exxon about US$2.5 billion. In 1994 a federal jury found that Exxon's 'recklessness' caused the grounding of the *Valdez* on Bligh Reef. It awarded US$5 billion in punitive damages against Exxon, a verdict the transnational giant appealed. Exxon is the world's largest public company, with $113.9 billion in sales in 1994, when it enjoyed $5.1 billion in profits. It has 6.6 billion barrels in oil reserves. But Exxon had been cutting costs since 1990, selling off $1 billion in assets per year and reducing staff by 50 per cent.

Despite its huge profits, the Alaska oil industry was almost totally unprepared for a spill emergency. Neither Alyeska Pipelines nor Exxon Shipping was prepared to respond to an emergency. They did not have the requisite equipment, such as barges, oil skimmers, and booms, on-site and ready to go. No dry runs for emergency spill response had been held in Prince William Sound to debug potential communications and equipment snafus. As a result, little oil was skimmed off in the moderate weather of the next two days. Chemical dispersants were not applied when the waters were calm and could not be, once the winds came up. After five days only 4,000 of the 240,000 barrels had been cleaned up.

Exxon's Frank Iarossi blamed the spill on the *Valdez*'s captain, Joseph Hazelwood. Hazelwood was a known alcoholic with several convictions in the previous five years, but Exxon kept him on, for he was an experienced and knowledgeable tanker captain. Even though icebergs were a concern, Hazelwood was in his cabin while a third mate, not certified for Prince William Sound, guided the ship through the difficult waters of the Sound. When the Coast Guard administered blood alcohol tests to the crew 12 hours after the ship left port, Hazelwood's blood had an unacceptably high alcohol level. Exxon later fired him. But it is far from evident that blaming operator error suffices to explain the problems contributing to the *Exxon Valdez* spill.

Emergency Unpreparedness

On paper, US law required oil pipeline operations like Alyeska to write up spill contingency plans, but Washington did not monitor their operational capability to live up to the plans. Interestingly, in this public sense the oil spill risk had not been 'legalized'. It was left to the state and the industry to handle it themselves. But oil price declines and shareholder pressures for higher short-term returns in the mid-1980s led Exxon to disband its local clean-up unit in 1987. The unit had failed three spill drills. Its senior environmental officer resigned. Alyeska also had reduced its oil spill staff. The mayor of Valdez had repeatedly offered to stockpile adequate clean-up equipment, but his offers were refused.

During the planning for the Alyeska pipeline in the early 1970s industry experts had anticipated that oil spills would occur only once in 241 years. No one, Frank Iarossi of Exxon Shipping said, anticipated a spill of this magnitude. In truth, the *Exxon Valdez* spill was not unpredictable. On the contrary, oil tanker spills in Prince William Sound were both predictable and predicted, repeatedly. In 1972 the US Coast Guard had expressed the concern that there might be as many as one per year. In the 1970s local Alaskan fishermen opposed having the Alyeska pipeline terminate in Valdez because of the earthquake risk and the ice from the Columbia glacier. They warned against using large tankers that would have difficulties navigating the tricky waters of the Sound. As salmon fisherman David Grimes later said, 'We predicted this very thing would happen. The preparation for this kind of spill was pathetic.' Environmentalists, too, had disputed oil industry claims that a major spill would not happen and that one could be cleaned up in 24 hours.

There had been other warnings. A previous smaller spill in the Sound totalled 40,000 barrels, and there had been a spill off Vancouver Island in 1988. But neither the industry nor government officials were responding to the signals. The spill risk was and continues to be high. Three million barrels of oil a day still move from Valdez to Seattle on single-hull ships through tricky Alaskan and British Columbian waters. Given all these warnings, the lack of preventive and preparatory measures indicates an extraordinarily optimistic view of environmental risk on the part of both government and the industry.

Indeed, on 28 April 1989 the *Exxon Philadelphia* lost engine power in the much more perilous waters of the Juan de Fuca Strait between Vancouver Island and Washington state. Almost four years later, in early January 1993, the oil tanker *Braer* ran aground off the Shetland Islands and spilled almost twice the amount the *Exxon Valdez* dumped into Prince William Sound. An underlying problem here is developing adequate environmental regulation of international shipping. On any number of conventional socio-economic measures, marine practice on the high seas is lax, especially in comparison to North American environmental regulatory standards.

In contrast to international marine practice, emergency preparedness is commonplace in the mining and chemical industries. It involves extensive operational and technical training with appropriate, available equipment. One presumes that emergency response preparedness is state of the art at Exxon's refineries and follows the 'responsible care' policy guidelines originally developed by the Canadian Chemical Producers Association. In California, unlike Alaska, mock accidents and clean-up response drills are now regularly staged in heavy oil traffic areas like the San Francisco Bay and the northern coast. For 10 years the California Coastal Commission has monitored oil industry spill contingency planning. Surprise inspections have uncovered performance deficiencies and disclosed unwarranted claims. Had such a system been adopted in Alaska it would probably have prevented the *Valdez* incident. In 1995 Joe Pesci of the California government Oil Spill Response group put it well:

> We're certainly much more prepared now than we were in 1990. But you can never prepare too much. You can never train too much. We know where the senstive areas are, where the sea otters are, where the endangered least terns or snowy plovers nest.

The spill damage in Prince William Sound would likely have been next to zero if the design of the *Exxon Valdez* hull was as technologically advanced as her navigation and cargo-loading systems. Unfortunately, Exxon had chosen to keep the old and cheaper single-hull tanker technology over more innovative triple- or double-hull designs. But single-hull oil tankers are in effect oversized tin cans. On being pierced their contents immediately pour out. So outdated a design involves an unacceptable environmental risk, especially in the tricky waters of the Pacific Northwest coast. Even today, no double-hull tankers are being built in the US, despite the stated requirements of the US Oil Pollution Act of 1990 and oil industry promises. Liquid gas carriers, one notes, have double-hull designs to reduce the catastrophic risk of an explosion. In a similar vein, airlines do not let alcoholic pilots fly their planes. So questionable environmental risk management was a significant factor in the *Valdez* incident.

Nor was the *Exxon Valdez* oil spill purely a US domestic matter. In 1972 Alaska rejected a safer land pipeline through BC on political grounds. Since 1993 international rules have called for double hulls on new ships. Notwithstanding all the talk about change and innovation, some oil companies still prefer the older and cheaper single-hull technology. Consequently, huge, spill-prone oil tankers continue to plough the hazardous waters of North America's Pacific coast. The environmental risks still remain less than acceptable.

Activists and Adversaries

Environmentalists have achieved a great deal in the last 30 years. They have helped end DDT and CFC use, stopped whaling, gotten the European Union to ban furs, generally raised public awareness of pollution and deforestation, and helped provoke the growth of environmental business and markets; but there are many problems about 'green' markets and product standards, as John Polak of Environment Canada's Ecologo Program notes: 'Who's to say a company is environmentally sound? Do you look at court convictions, recycling programs, or what?'³ Businesses, Polak believes, are moving up the learning curve and developing better green market criteria. This should help consumers to make more environmentally informed choices. The Ecologo label appears on many products. Ecolabelling should indicate the amount of environmentally hazardous substances, if any, and the ecosystem impact of their production and use. Consumers interested in green products certainly need such guidance if they are to make informed market choices. None the less, there are no universally agreed-on criteria for product ecolabelling.

Colin Isaacs, former director of Pollution Probe, has long maintained that environmentalists should co-operate with business, government, and the public. Green consumerism would use the marketplace to improve environmental protection.⁴ In 1989 Pollution Probe endorsed Loblaw's line of 'green' consumer products, even though they were not completely pollutant free. Probe also reaped royalties from the ads. The products ranged from unbleached coffee filters to disposable diapers. In an ad for Loblaw's disposable diapers Isaacs even argued for non-disposable cloth diapers, while saying that Loblaw's product was the least damaging disposable. On an environmental life cycle basis, disposable paper diapers, however, may be better than cloth diapers. Through their lifetime, cloth diapers may 'consume' six times more water and three times more energy than disposables do in the manufacturing process.

Ideologically minded environmental activists disagreed with Isaacs. Indeed, the diaper ads sparked a turf war between Pollution Probe and Greenpeace, the world's largest environmental group. Greenpeace originated in Vancouver almost 30 years ago. It spends $200 million on its media-savvy, high-profile campaigns and has about 1,000 staff in about 30 nations. It enjoys wide public support for its campaigns, notably its battle against whaling. Michael Manolson, Greenpeace's director, attacked Isaacs for the ads. Isaacs agreed that there are no environmentally perfect products, but for Manolson big business was 'more concerned with greenbacks than with saving the planet'. Greenpeace's success, Manolson felt, did not come from 'working with business. The environmental crisis is such that we cannot wait for just market forces. . . . Saving the world is more important than making money.' Manolson had not shown that any of the products Pollution Probe had endorsed were more environmentally harmful than the alternatives available. Some Probe activists rebelled and forced Isaacs's resignation as director.

Worse was to come. When Greenpeace's activism led it into a battle with Canada's Aboriginal peoples, it experienced what *The Globe and Mail* termed 'a Leftist activist's worst nightmare. A traditionally oppressed group—whose endorsement is vital . . . to your external legitimacy and to your confidence in the justness of your cause—allies with your opponents and skewers you with your own rhetoric.'

In the early 1980s Greenpeace was widely criticized for its campaigns against Newfoundland seal hunting and Native fur trapping. Many Newfoundlanders and Native communities sell furs to large auction houses in order to eke out a living. There emerged a curious alliance of the fur industry and hinterland trappers against Greenpeace's urban environmental activists. One result of the Greenpeace campaign, however, was a 97 per cent drop in seal pelt exports. Consequently, the already critical economies of Newfoundland and Aboriginal communities sank to new depths. Crime, family violence, drug abuse, and welfare rates skyrocketed. In Atlantic Canada, moreover, the seal population grew to large numbers after the end of the commercially viable seal hunt. Those seals eat young cod. Some argue that, in addition to overfishing and warmer ocean currents, the resurgent seal population contributed to the steep decline in the North Atlantic cod fishery.

Finally, Greenpeace met with Inuit hunters. The Greenpeacers were morally torn by their conflicting commitments to animal rights and to the Aboriginal peoples. They had to apologize to the Inuit, who later enjoyed some success in getting the European Community to rethink its ban on fur imports. In the view of Deborah Jones, an east coast journalist, Greenpeace 'had long ago blown its credibility over the witless baby seal issue [and other environmental] scare tactics.' In recent years Greenpeace has begun to rethink its old assumptions. It eventually compromised its hardline opposition and accepted Native subsistence trapping and hunting. Underlying these disputes is the lack of generally reliable environmental standards, as the debate over chlorine pollution shows.

It's Not the Chlorine

Problems about measuring environmental standards not only afflict green products, they also arise in relation to technical processes in industry. Here, however, there has been some progress up the environmental learning curve. Over the last 20 years, for example, many North American pulp and paper companies have radically reduced the amount of chlorine in the effluents discharged from their mills; but many have not. There are also concerns about acid rain or SO_2 outputs from mining company smelters and coal-generated electric utility plants. Greenpeace has long argued for zero chlorine discharge from Canada's pulp and paper mills. And demands for radical reduction in acid rain have been strong for the last quarter-century.

Environmentalists, business people, and the general public all want results. Companies should not pollute or harm ecosystems, but should protect and preserve them. Performance—actually reducing environmental damage and enabling ecosystem recovery—is what matters. The message to business, then, is to protect the environment and, lacking immediate results, to offer credible commitments to ecologically beneficent action. Many companies have improved their environmental performance; but this, too, poses the vexed problem of environmental performance standards. Corporate action plans require reliable quantitative environmental performance measures. Measuring performance, after all, is a common management practice. To this end, four environmental performance measures (EPMs), as shown in Table 7.1, are proposed.

All four EPMs are direct measures of environmental performance, applicable to both process and product technology. Each EPM is intended to be taken over an appropriate time period. Examples of each are commonplace, for today many firms—E.B. Eddy, Inco, Falconbridge, Transalta, Stelco, The Body Shop—have published environmental

Table 7.1: **Environmental Performance Measures (EPMs)**	
Pollutant *Load*	The *amount* of a pollutant discharged, as measured in kilograms, tonnes, etc.
Pollutant *Concentration*	The *proportion* of a pollutant discharged, to water, air, etc; usually a ratio or percentage.
Receiver Ecosystem *Harm*	Ecosystem damage as measured by *decreases* in species populations.
Receiver Ecosystem *Recovery*	Ecosystem rehabilitation as measured by *increases* in species populations.

reports with graphs and data describing their performance using these four measures.[5] *Load* is the first environmental performance measure. It states the amount, say, of sulphur dioxide emitted from smelter stacks over a day, month, or year. Both Inco and Falconbridge, for example, have reduced the sulphur dioxide load emitted from their Sudbury smelters by 90 per cent since 1970,[6] and both are publicly committed to reducing emissions much more. To achieve its pollution reduction goals Inco has spent hundreds of millions of dollars. First Inco built a 400-meter smokestack, and then it developed a new ore-processing system in its smelter. *Concentration* norms are preferred for measuring the organic chlorines discharged in pulp and paper mill effluents.

Harm EPMs are more important than either load or concentration values, for they indicate the extent of damage that pollutants caused in receiver ecosystems, such as the decline in fish populations near pulp and paper mills or of tree populations near sulphur dioxide emission sources.[7] Finally, ecosystem *recovery* measures are the most significant of all environmental performance measures, for they indicate that populations of affected species, such as fish, plants, insects, and animals, are increasing in receiver ecosystems. Reducing ecosystem damage and enabling its recovery are the two main objectives of environmental protection. The harm and recovery EPMs extend the 'do no harm' and 'act, learn, improve' maxims into the environmental realm. Reducing discharge loads or concentrations, in contrast, is merely an instrumental means to the primary goal of reducing ecosystem harms and enabling recovery. Load and concentration targets are therefore secondary sub-objectives, instrumental to enabling ecosystem recovery.

Unfortunately, pollution abatement is still generally seen to be the main goal of environmental protection. This approach stresses pollutant reduction over time in load or concentration terms. The 1994 Canadian Chemical Producers Association report, for instance, is appropriately entitled *Reducing Emissions*. It is dotted with numerous graphs showing declines in various chemical emissions over time, as measured in terms of loads and concentrations.[8] By late 1994, it claims, the total load of contaminants emitted by the member Canadian chemical companies had decreased by 50 per cent from 1992 levels. But carbon monoxide, carbon dioxide, and nitrogen oxide emissions, it acknowledged, remain too high.

As one might expect, stakeholders such as industry representatives, unionists, environmentalists, and government officials tend to disagree about desirable environmental performance levels. Their views tend to reflect their interests. This dissension raises concerns about demands of environmental activists for zero discharge—a highly stringent regulatory norm. While stringent regulations and tough enforcement may satisfy activists, they often are but the mirror image of poor regulations and lax policy. They reflect the legalistic remedies preferred by environmental law groups and the government legal enforcement 'environmental police' model.[9] Such approaches legalize environmental issues, but threat values are not always the best means for resolving complex social problems.

It is not clear, furthermore, that the legalistic zero discharge approach actually solves the environmental problems caused by the toxic effluents of pulp and paper mills, for example, or even correctly identifies these problems. Tracking the debate about the complex organic chlorines flowing out of Canada's pulp and paper mill discharges is quite revealing from an ethical problem-solving standpoint. Of the 145 mills in Canada, 46 use chlorine in the bleaching process; but many mills still lack primary (settling) and secondary (aeration) treatment of their highly toxic effluents. A few companies do produce pulp and paper virtually free of elemental chlorine, e.g., by using chlorine dioxide as a bleach, combined with secondary treatment of effluents. Thus the E.B. Eddy pulp and paper mill in Espanola, Ontario, now discharges around 0.8 kilograms of organochlorines per ton of effluent, and the Howe Sound, BC, pulp and paper mill is one of the first zero chlorine-based pulp and paper mills in the world.[10] The North American average is 1.5 kilograms; 15 years ago it was over six kilograms.

A 1991 Pollution Probe report argued that the organochlorines in pulp and paper mills are chronically toxic.[11] It expressed concern, however, that 27 Ontario pulp and paper mills discharge 61,750 tonnes of organochlorines per year and 275 grams of dioxins. Greenpeace has called for a zero discharge of all organochlorines. To date, however, only BC has required paper mills to achieve zero chlorine processing (by 2002). Near zero standards are in place in Ontario and Scandinavia. A Conference Board of Canada study opposed zero discharge and recommended that pulp and paper mills reduce their organochlorine discharges only to 2.0 kilograms per ton of effluent.[12] It also argued for the secondary treatment of effluents, a not insignificant point, as we will see.

Zero chlorine discharge is opposed by the paper industry because it may affect quality standards for paper brightness and strength and may lead to other contaminants being created and discharged.[13] The US Environmental Protection Agency guideline in this area is to protect the environment without imposing unacceptable costs. And the costs of zero organochlorine discharge are high, while the environmental benefits are not all that clear. Minute amounts of chlorine purify drinking water, but no one would drink straight Javex.

So in this case to call for more scientific research on the issue does not simply represent an industry bias. It represents a legitimate demand for the best available knowledge about the problem. Indeed, in 1993 an independent scientific report concluded that there is no correlation between organochlorine levels in Swedish, American, and Canadian mill effluents and levels of environmentally toxic contaminants in receiver ecosystems, or their bioaccumulation over time.[14] Instead, the research discovered significant receiver ecosystem damage next to mills not using chlorine and even near mills with secondary treatment facilities. The toxicity of mill discharges tends to correlate with proximity to the end-of-pipe point of discharge. In conclusion, the scientists not only call for more chemical, biological, and toxicological research to identify the toxic chemicals, but they also suggest that appropriate (but unspecified) innovations in pulp and paper technologies might hasten the recovery of fish populations in neighbouring rivers and lakes. In effect, the report focuses on receiver ecosystem harms and recovery rather than on pollutant loads or concentrations.

So the chlorine discharge debate supports the environmental problem-solving strategy proposed above. Diagnose ecosystem problems, reduce harmful impacts, and then encourage ecosystem recovery. The point is zero harm rather than zero discharge, and the goal is ecosystem recovery. Or, in Weyerhauser's words, 'No Effect'.[15] On that basis, and with a little help, restoring ecosystems becomes possible. In the business world, however, environmental performance and values do not stand alone. They need to be integrated with technological, economic, and social performance measures.

II New Tales: Environmental Management

Integrated Environmental Performance

The ethically preferred environmental performance level is zero ecosystem harm and subsequent recovery. This requires firms to access and use the best available knowledge and technology. An organization's value system should reinforce environmental values. These considerations show the need for business to integrate environmental performance with other business performance measures, such as technological, economic, and social performance indicators. This section examines how environmental and economic performance are linked with the help of these three indirect environmental performance indicators: technological, economic, and social. They are presented in Table 7.2.

1. *The technological indicator.* Technology is the first indirect environmental performance indicator, for the direct causes of environmental harms and pollutants are usually technological in the broad sense. They are products, machines, chemicals, materials, processes, or systems of various sorts. So improving the product and process technologies, their materials and designs, represents a step forward in reducing environmental harms and restoring ecosystems. In this spirit, for example, the Canadian Chemical Producers Association 'responsible care' policy stresses pollution prevention over end-of-pipe reduction approaches, plus research on less toxic process input substitutes.

Table 7.2: **Indirect Environmental Indicators**	
Technological	Process technologies and product design
Economic	Production, sales, returns, etc. data
Social/ Organizational	Stakeholder/organizational views, communication

Solving environmental problems usually requires a search for the best available technologies, an approach familiar from Chapter 6. This has been the experience of innovative companies like Inco and Falconbridge in mining and E.B. Eddy in pulp and paper.[16] A famous example of a company committed to environmentally driven technological innovation is 3M.

3M: Profit from Preventing Pollution

3M, the maker of Scotch Tape and Post-It notes, has adapted its innovative learning culture to environmental purposes. 3M's '3P' (Pollution Prevention Pays) program began in 1975. It resulted in eliminating CFCs and PCBs and reducing contaminant emissions by 134,000 tons, waste water by 17,000 tons, sludge and solid wastes by 426,000 tons. It has saved 3M over US$500 million. 3M intends to reduce its contaminant discharges 67 per cent further by 2000.[17]

Many small businesses, Pollution Probe reports, have followed a similar strategy of developing pollution-preventing technological process and product innovations that have reduced costs and increased profits.[18] In many cases the new technologies paid back the investment in a few years, well ahead of the six-year, 15 per cent conventional return norm. For example, in 1977 Uni-Rent of Whitby, Ontario, upgraded its old dry-cleaning equipment, reducing carcinogenic solvent fumes and decreasing consumption from 700 to 300 gallons a month. Uni-Rent thus saved $50,000 a year. There are many other examples of similar innovations that helped firms to recover and reuse costly oils, paints, chemicals, plastics, solvents, and inks, all of which had previously been discharged as wastes into local ecosystems. Clearly, good design principles can enable the separation, recovery, and reconditioning of used materials, fluids, and parts, and facilitate their reuse.

Even automobiles are recycled.[19] In Germany, VW, BMW, and Mercedes have all been building recyclable automobiles for over five years. This has affected the whole technology and product life cycle, from design and development through production, operation, and disposal. The result has not only been to recover and reuse water, chemicals, and other materials in production. It has also meant redesigning the automobile itself, using fewer and more standardized parts and sharing parts across models. Society benefits, too, inasmuch as the pressure on junkyards and landfill sites is reduced.

2. *The economic indicator.* The second indirect environmental indicator is economic. This means that businesses should consider the benefits as well as the costs of environmental management. Indeed, it is dawning on many businesses that environmental products and services represent an opportunity to improve competitiveness, returns, and profits.[20] By 1990 the environmental business sector in Ontario was already larger than the forestry or mining sectors. The environmental sector of the Canadian economy, with 100,000 employees, has been growing about 6 per cent a year. There are 5,000 firms in the Canadian Environmental Industry Association, selling environmental services, technologies, and products. By the mid-1990s it was bringing in about $11 billion in revenues, up from $6 billion in 1990.[21] Again, many of the new environmental firms, like Altech and Ballard, are technologically innovative.

Two Innovative Environmental Businesses

Altech Technology Systems of Toronto, a group of scientific and engineering professionals headed by environmental economist Alex Keen, offers a range of environmental consulting services and innovative technologies. Altech tries to link environmental protection and economic benefits, and develop marketable, leading-edge scientific solutions for environmental problems. Its products include soil washing treatment for contaminated land, closed-loop wastewater processing, and water treatment systems.

Another interesting company is Ballard Power Systems of Vancouver. Ballard has developed hydrogen fuel cell energy technology for automobiles, which is a possible replacement for fossil fuel systems.

The existence of environmental businesses and the growth of the environmental sector in the economy demonstrate the importance of indirect environmental indicators such as stable or increasing revenues, sales, profits, production, returns, growth, and reduced or forgone losses. These economic measures, we have seen, should be correlated with improved environmental welfare as shown by reductions in pollutant loads, concentration, or ecosystem harms, and by ecosystem recovery. Since both economic returns and environmental improvements take time, benefits to both should be measured over time, too. In this way exchange values take environmental form, literally, for economic benefits interact with environmental benefits. Hence the Good Environmental Performance Pattern shown in Figure 7.1.

The pattern in Figure 7.1 exemplifies a long-term 12-year trend of interlinked economic and environmental benefits. What makes the pattern a good one environmentally is that pollutant reduction and ecosystem recovery correlate with rising or stable

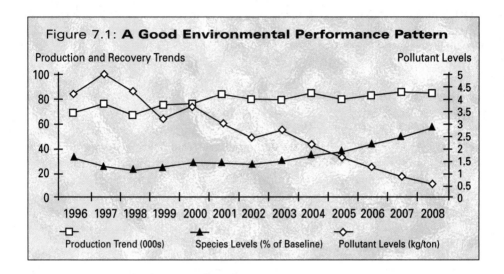

Figure 7.1: **A Good Environmental Performance Pattern**

production levels. This is normally not achievable without significant technological innovation, the first indirect environmental indicator. Such a pattern is evident in the performance of businesses like Falconbridge, Inco, E.B. Eddy, and 3M, where economic returns have slowly increased or been stable, while pollutant load or concentrations decreased and ecosystems recovered.

The time frame extends more than a decade because it often takes years for this kind of performance pattern to become evident. Nor are the trends all that constant. Rather, there are some ups and downs, as one would expect; but the variation is not extreme. In contrast, the short-term high returns typical of a profit-maximizing financial approach to business are not shown, for they tend to collapse into losses, as evidenced in the classic boom/bust cycle of the resource industry. Similar instability is shown in population overshoot and collapse patterns in stressed ecosystems, but here we see the relatively stable pattern of ecosystem recovery. Thus, a good environmental performance pattern correlates with desirable long-term business performance trends. Also, economic and environmental performance improvements are interlinked over the long term. This approach to 'steady state' economics is what one should expect of good, integrated environmental performance.[22] It is a small-scale model of sustainable development.

3. *The social indicator.* Business responsiveness to social issues is what social indirect environmental indicators reflect. Any business that achieves long-term environmentally satisfactory performance likely also has an environmentally responsive organizational culture, takes stakeholder concerns seriously, and is fairly responsive to social issues. Canada's National Roundtable on the Economy and the Environment, for example, is based on extensive stakeholder consultation.[23] It brings environmentalists and government and business representatives from each major economic sector together in

Ottawa to discuss industry-specific environmental problems and search for solutions. The sustained correlation of technological and economic indicators with improved environmental performance usually is a signal that a company also ranks high in terms of social and organizational performance indicators. (The subject of social performance will be explored in the next chapter.) From the governmental side, good regulations are designed to encourage industry to use the cleanest technology at the lowest cost. E.B. Eddy, 3M, and Falconbridge each try to keep ahead of regulatory requirements.

But multi-stakeholder processes are complex. They may not achieve the best results in either environmental or economic terms. Resolving stakeholder differences is not the same as solving environmental problems. Instead, the key norms for evaluating environmental problem-solving are the four direct environmental performance measures, especially reduced ecosystem harms and enhanced ecosystem recovery. They are also relevant to evaluating environmental policy, whether public or private. The three indirect environmental indicators, economic, technological, and social, are less useful than the four direct environmental performance measures in determing the level of environmental performance in government or business. Furthermore, to better integrate environmental and business performance, companies need to develop their own management systems.

Proactive Environmental Management

Business performance correlates with environmental performance in unexpected ways. Many firms have been developing their own integrated environmental management systems, using environmental performance measures and indirect socio-economic and technological indicators. Such environmental management systems have enabled these firms to keep ahead of ever tougher regulatory standards and to achieve the good environmental performance pattern presented above.

A key element in proactive environmental management is to formulate good environmental policies. They should go beyond vague value statements that espouse care for nature or compliance codes that commit the firm merely to obey the law. Care for nature is, after all, only the beginning of environmental performance. For care to be credible, it must go beyond nice words and good intentions. Companies also need to develop detailed environmental performance codes specifying appropriate environmental practices throughout a company's operations. A model for such codes is found in the 'total commitment' policy of the Canadian Chemical Producers Association, a unique Canadian initiative that has been adopted in 36 other countries. Corporate commitment to follow the guidelines by the 63 member firms of the Canadian Chemical Producers Association is a stated condition of membership. The 'total commitment' policy involves several 'codes of practice' covering manufacturing, R&D, transportation, distribution, waste management, community awareness, and emergency response preparedness. It covers the whole life cycle from production to sale to disposal. The overall purpose is to ensure that products and operations do not involve unacceptable health, safety, or environmental risks to employees, customers, the public, or ecosystems.

One finds such codes in environmentally proactive firms. They specify environmental values, norms, and specific measures and targets throughout the organization, from board oversight systems to corporate and divisional policies. Falconbridge, for instance, has its own internal environmental code of practice, which is supplemented by an extensive environmental management system.[24] Despite the recent recession, overall environmental staffing at Falconbridge increased. There is environmental commitment at the top, in both the board and executive suite. Sudbury's Environmental Service Department acts as a resource to help the mines, mills, and smelters to live up to their environmental responsibilities. There are, in addition, environmental technicians in most business units.

At Falconbridge the management of each business unit is responsible for the environmental performance of their unit, as it is for health and safety. Operational management is evaluated in terms of the unit's compliance with both corporate policies and government regulations. Environmental responsibility in effect extends to the fingertips of the organization and is expected of each employee. If he sees an environmental problem, the acid plant control room operator, for example, can shut down the plant. And, as one environmental services manager said, 'if they suspect something they're not too shy to shut it down, which is good.'

Indeed, emergency preparedness is commonplace in modern mining management at both Inco and Falconbridge. Staff training in responding to health and safety mine emergencies has been extended to environmental incidents, too. If Exxon and Alyeska had developed and maintained the environmental emergency preparedness and skills commonplace in the Sudbury mining community, there would likely have been at worst only a minor incident at Valdez. Not only are Falconbridge and Inco well prepared for emergencies, they also have been working for years on environmental rehabilitation. For over 40 years Inco has worked on the revegetation of the Sudbury area and its huge tailings area, with the help of world-renowned experts in the new field of restoration ecology such as Keith Winterhalder and John Gunn of Laurentian University. Indeed, in 1992 Sudbury received a United Nations Local Government Award for its world leadership in ecosystem restoration.[25] Falconbridge's Mark Wiseman has conducted extensive research into preventing contaminant leaching from mill tailings and even reversing acid drainage.

At both Inco and Falconbridge site reclamation is now linked back into early mineral exploration and site development. Environmentally responsive mining means that there is minimal receiver ecosystem harm over the whole mining life cycle, from site exploration to mine design, operation, and closure. This has yielded economic benefits, such as operational savings in waste management, recycling, and mine closure. Ecosystem reclamation is even linked back into mine design itself. Local ecosystem impacts are minimized from the first. As a result, returning the site to near-original conditions on closure is easier and cheaper. In ore processing, waste rock is reused as much as possible, for example, as mine backfill. Pollutants in the ore, such as sulphides, are rejected as soon as possible in the milling and grinding process. The results are enhanced metal recoveries and other efficiencies. The pure sulphur by-products are used as energy for processing or to make acid for sale on the market. In addition, Falconbridge is developing its own Product Stewardship program to develop partnerships with suppliers and customers to help them take responsibility for the environmentally safe transportation, distribution, use, and disposal of Falconbridge products.

One section of Falconbridge's environmental code of practice considers the research, development, and planning of new products, processes, and plants, as the 'Responsible Care' guidelines suggest. All major capital appropriations for acquiring or developing new technology are subject to review by Environmental Services to ensure they comply with policies and regulations. Both Falconbridge and Inco have acquired and/or developed innovative mining, milling, smelting, and tailings control systems and technologies.

Both companies have extensive internal environmental audit systems that go well beyond regulatory compliance into detailed analyses of strengths and weaknesses in divisional operations.[26] In both firms the aim is not just legal compliance, for the audits are management tools. They are designed to support business unit performance in waste reduction, materials handling, emergency preparedness, etc. They try to link general environmental policies with detailed, specific operational problems. The audits are designed to help each business unit continually improve its environmental performance. To this end, audits identify operational environmental problems in detail. Audits are early warning systems. They also seek to develop solutions to environmental problems. As Bob Michelutti, Environmental Services superintendent in Falconbridge's Sudbury division, says, the solutions should not only be cost-effective but also offer 'environmental value-added' results.

Audits focus on a business unit such as a mine or selected aspects of a larger operation such as a smelter. They are scheduled by corporate management and performed by outside teams, independent of unit management. Audit results are discussed with business unit management and employees, and plans for improvement are developed. Environmental staff periodically check progress on audit response. There are wholesale unit audits, issue-driven environmental reviews, and ongoing 'mini-audits' or local spotchecks. Employees are well trained in environmental work practices, as they are in health and safety and in skilled mining techniques. While there are still some minor exceedances, the frequency and seriousness of incidents have decreased sharply over the years as a result of the growing sophistication of each organization's environmental management system.

And there are growing returns from environmental management and business. 'A lot of times where you get an environmental benefit,' Bob Michelutti says, 'you get an economic benefit as well.' Falconbridge has even run a profitable and growing metals recycling business for several years now. The markets for green products, like recycled metals and papers, are increasing. About a third of newsprint should be recycled paper by now, but this varies with the ups and downs of virgin fibre newsprint prices.[27]

One area that may need improving is environmental accounting. Because the old economics assume that the environment was only a 'negative externality' to the firm, conventional accounting has tended to count only the costs of environmental management.[28] Normally, these covered a wide range of expenditures:

- ❖ regulatory and policy compliance
- ❖ liability insurance
- ❖ waste management
- ❖ incident clean-ups.

The sophisticated environmental management systems at firms such as Inco, Falconbridge, and Eddy have certainly reduced these costs and realized operational and process efficiencies. But their environmental accounting methods may not recognize the savings accrued or the returns from related energy efficiencies, new technologies, or environmental product sales, such as from the metal and paper recycling businesses. Instead, economic benefits are sometimes shifted into another accounting allocation category. As one Falconbridge executive said, 'You always have this dilemma of deciding whether it's environmental or production. We produce sulphuric acid, for environmental reasons; but [it] is also saleable, so that's production.' Neglecting to include the benefits of environmental management and the returns from environmental businesses skews environmental accounting towards the negative, cost side of the ledger. The book costs of environmental management are therefore quite likely higher than the actual costs; and the benefits of environmental business are probably higher than stated in the accounts. As green markets grow and companies move up the environmental learning curve and away from old, dirty industrial systems, one might expect the costs of environmental management to decline further and the benefits of environmental business to rise.

Summary

We have seen the problems of old tankers and polarized environmental activism. The diaper and chlorine issues showed the need for good science and environmentally friendly innovation in both processes and products. This, in turn, requires appropriate *direct environmental performance measures*, supplemented by *indirect technological and socio-economic indicators*. Both together yield a good environmental performance pattern in which ecosystem recovery correlates with economic benefits. This approach of combining economic benefits with environmental protection is a form of reciprocity between business and nature. It further requires integrated, proactive environmental management systems.

But there are limits to what businesses on their own can achieve. There are, for instance, over 1,000 abandoned mine sites in Ontario alone. The Canadian government has identified over 10,000 contaminated sites:

- ❖ leaking gas station storage tanks
- ❖ the polluted waters of the St Lawrence and countless lakes

❖   thousands of abandoned mine sites
❖   uncounted urban factory sites, waste dumps, and scrap yards.[29]

Many pose a significant health, safety, or environmental risk. Together they represent the country's 'pollution stock'. Most of that stock was created under earlier, lax environmental laws and regulations. Both government and business were responsible for the original pollution flows that led to these huge stocks of contaminants.

Cleaning all the polluted sites in North America, however, will likely cost in the trillions. This is an immense project. Here government action, in collaboration with business and other stakeholders, is required.[30] Such co-operation was implicit in the indirect, social performance indicator. The scale of the detritus left by the old industrial economy is a clue to the magnitude of the problem of the transition from the old, environmentally damaging industrial, *laissez-faire* world to a spaceship earth, steady-state environmental economy. The long-term shift to sustainable development is like turning a huge 200,000-ton ship around. It is laborious and slow at first, but the ship's momentum makes the turn easier and faster as time goes on. Similarly, the more businesses turn away from the industrial-era technologies and business practices, the faster the economics of spaceship earth become visible, easier, and more rewarding, as Kenneth Boulding foresaw 30 years ago.[31] Here again, business/government co-operation is needed, a theme to be developed in the next chapter.

Chapter 8

Social Values

I am mystified by the fact that the business world is apparently proud to be
seen as hard and uncaring and detached from human values. . . . I personally
don't know how the hell anybody can survive running a successful business in
the nineties without caring. I don't know how they keep their soul intact.

Anita Roddick, *Body and Soul*

The business of business is business in society.

Max B.E. Clarkson[1]

The Ship's Flag

*Fluttering from the stern of Sandro's ship was the flag of Genoa, its home port. Most ships that transport
goods through the lakes and rivers of Canada fly the Maple Leaf, the flag of their home nation. The ship's
flag symbolizes its relationship with its own society and its government. Every business is the creature of
society. Every business belongs to a society, follows its customs, and obeys its laws. Commercial shipping,
like any other business, is governed by an extensive complex of laws and regulations governing water traffic, trade, transport, smuggling, immigration, labour, health, safety, and the environment.*

Every company, Chapter 8 aims to show, should contribute to society's welfare. Part I
begins with an old tale of lax regulatory enforcement that led to a disastrous fire in the
community of St Basil le Grand, Quebec. This evokes a discussion of the old nineteenth-
century free market idea of *laissez-faire* or, in modern parlance, deregulation. Should
governments merely let businesses do what they will, within broad moral and legal limits? This idea, we will see, is as dated as the reverse belief that the State should run the
economy. Instead, in large, modern economies the relationship between business and
government is complex and changing.

Accordingly, Part II proposes a more complex and co-operative view of the relationship between business and government. Businesses, for their part, should improve
the quality of their relations with external stakeholders and thereby their social performance. This should help companies to identify the social problems that affect them and
to act proactively to solve them before they develop into full-blown crises. To this end
they need to develop an ethical approach to issues management. Thus Canadian businesses, for example, can and should develop mutually beneficial relations with
Aboriginal communities and work to avoid the potential crisis of Quebec independence. Finally, the example of The Body Shop suggests that a new 'social market' business paradigm is emerging, albeit imperfectly.

I Old Tales about Social Irresponsibility

St Chernobyl le Grand

The first story is about government irresponsibility. The nationalist passion of Quebec governments for expanding their State powers is well known. Less evident is their extraordinary disinterest in enforcing their environmental laws, as shown by the historic neglect of the massive pollution of the St Lawrence River.[2] Quebec's 1984 environmental law had set a goal of eliminating PCBs in 10 years but mandated only nominal efforts to regulate the storage of PCBs and other toxic wastes. PCBs are relatively inert oils used for cooling electrical transformers, but if they burn they give off toxic fumes. On 24 August 1988 events finally took an all too predictable, and explosive, turn in the small town of St Basil le Grand. A metal warehouse that had held 117,000 litres of PCBs went up in flames. Security had been so lax that a disgruntled town worker, Alain Chapleau, had little difficulty in breaking in and torching the place. The resultant fire raged for several days. Since PCB fumes are toxic the Quebec government reacted with belated urgency and evacuated 3,300 residents in nearby neighbourhoods. They were not to return for three weeks. The locals renamed their little town 'St Chernobyl le Grand'.

The warehouse was a well-known dump and eyesore in the town of St Basil le Grand. Town residents had complained about it for years. They wanted the site condemned and the PCBs destroyed. An accident, spill, or fire, they had often protested, was merely a matter of time. They had complained that there was no adequate fencing around the warehouse, no sprinkler system, and no full-time guard. The town officials had asked the Quebec government to get the warehouse removed, but Quebec's environment ministry did not respond. Like the residents of Valdez, Alaska, the local community's concerns were dismissed in favour of superior expertise.

The owner of the warehouse was Marc Levy, a former federal government employee. (He had worked for Environment Canada!) Levy had operated the warehouse without a permit for two years, even though it did not conform to regulations for the safe storage of hazardous wastes. He also owned a smaller warehouse near Quebec City. The warehouse fence and building at St Basil le Grand had been dilapidated, and storage was haphazard. Barrels were piled on top of each other. Flammable solvents were stored beside PCBs. The amount stored exceeded the legal limit of 91,000 litres. Indeed, as many as 440,000 litres of PCBs may at times have been stored in Levy's warehouse. Louise Lapierre, Levy's secretary, later testified that Levy routinely falsified warehouse inventory reports to the government so as to show lower figures that were within the regulatory limits.

It was intimated that he had good connections with the government, for he always knew in advance when inspectors were coming. As Louise Lapierre put it, he 'did some housework' beforehand, such as masking or moving the excess PCBs. She guessed that Levy was making $500,000 per year from both warehouses. Quebec's environment ministry conceded that inspectors had accepted the warehouse owner's word on the volume of PCBs stored. 'He had good connections', Ms Lapierre added. 'He could always find someone to call and settle things.'

Levy was last seen in Florida, just after the fire. He never did return to Quebec, so the Quebec taxpayers had to pay clean-up costs of over $10 million. Belatedly, the province built a fence around the Quebec City PCB warehouse. Quebec then developed tougher new regulations for PCB storage inspection and disposal in a law that would implement the 'polluter pays' principle. Even if the business sold suspect contaminants to others, the government would be able to impose up to a $1 million fine on the firm. Presumably, environment ministry inspectors now make unannounced visits to waste storage sites.

Government as the Enemy

Andrew Carnegie, the corporate robber baron who created Carnegie Steel in Pittsburgh, was noted for his philanthrophy. In 1889 Carnegie expressed the common view that the poor were responsible for their plight:

> It were better for mankind that the millions of the rich were thrown into the sea than so spent as to encourage the slothful, the drunken, the unworthy. In bestowing charity the main consideration should be to help those who will help themselves. Neither the individual nor the race is improved by alms-giving. Those worthy of assistance . . . seldom require assistance.[3]

Carnegie did not see much of a role for government in the free market. Instead, he assumed that markets were self-regulating efficient economic systems, autonomous of governmental control.[4] In his day owners employed workers 'at will', worked them long hours in unsafe conditions, and paid them subsistence wages. The owners then enjoyed the high profits merited by their hard entrepreneurial exertions. The market being truly free, companies were not prevented from destroying the ecosystems near towns like Pittsburgh, Hamilton, Sudbury, and many other places. Consumers had constantly to be on guard against fraudulent claims and unreliable, unsafe, and overpriced products. Government's role was to reduce costs and taxes, and stay out of the way of the sole engine of welfare and prosperity, business.

The economic catastrophe of the 1930s, however, showed the danger of such a *laissez-faire* attitude on the part of business to society's problems. It radically changed society's view of free markets. Many called for a wiser, less socially objectionable form of capitalism. John Maynard Keynes, the great British economist, stated the issue well: 'Our problem is to work out a social organization which shall be as efficient as possible without offending our notions of a satisfactory way of life.'[5]

He was right. In that terrible crucible of bankruptcy, unemployment, and despair, the welfare state was born. Sixty years ago, social concern, democratic politics, and government intervention tried to solve the daunting problems of the Depression. Socially committed corporations such as Kellogg's, Sears, and many others, as we saw in Chapter

4, worked with governments to alleviate the unemployment crisis. Modern govern-ments created social insurance and assistance systems to reduce the risks of any future socio-economic crisis for the majority of the population. For the last 30 years, as Chapter 7 showed, we have learned in addition how the natural environment itself was damaged by 'free' industry. The Quebec government's attitude to PCB warehousing sym-bolizes the dangers of *laissez-faire*.

For a long time, however, this history has been neglected and forgotten. The world has changed tremendously since the Depression of the thirties. In the last half-century the welfare state has grown and developed in close concert with equally large corporate capitalism. Both large government and large business have, of necessity, developed modern administrative management systems. All developed economies, moreover, are mixed; none is purely State-run or a totally deregulated free market.

Governments provide numerous public services: in education, health care, social assistance, crime and security, communications, transportation, R&D support, and infrastructure and environmental protection. When well designed and efficiently deliv-ered, these services are of great benefit to modern societies. Many are essential to the development of modern knowledge-based economies. Nor are taxation levels in Canada that high. At 35.6 per cent of GNP they are under the 38.5 per cent average for the 26 OECD nations; the US is just under 30 per cent—but this climbs significantly if its health care costs, which are 150 per cent higher than Canada's, are included.[6]

In addition, governments are major economic players in every developed nation. Canada has many government enterprises, including 29 large enough to make it into the *Financial Post 500*. Ontario Hydro and Hydro-Québec each have workforces over 20,000 employees, assets around $50 billion, and annual revenues of about $8 billion. Other Crown corporations, from Canada Post and the CBC to Quebec's Caisse de Depot, Canada's Export Development, and BC's auto insurance corporations, have equally impressive employment levels, assets, and revenues.

Since 1980, however, we have seen the re-emergence of entrepreneurial values, the growth of international business, and the slimming down of government. Business and government, like business and morality, are once more seen by many as polar adver-saries. Today the old nineteenth-century tale of *laissez-faire* government, in conjunction with the free market, is resurgent. But society, Kenneth Boulding warned, should be mistrustful about the promises of 'cowboy capitalism'.[7] Downplaying the risks of finan-cial euphoria, untested new technologies, and reactive downsizing is not socially cred-ible. Recalling past crises provides a healthy corrective to the current fad for blaming society's ills on government and promoting business as the solution for social problems. But neither *laissez-faire* nor statism is credible on its own.[8]

Certainly the world has changed. Both governments and businesses have to adapt to the changing times. They have to change and improve their relationship, for the good of society. Public concerns about the social, economic, and environmental impacts of business are at least as legitimate as business concerns about government waste. In a groundbreaking 1975 study Lee Preston and James Post argued that business and gov-ernment are interdependent.[9] Business should therefore co-operate with governments in responding proactively to socio-economic change. This view throws a new light on the creative approach of the Ontario NDP government in bringing business, labour, and communities together to help save firms like Algoma Steel from bankruptcy and thereby preserving jobs and communities. Indeed, management expert Henry Mintzberg has criticized the current attack on the legitimacy of government, for, he writes, the end of the Cold War did not signal the victory of either business or government. 'Capitalism did not triumph at all; balance did. We in the west have been living in balanced societies with strong private sectors, strong public sectors and great strength in the sectors in between.'[10] In between business and government, he adds, one finds the professions, co-operatives, non-profit organizations, and voluntary organizations in health care, education, and many other fields. Mintzberg's point is that each sector has its special place, its strengths, and its weaknesses.

Part of that balance, of course, is that the State should listen to public demands to eliminate waste and develop more effective laws, policies, and administrative practices. Government waste is not a public good. On the contrary, Hernando De Soto, a Peruvian economist, argues, to the extent that government policies and laws are efficient and effective, they benefit society: 'When legal institutions are efficient, rulers can reap major benefits with minor actions. To do so, they must discard the bad laws of mercantilism, which seek to regulate every issue, every transaction, every property, and replace them with efficient laws.'[11]

Underlying both De Soto's and Mintzberg's views is the continuing truth that government alone is the legitimate representative of the public and defender of the common good. Only government has the authority to identify and solve society's problems. Only government is democratically accountable to society as a whole. On the other hand, government is not a private business. It should respect the legitimacy of business and the need for competitive markets. Business and government, then, each have their place. Each, Mintzberg suggests, has its own role to play: 'Business is not all good; government is not all bad. Each has its place in a balanced society alongside co-operative and non-owned organizations. I do not wish to buy my cars from government any more than I wish to receive my policing from General Motors.'

Nor is business government; its authority is limited to the private sphere. But does it have any social role? The first, clear answer is not to refer to the old business/ethics dichotomy and demand that business altruistically solve our social problems. The second, fuller, and more positive answer is that businesses indeed have a social role to play, as Part II will explain.

II A New Tale: Business in Society

For decades now there has been vague talk about corporate responsibility. While many companies and business commentators reject such talk as incompatible with their primary responsibilities to their shareholders, a good number of firms take a different view. They accept, as Xerox's code suggests, that they have some social obligations. Business, after all, is a creature of society. But social responsibility is an ambiguous and amorphous concept. Increasingly, it is replaced by the notion of social performance. This means, we will discover, at least three different things:

* ❖ proactive responsiveness to the problems and issues impinging on a company
* ❖ ethical issues management
* ❖ the new, emerging concept of the social market.

We will take them in sequence.

Social Performance

> ### Xerox on the Social Obligations of Business
> We believe that a company has a powerful social obligation to its community, its country, and the environment that sustains it. You can't just take profits out—you've got to put something back.
>
> Xerox Canada, *Business Conduct Guidelines*

Social performance is necessary, Boulding claimed, because business needs to prove its legitimacy if it is to be integrated into society. Indeed, as employment levels decrease and environments are degraded, the social legitimacy of business comes increasingly into question. So businesses should not shirk their responsibilities as partners in society. Companies, the previous chapters have shown, are responsible for ethical performance in their own spheres of ownership, investment, management, employee and consumer relations, technological change, and environmental protection. The first ethical duty of business is to do no harm. Companies are responsible for minimizing stakeholder risks. This is the heart of business ethics.

> ### Business Needs Legitimacy
> To survive business must be perceived as legitimate by the rest of society. No institution or organization can survive if it loses legitimacy. Integrative power is the ultimate power.
>
> Kenneth Boulding, *Beyond Economics*[12]

Thus, social performance first means that each business should solve the problems resulting from its operations. Rather than add to society's already overwhelming stock of problems, business should help reduce them. The fundamental underlying principle on which social performance rests has been stated well by Max Clarkson. Business, for Clarkson, is inextricably connected to society. He summarizes his view:

1. Business and society are not in separate compartments, one economic and the other social. Business corporations operate IN society.

2. Managers and their organizations will be held responsible by society for the results and consequences, both direct and indirect, of their decisions and actions.[13]

It will become more difficult, Clarkson adds, for managers to avoid responsibility for the problems they cause by hiding behind the impersonal walls of the corporation, as we have seen in the old tales told throughout this book. Every organization is responsible for solving the problems it causes. So management, more and more, will have to frame decisions in explicitly ethical terms. Hence the need for the core ethic and techniques presented here.

Social performance is complex. EthicScan in Canada and *Business Ethics* magazine in the US each consider a wide range of measures when ranking the social performance of Canadian and US firms.[14] Three components in social performance especially must be considered. We have seen much about the first—*solving the organization's own internal ethical problems*. The second component is *solving problems that transcend organizational boundaries*, for example, when external stakeholders are directly affected. This was the case for most of the people of St Basil le Grand, who were not members of Marc Levy's company. Nor were the fishermen and people of Valdez, or the species in the local ecosystems, members of the Exxon or Alyeska companies. As problems spill beyond organizational borders, external, and often indirect, stakeholders become involved. 'External' interest groups involve themselves in issues: environmental activists (in Alaska and Quebec), politicians, lawyers (notably in the breast implant and tobacco industry cases), and the media. This is one reason why social problems are termed issues, and why solving them involves responsive social performance.

The third component of social performance is that companies need to *respond to social problems as soon as they emerge* and prevent them from developing into full-blown crises. This theme will be developed in the next section, on the management of ethical issues. This complex and multilayered concept of social performance is spelled out in Table 8.1.[15]

The general idea of the table is to display the full spectrum of four classic stances that companies can take towards an ethical or social problem, internal or external. The previous chapters were concerned with internal problems. This chapter and the next two are concerned with external, expressly social problems. Company stances range, in ascending degree of responsiveness, from hostile and legalistic to accommodative and leading edge. The hostile and legal postures are reactive and enforced. Short-term, reactive approaches reflect these attitudes, and reactive firms tend to respond only as forced to by the law. They represent the old short-term profit-maximizing approach that spawns the business vs ethics dichotomy.

Hostile firms take adversarial positions on social issues, exacerbate conflict, and polarize stakeholders, as clearly happened at the Westray mine. Many verge on violating the law or do break the law, such as Nick Leeson's secret account at Barings, Marc Levy's PCB warehouse, and National Film Recovery System's cyanide poisoning of workers, or come very close to gross negligence. Such firms often deny the existence of the

Table 8.1: **The Social Performance Spectrum**

		I	II	III	IV
1	General Stance	hostile resistance	legalistic compliance	accommodative mediator	leading edge
2	Experience	ignorance	legalistic interpretation	experience, familiarity	expertise, innovation
3	Responsiveness		+ Reactive ← + Enforced ←	→+ Proactive →+ Voluntary	

ethical problem they face and deem stakeholder groups as illegitimate. Radical stakeholder activists like Greenpeace take the mirror-image position of demonizing business, as the chlorine and diaper stories show. Generally, the more reactive the posture, the more businesses and stakeholders will be adversaries, emotion will override information, and pet agendas and special interests will control the issue.

The legalization of social issues characterizes the second group of reactive firms. At one extreme this has shown up in dubious legal strategies: stonewalling in the tobacco industry, and litigation based on dubious science in the breast implant story. Opposition to government regulation is a common stance here, as in the textile and chemical firms studied by Jackall (Chapter 3). Legalization takes milder, mainstream form in those businesses, possibly the majority, that interpret ethics in primarily legal or regulatory compliance terms. Legal considerations therefore colour their understanding of ethical and social problems.

The accommodative and leading edge postures are proactive and voluntary. Proactive firms make informed choices in searching for solutions because they are willing to gain experience, skill, and knowledge about social problems. They voluntarily choose to solve problems and search for solutions. Accommodative firms on their own initiative respond to problems, as Falconbridge, Inco, E.B. Eddy, and 3M have done in dealing with environmental issues. They also discuss concerns with affected stakeholders. The M&M meats franchise, for example, has an advisory council for franchisees. Algoma Steel has developed a much more inclusive form of corporate governance. Many Canadian corporations, we will shortly see, are discussing accommodative business relations with Aboriginal communities. Finally, a few companies take leading edge positions on ethical and social problems, well ahead of their industry, governments, and even interest groups. Levi Strauss has for a long time been a leader in employment equity. Procter & Gamble withdrew its superabsorbent Rely tampon from the market in response to early, unproven warnings about toxic effects on women using it. And The Body Shop has been creative in trying to integrate retail and social values in its business, a commercial innovation that can be termed the 'social market'.

The best, most proactive firms, then, try to act with foresight, respond to early problem reports and warning signals, and continually improve their performance. They are socially intelligent, but no firm is perfect. Ethics are about achievable levels of social leadership, not impossible ideals. Every good firm has its flaws. No single athlete, after all, wins all the gold medals in the Olympics. The greatest of athletes excel in ten events, in the decathlon. Similarly, different firms, or business units, perform at various levels of achievement in diverse business areas, from production and employee relations to customer satisfaction and ethics.

Ethical Issues Management

Accommodation with stakeholders is the first step in developing responsive and proactive social problem-solving. To ensure that a problem does not escalate into a full-blown crisis, or that an issue is not hijacked by some interest group, ethical issues management is required. Issues management, as Heath and Nelson warn, is not merely a matter of public relations and manipulating an issue purely to ensure that the firm wins the media battle for public opinion. Rather, it requires companies to integrate business and social performance.

Reciprocal Accommodation

Issues management [is] designed to adjust the company to the public and help the public understand the complexity and requirements of the company. No other corporate function more completely stresses the inseparability of ethical corporate behaviour [and] the production and delivery of goods and services.

R.L. Heath and R.A. Nelson, *Issues Management*[16]

To respond proactively to social issues that impinge on their operations, businesses need to be sensitive to early warnings about emerging problems and listen to stakeholders as well as communicate their message to the public. To do this requires some understanding of how problems turn into social issues and crises by moving up the issue life cycle, as presented in Table 8.2.[17]

Ethical issues management begins with sensitivity and responsiveness to early warnings, to seemingly insignificant problem reports (Phase 1). Problem-reporting is encouraged and feedback is listened to. Such responsiveness can advance the problem-solving process and prevent a problem from being transformed into a social issue. In this way the ethical problem-solving approach (see Chapter 2), complements ethical issues management.

Hard-headed unresponsiveness to issues helped breed the crises in Barings, Dow-Corning, Exxon, Westray, the tobacco industry, and St Basil le Grand. So from the first, careful attention to problem reports is of great importance. They often represent early warnings of small problems that can escalate out of control if the warnings go unheeded. If these organizations had all responded to early warnings about financial mismanagement, mine safety, smoking risks, implant failures, possible spills or fires, and dubious PCB storage practices, we might not be reading about them today. And some people would still be alive. A real difficulty none the less, for companies and stakeholders alike, is how to discriminate signals of real problems from noise or false warnings. Avoiding groupthink and responsiveness to negative feedback are ethically important qualities, signs of socio-economic problem-solving intelligence.

Table 8.2: **The Issue Life Cycle**

Phase Number	Phase Description	Number of Reports
1	Beginning: latency	No reports
2	Dawning perception	Few reports
3	Open debate	Many reports
4	Critical mass	Rapidly increasing
5	Full-blown crisis	Exponentially increasing
6	Resolution, victory, or disinterest	Decreasing

In Phase 2 reports increase and the perception of a possible problem dawns, as happened with the Rely tampon. If such perceptions are ignored, the issue may become critical and begin to run out of control. As problem reports increase, it becomes easier to perceive the problem and even to solve it. If no action is taken, however, problem reports will multiply and eventually erupt into the public arena (Phase 3), as they did with the breast implant case and environmental problems near industrial plants. Public debate ensues. A crisis is emerging. Organizations find themselves suddenly responding to hostile questions and attacks. Openness to feedback and willingness to act and solve the problem are essential to preventing a crisis from developing further. When some bottles of Tylenol were poisoned and seven people died, Johnson & Johnson immediately withdrew the product from the market and redesigned the Tylenol bottle cap to make tampering much more difficult.[18]

Stonewalling or taking a legalistic compliance approach does not solve problems. Rather, it exacerbates them and polarizes the debate to the point of critical mass (Phase 4). At this point it becomes difficult to separate signals from the noise and true from false reports and warnings. Thus the debates about disposable diapers and zero chlorine discharge became battles between environmental activists like Greenpeace and business, other environmentalists, and other stakeholders, such as consumers. Both extremes downplayed or ignored the best available research on pulp and paper effluents. Even at this late date solutions can be found, as they were in the chlorine debate. There a critical mass issue did not explode into a full-blown crisis.

The consequence of resisting or denying an issue that has reached critical mass is that a full-blown crisis may develop (Phase 5). This can be very costly for any business or organization. The hotly contested debate explodes beyond anyone's control. Accommodation with stakeholders becomes close to impossible. Polarized positions are simplified and then exaggerated by the mass media.[19] In such situations heat replaces light. The issue grows, multiplies, and takes on a life of its own beyond the control of any of the stakeholders. Panic, fear, and perception rule. This is now threatening to happen for the the tobacco industry. Just over a decade ago, for example, Nestle resisted responding to critics about exporting infant formula to developing nations. The issue eventually became a full-blown international crisis.[20]

In a full-blown crisis moral intelligence loses. Information, experience, expertise, and knowledge tend to be ignored or discounted. Decision-makers and knowledgeable experts and observers, however responsible or in the right, can lose the moral and cognitive high ground. Careful analysis, accurate data, consulting stakeholders, and solving problems are not exciting. So productive developments are all too often treated as boring and downplayed by the mass media.

An important lesson from major crises is that no single stakeholder should be allowed to dominate an issue or define the problem to the exclusion of other standpoints. Activist groups, unfortunately, tend to elaborate their grievances into absolute demands for instant satisfaction and play to the media's penchant for polarization. They are not interested in accommodation. Instead, they assert a form of sovereignty over their favoured issue.[21] In Tom Wolfe's novel, *The Bonfire of the Vanities*, the 'hero' was an arrogant Wall Street trader who saw himself as 'master of the universe', but he got caught in a scandal where accusations, media hype, and political grandstanding all reduced the chances of real problem-solving to nil. This is a growing occupational hazard in contemporary politics. In developing its fiscal, employment, and pay equity policies in the early 1990s, for example, the Ontario NDP government found itself caught in a tangle of warring unions, Natives, Blacks, gays, and women's activists, all traditional NDP supporters and all demanding their rights to the exclusion of other stakeholders.

At this point we enter the sixth and last phase of the issue life cycle. One of three outcomes may occur. Media or public interest may wane, one side may claim victory, or the problem may actually get solved. The first happens as media attention is diverted to some other, more sensational issue. The decline in media reports will raise communications problems for those organizations and stakeholders who have not effectively communicated their position. In this case the public memory of an issue will likely be one-sided. Few will have learned anything about solutions or even understand the original problem.

The second outcome, victory by one side, can be just as bad. Corporate tragedies become inevitable as full-blown crises develop.[22] The company at fault may face a considerable 'rear-end load' of delays and costs for those hurt by the problem, especially if it is demonstrably wrong and is responsible for imposing significant harms on others. For several firms, we have seen, full-blown crises led to catastrophic results: Dow-Corning, Barings, A.H. Robin, National Film Recovery Systems, and Johns-Manville. Each stonewalled a problem until it lost control of the issue and eventually went bankrupt. The same scenario now seems to face the tobacco industry. Greenpeace won its case over the Newfoundlanders and Inuit seal hunters, especially with the European public, but the seal hunters' communities suffered significant socio-economic losses as a result.

Only the third outcome truly resolves the issue, because it solves the underlying problem. It usually requires a responsive approach to the problem from the first, but sometimes crises force businesses to solve their problems. Nestle, for example, ultimately came round and accepted the World Health Organization code for marketing infant formula in developing nations, which largely resolved the issue. There were far fewer media reports about the solution than there had been about the crisis.

Cultural Relations

Canadian businesses have always had to deal with sensitive issues relating to the cultural diversity of the country. The two most notable cases are developing appropriate relations with Canada's Aboriginal communities and with Quebec nationalism. In both cases the ethical problem for business is less that of relativism than of cross-cultural understanding, developing reciprocally beneficial relations, and minimizing socio-economic risks. A special concern in the Quebec case is the delicate matter of dealing with an openly secessionist government. Here, core civil rights values become prominent. We will begin with the issue of Aboriginal relations, and then turn our attention to Quebec.

The first cultural relations challenge for Canadian business is how to develop appropriate business relations with Aboriginal communities. The Canadian constitution recognizes Aboriginal rights, and the government for some time has been negotiating Aboriginal land claims with First Nations; but most Aboriginal communities are small and have few socio-economic resources. Modern industrialization, furthermore, threatens Aboriginal cultures, for they are based on tribal ownership of the land. The land is inhabited by small populations for whom sharing resources is unproblematic. In contrast, large modern societies have developed more restrictive private property systems to control access to scarce resources. In addition, Canada's northern frontier, as Mr Justice Thomas Berger argued in his 1977 report on the Mackenzie Valley pipeline, is the homeland of many Native peoples. Berger recommended mutual accommodation and the gradual development of the dual, Aboriginal/Canadian, northern economy, 'based on modernization of hunting, fishing, trapping, . . . on small enterprise and on the orderly [development of gas and oil resources]. This is no retreat into the past;

rather, it is a rational program for northern development based on the ideals and aspirations of northern native peoples.'[23]

Pamela Sloan and Roger Hill's case studies of 36 Canadian businesses show that business is learning how to accommodate the different ways of Aboriginal communities. Of the firms Sloan and Hill studied, 18 are federal or provincial Crown corporations, 16 are privately owned, and two have mixed ownership. Of the 36 businesses, 17 are in the resource sector (energy and resources, forestry, mining), nine represent government services, from revenue to the RCMP, five are banks, and five are involved in telecommunications and transportation. Many of the firms offer Native pre-employment training programs and jobs, often adapted to the Native hunting and fishing economy. Some support Native business ventures through special contracts, tenders, procurement arrangements, and joint ventures.

Different firms take different approaches. Hydro-Québec tries to mitigate the negative impacts of the massive James Bay project on the local Cree community by helping them relocate and maintain their hunting, fishing, and trapping economy. Hydro-Québec also has programs to help southern Montagnais to enter the company workforce and special tendering for Montagnais contractors. Ontario Hydro, in co-operation with Ontario Native communities, has developed a 'team-based joint problem-solving' process to identify Aboriginal concerns in regard to Hydro operations on or near their lands. The aim is to develop consensus, mitigate impacts, and negotiate alternative solutions. Most programs go beyond general value statements to set specific goals and targets and to monitor the results. In most cases there has been measurable improvement over time, for example, in the number of Native trainees graduated, the number employed, and the number and size of business contracts tendered to Aboriginal contractors. A central theme is that corporate/Aboriginal relations should rest on understanding, respect, and mutual benefit.

Bridging cultural gaps through communication and understanding is a key theme. Toronto-Dominion Bank's Nakoda Circle program brings Aboriginal employees together from across Canada to advise senior managers on Aboriginal business concerns, work, and traditional culture. TransAlta Utilities is committed to building positive long-term relationships with Aboriginal communities, based on mutual benefits and trust. Aboriginal people are seen as business associates and stakeholders important to the corporation's future. Manitoba Telephone has half-day 'Walk a Mile in My Moccasins' cultural exchange workshops to help Manitoba Tel managers overcome cultural barriers with Aboriginal communities. BC Hydro has a three-stage cross-cultural training program, moving from understanding general differences to work-related problems with specific Aboriginal cultures. In response, the Salish and Squamish peoples awarded BC Hydro a 'talking stick' at the first potlatch ever held for a corporation.

The second cultural relations issue is the critical and highly political matter of Quebec independence. There is much less of a cultural gap between English and French Canadians than between Canadians and Aboriginal cultures. Quebec, with a population of about 6 million, is the home province of French Canada, but there are a million more French Canadians outside Quebec. There is extensive trade between Quebec and the other provinces. The main problems are Quebec's language law requiring French-language signs and rising concerns about its push towards independence.

Both English and French are Canada's official languages. For over 20 years now French has been accepted as the language of work in Quebec.[24] It is used extensively in neighbouring regions of Ontario and New Brunswick, a province which is also officially bilingual. There is controversy about details of the Quebec language law, which requires French to be more prominent on commercial signs than any other language; but most businesses have been willing to comply with the regulations. Concerns about 'the language police' are widely shared, including among the Francophone population. This is a minor irritant compared with the much more vexed matter of the stance Canadian businesses should take towards Quebec independence, an issue that approached critical mass in 1995 at the time of the most recent Quebec referendum on independence. The issue has smouldered just under the surface of Canadian politics ever since.

There is a large French business sector in Quebec. The closer a firm or stakeholder group is to the Quebec government and the more its business is purely in Quebec, the stronger its support for independence. Thus, Crown corporations such as Hydro-Québec and the Caisse de dépôt investment fund and the public service unions all support sovereignty. On the other hand, private Quebec firms that do business in English Canada and internationally tend to be federalist. Many English as well as French Quebec commercial interests, however, call for more autonomy for the Quebec provincial government. Their constitutional preference for decentralization, like states' rights in the US, is historically associated with *laissez-faire* economics—but only on the federal side. Provincially, nationalists have always favoured the strong, interventionist State.

Laurent Beaudoin is CEO of Bombardier Ltd, with 2,700 employees in Quebec, one of Quebec's most successful and innovative manufacturers. Bombardier has an increasingly international, high-tech market, including high-speed trains and executive jets. Beaudoin has consistently attacked the sovereignists, stating that Quebec independence is not just another social issue. It goes right to the very survival of Canada, and of Quebec.

Quebec nationalists, however, prefer to treat the issue as purely an internal family matter. On the one hand there is a Canada-wide democratic consensus that if the great majority of Québécois freely decide to leave in response to a clear question and a full airing of the likely consequences, then they will have made an informed choice, and democracy has spoken. The governments of Canada and Quebec should then negotiate mutually acceptable and constitutionally legitimate terms. On the other hand, the ruling Parti Québécois (PQ) regime in Quebec continues to try to disguise its independence project by linking it to vague talk of a future equal partnership with Canada. This is good political marketing, if somewhat disingenuous: stress the benefits and downplay the risks. So in the 30 October 1995 referendum on independence, to entice the soft nationalist vote the question linked sovereignty to a vague notion of an offer of a new equal partnership with Canada. The ambiguous question, many felt, soft-pedalled the independence option. The result was that the PQ almost won the day. Quebec and

Canada barely avoided a full-blown political and constitutional crisis.

Notwithstanding the soft question, the PQ government was ready to declare independence unilaterally and secede from Canada if its terms for separation were not immediately agreed to by the Canadian government. The Supreme Court is currently deliberating the legality of the independence option. The PQ provincial government, however, has refused to participate in the Supreme Court hearing and now openly favours a unilateral declaration of independence outside Canada's constitutional framework.

The PQ also maintains that Canadians have no say in the matter of Quebec independence. It is a purely in-house affair, or *en famille* as one says in French. Moreover, several PQ leaders, including a former Premier, have expressed racist sentiments. Understandably many Canadians, including Québécois, feel that Quebec's secession would put their welfare at significant risk. As direct stakeholders in that decision they have demanded a say in the matter, but Quebec nationalists deny that Canadians outside Quebec should have anything to say in their independence decision. None the less, many both within and outside Quebec argue that in any future independence referendum the question must be clear and unambiguous and the voting procedures utterly fair. It is commonly agreed that any subsequent divorce negotiations would be very unpleasant. Many Canadians inside Quebec want to remain Canadians, even if that means partitioning Quebec.

This critical and divisive political issue poses difficult choices for any business with investments in Quebec. The core civil rights value and the 'do no harm' and 'informed choice' maxims suggest that the case for Quebec independence and the break-up of Canada would have to be extremely cogent and pressing. But in fact, the use of French in Quebec is not declining and the people of Quebec are in no way oppressed by Canada. On the contrary, Canada is generally recognized as one of the most democratic and civil of nations. In addition, there is little, if any, evidence that independence will enhance the position of the French language in North America or bring greater prosperity to Quebec. On the contrary, the PQ's own 1995 studies of the consequences of separation suggest it may involve significant costs.

In response to the close referendum vote and the continuing commitment of the PQ government to sovereignty, capital and people, including many Francophones, have already started to leave Quebec. Montreal has the highest urban unemployment rate in the country. Property values are depressed. Dick Pound, a prominent Montreal corporate lawyer and member of the International Olympic Committee, has said that an independent Quebec would be 'a rapidly shrinking, marginalized ghetto'. Many Quebec firms feel that a vote for Quebec sovereignty involves significant economic risks. Paul Desmarais, CEO of the Montreal-based Power Corporation, declared that 'It's self-evident that the separatists . . . haven't made a case as to why we should separate. It's up to them to tell us why we should get out.'

Some firms are already thinking of developing operations outside Quebec. Allan Segal, CEO of Peerless Clothing, which sells 95 per cent of its product in the US, was worried about his new Montreal factory, which has 2,400 employees. Peerless's access to the US market would be at risk, for NAFTA would be renegotiated. So Segal plans to diversify his operations. His fears about NAFTA access were confirmed in the summer 1996 hearings of a US congressional subcommittee.

In a 15 January 1996 speech, Matthew Barrett, the chairman of the Bank of Montreal, gave prominent voice to these concerns. The bank released the results of an internal report that forecast economic chaos in the five years following Quebec independence, even with a new partnership. There would be high interest rates, massive population and capital outflows, reduced capital inflows, and the Canadian dollar would plummet. The result could be a $150 to $200 billion decrease in Canada's GDP, or a loss of about $20,000 for every family of four. Interest rates would rise, critically worsening the serious public debt, especially for Quebec, which already has about the highest public debt in Canada. Quebec might suffer an immediate 7 per cent fall in its GDP. Barrett concluded, 'These are sobering numbers. Quebec is particularly hard hit, and a serious hit for the whole of Canada. . . . We can no longer afford to be disengaged or tuned out. We have to accept the true seriousness of the risks we are running.'

Barrett called for an innovative federal response to Quebec. Lucien Bouchard, the Premier of Quebec, dismissed Barrett's report, terming it 'irrational and irresponsible. I think we have better things to do right now than to engage in phony debates that are based on absolutely freakish numbers, derived from absolutely no analysis, on nothing concrete.'

Premier Bouchard has already declared that Quebec is not bound by the Canadian constitution. Any declaration of independence by Quebec will therefore likely be unilateral. This will exacerbate the socio-economic problems it claims to solve. So here, the risk-minimizing, 'do no harm' values suggest that businesses should do all they can to prevent the smouldering critical mass of the Quebec independence issue from exploding into a full-blown crisis. They can encourage all parties to follow the civil, democratic, and constitutional values that Quebec and Canada share, stressing the need for informed choice and mutual accommodation, and especially the obligation to minimize the risk of a national crisis. Both the Aboriginal and Quebec issues, then, require companies to take proactive positions on social issues.

The Social Market

Today, many businesses contribute to resolving social issues through responsible business practices. Edward Newall of Nova Corporation and former chairman of the Business Council on National Issues claims that one major social problem that business should help to solve is poverty.[25] Across North America numerous firms are contributing, each in its own way, to improving education, reducing sexism and racism, protecting the environment, and so on. Joan Kroc, the wife of the founder of McDonald's, has spent over US$30 million on the campaign for world peace, AIDS research, and the homeless—about 5 per cent of her estimated fortune of $600 million.[26] Of the 472 major Canadian firms surveyed in the *Corporate Ethics Monitor*, 38 per cent donate on average about 1.4 per cent of their profits to charitable causes, and support education, social welfare, and the arts. So there is some sense of social obligation in the business community. That sense of social values has been taken a step further by The Body Shop. It began with a classically creative entrepreneurial idea.

The First, Entrepreneurial Step

I was annoyed by the fact that you couldn't buy small sizes of everyday cosmetics. . . . I was paying a lot of money for fancy packaging which I didn't want. So I opened a small shop to sell a small range of cosmetics made from natural ingredients in five different sizes in the cheapest possible plastic containers.

Anita Roddick, founder of The Body Shop

Anita Roddick is not a do-gooder who disdains business and selling her goods in the marketplace. On the contrary, she brags, 'I know how to trade.' Roddick certainly is an entrepreneur. (Her husband, Graeme, is the manager who keeps things under control.) Twenty years ago she opened her first Body Shop store in Littlehampton, England, because of her dislike of commercial cosmetics and marketing practices.[27] Roddick says she saw women in developing nations using local natural products, like pineapple, and sensed the market potential for low-price, natural products designed more for healthy skin care than for beauty.[28] Body Shop products were sold without the marketing hype and high prices typical of cosmetics retailing. Customers could recycle their own containers. In addition, The Body Shop has moved away from the hard commercialism of the cosmetics industry. It does not advertise. In each shop consumers can find information on product contents and on current social campaigns.

It has also rejected animal testing on cosmetics, refusing to buy from suppliers that tested materials on animals in the last five years and monitoring its suppliers to ensure compliance. That policy has been independently shown to meet rigorous, international quality control standards. In 1994 the International Federation of Animal Welfare favourably reviewed the policy against animal testing, and also found it effective in increasing social pressure to end animal testing. As well, The Body Shop has followed proactive environmental management methods and done extensive social and environmental audits. It supports social issue campaigns in its stores, and has developed an international Trade Not Aid program that helps small suppliers in the developing world to become self-reliant. The result, Roddick contends, has been to create a new social model of business: 'What we are trying to do is to create a new business paradigm, simply showing that business can have a human face and a social conscience. Why should we expect less from it, in terms of social ethics, than we do from ourselves and our neighbours?' This is echoed in Body Shop International's mission statement. The company's 'Reason for Being', it states, is 'to dedicate our business to the pursuit of social and environmental change.' Together, these statements suggest a new entrepreneurial idea, that of *the social market*.

Instead of associating skin care with the beauty myth, from the first The Body Shop connected its retail trade to social and environmental issues and campaigns, for

Roddick's aim was not only to survive as a business but also to 'keep our soul intact'. In 1988 Body Shop International deliberately located its soapworks factory in a depressed Glasgow neighbourhood. From the first the company has been environmentally proactive, using biodegradable material in its plastic bottles and packaging. The Body Shop Canada has an in-house greenhouse, biological wastewater and sewage treatment, and high efficiency lighting. It operates an award-winning internal recycling program. Since 1992 Body Shop International has published three independently verified environmental audits along with its financial statements. In his independent audit Kirk Hanson awarded the company five stars (out of five) for energy conservation and four stars for environmental management, reporting, and pollution abatement. It is now moving toward life-cycle environmental manufacturing. The Body Shop's *Environmental Statement 1995* is detailed and comprehensive, and approximates the quality of internal environmental auditing done at Inco and Falconbridge.

Body Shop Canada is owned by a woman, Margot Franssen, and 56 per cent of the executives are female, as are 76 per cent of administrative management and 90 per cent of the workforce. The company offers day care on site, extended maternity leave, flex-time scheduling, employee training, profit-sharing, and health care support. Body Shop Canada requires each store to take on a community project to which staff must devote 16 hours of paid time per month. The stores supported campaigns against whaling, child poverty, domestic violence, nuclear tests, and animal testing, and for women's rights, the YWCA, saving tropical rain forests, and protecting endangered species. It also donates products to the Daily Bread food bank and battered women's shelters. Body Shop International opposed the Gulf War, even producing a corporate video. Recently, it ran a campaign against Shell's involvement in Nigeria, the story that opens the next chapter. In the US, Body Shop stores promote voter registration. In this way social values have penetrated retail trade.

Body Shop Canada commits 20 per cent of its profits to local projects in high-risk neighbourhoods, such as Toronto's unique Dufferin Mall. In a 1993 visit Anita Roddick contributed $20,000 to the Sierra Legal Defence Fund, Habitat for Humanity, Street Kids International, and the Dene Cultural Institute. Since 1993 the Body Shop International Charitable Foundation has distributed over US$400,000 to various social and environmental groups. In 1994 donations reached 2.87 per cent of its pre-tax profits, well above the UK and North American average.

Since it was founded over 20 years ago The Body Shop has grown a great deal. In 1995 Body Shop International had 572 franchisees with 1,375 stores in 45 nations (there are 113 Body Shop stores in Canada). Sales were over US$440 million. In 1995 Body Shop sales were up in most markets except the US, where it faces strong competition from Soapberry and Bath and Body Works. Indeed, the company is now facing competition on a product quality/good value basis. Some popular writers on cosmetics express concerns about the quality of several Body Shop products, noting that they often use the same basic synthetic chemicals as most hair-care products. One, Paula Begoun, does not feel the natural ingredients add much value. Another, Debra Dadd, is more environmentally inclined. She is unhappy that some of the product ingredients are not natural.[29] As we saw in the last chapter, without widely accepted product standards, it is difficult to verify such product claims. The Body Shop, however, only claims that it uses natural ingredients as much as possible, for transportation and shelf life still require the use of some synthetic preservatives.

The Body Shop is not without its critics. Whenever outspoken people boldly proclaim that they are rejecting the conventional business model in favour of something as soft and dubious as integrating business and social values, one should expect criticism. And The Body Shop has provoked controversy. In 1994, Jon Entine, an advocacy journalist, criticized The Body Shop for exaggerating its natural product claims and animal testing policy and for uneven product quality. The last claim does seem to have some merit, as we just saw. But long-time consumer advocate Ralph Nader has some reservations about Jon Entine's criticisms: 'He sounds like the mouth that roared. Apart from his inclinations toward fiction, the author seeks to make smaller and better companies perfect. Maybe next time he should go into the trenches and go after the likes of GE and Monsanto.'

In response to these criticisms The Body Shop commissioned an independent audit by Kirk Hanson of the Stanford University School of Business, which it published, unedited, in the spring of 1996. Hanson's findings were mixed. He found that The Body Shop outperformed comparable firms in the industry in 16 areas, was about the same in 22, and did poorly in two areas. The company did a good job on employee wages and benefits and women's opportunities. But Hanson found the company overly defensive in response to criticism, with a deplorable tendency to exaggerate and overstate its case. Finally, The Body Shop has had poor relations with its employees, franchisees, and the public. Overall, it needs to improve communication with its stakeholders, a failing admitted in its own *1995 Social Statement* (independently verified by the New Economic Foundation in London). In it Body Shop International reports that many stakeholders felt that the company's statements did not accurately describe its business practices. None the less, most stakeholders said they believe that the company lives up to its mission, an important expression of confidence. The problem, Hanson concluded, is that 'Until recently, it has given more attention to its "social campaigns" than it has to improving the social impact on its day-to-day business dealings.'

Body Shop International openly acknowledges that there is some validity to many of these criticisms. In fact, The Body Shop has opened its doors to independent outside evaluation to an extraordinary degree. No other firm, especially in the cosmetics industry, has been as transparent in disclosing its inside operations and audits to outsiders. Furthermore, very few firms, if any, have so closely integrated their business trade with environmental, social, and international aid campaigns.

When taken together, its environmental audits, social statements, social campaigns, and efforts to change the skin-care market all represent an impressive social performance achievement on the part of The Body Shop. It has offered a good product concept (now in need of some upgrading) with in-store and in-house social campaigns. Despite all the problems, Anita Roddick's social entrepreneurship seems to have been successful. Indeed, Hanson gave the company high marks for its values statements, donations, and animal welfare and environmental positions, concluding that 'The Body

Shop demonstrates greater social responsibility and better social performance than most companies of its size.' By and large, the company has lived up to its self-set mission of integrating business with social and environmental change, and remains a leader in social and environmental performance. In so doing it has created a new business paradigm, the social market. If other firms do any or all of these things better than The Body Shop, that, of course, would be wonderful. It's about time businesses competed on ethical as well as market values.

Summary

To review, this chapter began with an old story of lax government regulation and all-too-free enterprise in the PCB warehouse fire at St Basil le Grand, Quebec. Concern for the public was totally lacking, to the point that the owner of the warehouse fled the country, without paying for any of the damage the fire caused. This demonstrated the need for improved government regulations and ethically more satisfactory relations between business and government. It also showed the need for a more proactive, crisis-preventing approach on the part of business. From this comes a clearer concept of social performance, according to which a business should solve the social problems caused by its operations. Similarly, Canadian businesses need to adapt their approach to different cultures, as several have succeeded in doing with regard to Aboriginal peoples. Finally, The Body Shop exemplifies the new, and controversial, 'social market' that social performance implies. This market extends well beyond national boundaries. Indeed, the subject of the next chapter is the ethical complexity of international business.

Chapter 9

International Values

All these merchants observe the laws of the city, and moreover live and conduct themselves freely, and are of use to the world . . . merely by means of [their] trade.

> Ludovico Guicciardini, Florentine diplomat,
> at the 1560 Antwerp trade fair

Reciprocal dependence and peace are the natural effect of trade.
> Michel de Montesquieu,
> *The Spirit of the Laws*, 1748[1]

Ports of Call

Sandro knew what Guicciardini was talking about. His ship flew the flag of Genoa, but it docked in the ports of many nations, from France and Spain to the Low Countries. In them all he traded peacefully with peoples of many languages. Sandro's cousin in Venice even traded with Muslims, Asians, and Africans. No flags ruled on the seas—they were free for ships, sailors, and for pirates, too. Sometimes Sandro longed for the protection of Genoa, or even the English. He had met all too many corrupt officials and merchants in his travels, but of course there were honest ones as well. He saw terrible poverty in the streets of Marseilles, Barcelona, and London, often beside unimaginable wealth. Antwerp and Hamburg, which he had voyaged to twice, were lively, democratic cities, whose volatile politics, Aldo said, reminded him of the unending squabbles in Florence and Bologna. In every port Sandro sold Aldo's wares and loaded goods to bring back for Aldo to sell, making their financial partner, Cosmo, happy, too. And Sandro made many friends in every port. It was a good life. As long, that is, as no one was at war. Peace was good for business.

Like Sandro, in Part I we will see some of the vexed problems still encountered in international business: oppression, poverty, exploitation, and instability. We begin with two contrasting tales about ethical controversies in foreign direct investment. Shell's operations in Nigeria are compared with Sherritt-Gordon's mine in Cuba. Then we shift to two tales about ethics in global trade: the problem of foreign suppliers to multinational retail firms using child labour in poor, developing nations, and, finally, the problem of economic instability in response to highly volatile global financial trading. All raise ethical questions about large multinational corporations (MNCs) and international trade. Free trade does not always deliver the socio-economic goods. Instead, it often seems to be accompanied by exploitative labour, environmental degradation, dependency, and financial instability. All show that the old talk of ethically neutral free trade is naïve at best.

Part II begins by making the case for 'social trade' in international business. It extends the community of interests to external stakeholders, direct and indirect, outside the home nation of the firm. The aim of international commerce and therefore of foreign investment, it is argued, is to bring benefits to other nations, to enhance their socio-economic welfare, in return for being allowed to do business there. In international business as everywhere else, the maxim must be to *do no harm*: foreign businesses should not make things worse for their host nations. For international business is a form of trade, and trade is based on reciprocal exchanges, on mutual benefit. Just as international business in effect extends business from domestic to foreign markets, so social trade extends exchange values and the social market approach to distant lands. An important lesson, reinforced in the conclusion, is that businesses make a socio-economic and ethical difference through the way they do business, through trade rather than aid. This social trade path to development involves encouraging local skills and entrepreneurship.

I Old Tales about Politics, Children, and Money

Part I presents four different tales about ethically dubious forms of international business. First there are two controversial cases of foreign direct investment, in the oilfields of Nigeria and the mines of Cuba. They tell contrasting stories about the ethics of foreign direct investment in countries with undemocratic regimes where civil rights are in question. Next, there is the problem multinational retail firms are experiencing with the exploitative child labour practices of distant suppliers. Fourthly, the growing risk of volatility in international financial flows is shown to be open to an international solution that, it is argued, would be in the interest of business to support. Reflection on all four cases shows the need for a social trade approach to international business. First, to Shell in Nigeria, and then to Cuba.

Investing in African Oppression

With 112 million people Nigeria is Africa's most populous nation, one beset by old tribal tensions between the Christian Ibos in the east and the Yoruba in the south, and the Muslim Hausa and Fulani in the north.[2] These tensions led to an Ibo secession attempt and a bloody civil war in 1967. The current military regime of General Sani Abacha, of the northern Hausa, at first had sought to end tribal violence and restore peace and order. Today, however, the Abacha junta has annulled elections, abolished parliamentary and regional governments, shut down newspapers, and jailed most of the opposition, including the winner of the 1993 presidential election. Amnesty International reports that in 1994 the Nigerian regime arbitrarily detained about 600 Ogonis, a tribe that lives in the oil-rich delta region—100 people were publicly executed and another 50 'extrajudicially' murdered by the military.

The Nigerian economy is corrupted by nepotism, extortion, the drug trade, bribes and kickbacks, inflated government megaprojects, and notorious fraud scams. This has weakened its already poor economy (£23 billion in debt) and chilled international investment. Despite all these problems many foreign firms continue to invest in Nigeria. Britain had a 1994 trade surplus of £333 billion with Nigeria. Multinational corporations like ICI and Wellcome have divested and left; but Cadbury, Guinness, Lever Brothers, and Paterson are still there, as are French MNCS Michelin, Peugeot, Boygues (oil), and Berger (construction). Vickers PLC sold Nigeria 80 armoured tanks, but their delivery has been embargoed.

Canadian refineries, owned by Irving, Ultramar, and Imperial Oil, import about $600 million in Nigerian crude, or 12 per cent of Canadian oil imports. In 1994 the Canadian Energy Research Institute warned that oil industry investment in Nigeria was highly risky due to military government corruption. Two Canadian oil firms, Abacan Resources and Profco, do work in Nigeria. 'You can't get involved in politics', declares Wade Chewayko, president of Abacan Resources (Canada). 'You don't side with anyone. You're there just to do business.' His view is echoed by Shell Nigeria local management, but not by local villagers.

Message to Foreign Investors: Bring Stability and Civilization

You need a stable environment [for foreign investment]. Dictatorships can give you that. Right now in Nigeria there is acceptance, peace and continuity.

N. Achebe, general manager, Shell Nigeria

Shell brought civilization to Nigeria. I don't see why they can't bring civilization to us. Shell promised to build schools and to make a sea wall because the town is flooded every year. Nothing was done.

Edwin Ofonih of Oloibiri, Nigeria

Shell is certainly not a newcomer. It has been in Nigeria for 50 years. Its operation is a division of Royal Dutch Shell, a Dutch/British multinational, whose US$128 billion in assets are almost four times larger than Nigeria's GNP (US$32.9 billion). Shell had sales of US$107.8 billion in 1995 and a 6.3 per cent profit rate (US$6.8 billion, the highest for any MNC). Shell's 180 executives in Nigeria live in air-conditioned homes in the well-manicured 'Shell Camp' in Port Harcourt. Shell has a 30 per cent stake (the major foreign share) in Nigeria's state oil consortium, along with Elf of France, Agip of Italy, and the state-owned Nigeria National Petroleum Company.

For 30 years the Nigerian consortium has run the Ogoni oil fields, which pump over half of Nigeria's output of about 2 million barrels of oil per day. The oil brings Nigeria revenues of US$10 billion a year, of which the government keeps 70 per cent. The government had decreed that 3 per cent of the total revenues should flow back to local communities; a proposed increase to 13 per cent has not yet been ratified. It is not clear whether either has been fully implemented. The oppression and corruption in Nigeria have put pressure on foreign firms to support community projects. But, Shell protests, the more the company builds local hospitals and schools, the more it replaces the junta as a target for dissent.

The repressive approach of General Abacha's military junta has exacerbated tribal and regional tensions. Five hundred thousand Ogoni live in the southeastern delta, where the oilfields are. Ken Saro Wiwa, an internationally acclaimed author, led the Movement for the Survival of the Ogoni People, which opposed the military regime and talked of secession. In November 1995 the military junta arrested nine Ogoni opponents, including Saro Wiwa. After a show trial they executed all nine. Before he died Saro Wiwa accused the Abacha regime 'of practicing racism against the Ogoni people. I appeal to the international community who buy oil from Nigeria to come to the aid of the Ogoni people and stop this genocide.'

Critics contend that Shell could ensure that much more of its billions in oil revenue and the benefits from its operations go to the Nigerian people, including the Ogoni. Shell, they feel, has some responsibility to support civil rights in Nigeria. Despite its influence, however, Shell seems to have done little to protest the oppression or prevent the executions. Shell withdrew from Ogoniland over two years ago, but it has not abandoned its Nigerian operations. The official company line is that as a private firm it should not support Ogoni secessionism or interfere in Nigerian domestic politics.

Pollution from the oilfield has harmed the rural ecosystem and economy, as the comment of an Ogoni villager suggests:

> In the old days in Gokana you could fish, farm and survive without money. But oil exploration spoiled the creeks and the seas and you can't fish like you did before. We used to have a lot of land, but Shell made much of that unusable.

In reply, Shell claims that it has begun to repair the environmental damage, but that sabotage caused about 70 per cent of the oil spills in Ogoniland, much higher than the 28 per cent average in other areas. Claude Ake, of the Niger Delta Environmental Survey, tried to negotiate an environmental clean-up in the Niger Delta with the oil companies. He urged them to enter a dialogue and improve their poor relations with local communities. But Shell resisted his solicitations. Ake explains:

> I was taken aback by their unwillingness to accept responsibility. Frankly I would have expected a much more sophisticated corporate strategy from Shell. No one is calling for altruism, just a certain pragmatism. . . . All this could have been avoided for no money whatsoever.

From Canada and the 52 Commonwealth nations to the European Community parliament, there is talk of international sanctions against Nigeria, such as those that had been successful in South Africa a decade ago. Options discussed include an international embargo against Nigerian oil exports and a freeze on the military leaders' foreign assets. Shell, Elf, and Agip are entangled in a growing debate about the moral obligations of multinationals to respect civil rights in host nations and support local development.

Investing in Cuban Socialism

The same issues arise in different form as we travel from Nigeria to Cuba. The contrasts, however, are dramatic, even though neither country is a democratic regime or a developed nation. Cuba, with 11 million people, is the largest island nation in the Caribbean.[3] It is a dictatorship and the press is censored, but the country is still ruled by law and the government is much less corrupt and oppressive than that of Nigeria. Cubans are healthier, more literate, and less poor than Nigerians, with four times their average income. The government imposes high taxes and extensive regulations on small private enterprises like bed and breakfasts, restaurants, taxis, and street vendors. President Fidel Castro has none the less begun to welcome foreign investment, within limits. The US State Department, however, advises foreign businesses not to invest in Cuba.

In December 1994 Sherritt-Gordon Mines, a Canadian firm, negotiated a joint venture with Cuba's state-owned General Nickel SA to mine cobalt and nickel at Moa Bay. The deal also provides Sherritt's Saskatchewan refinery with needed natural gas for the next 25 years at a stable price, in contrast to Canadian gas. Sherritt International of Toronto is the first foreign company to gain access to state-controlled Cuban sugar, real estate, and finance industries. The Moa Bay operation employs 1,700 Cubans. Workers are paid about US$9,500 a year in Cuban pesos, with bonuses in US dollars. Ian Delaney, Sherritt's CEO, terms his company 'the Canadian Pacific of Cuba' because of its potential impact on Cuba's future development.

The Sherritt/General Nickel joint venture reflects the dual, foreign capitalist/domestic statist Cuban economy. Other Canadian firms have invested in Cuba, too: Pizza Nova of Toronto, Delta Hotels, Redpath Sugar, and a few western oil and gas development firms. They all had to negotiate with a socialist government that does not recognize private enterprise in Cuba. For example, Delta runs a hotel for Cubanacam (the State-owned tourism authority), but it could not contract directly with individuals to supply fresh fish. So Delta got the Cuban government to agree to allow a fishery co-op to be formed to act as its supplier.

In contrast to its good relations with Vietnam and China, the US government is quite sensitive about having a Communist state as a close neighbour. Its attitude to Cuba reflects a historical pattern in US/Latin American relations. Washington intervened to overthrow democratic, reformist regimes in Guatemala in 1954, in Chile in 1973, and in Nicaragua in the early 1980s, all because of perceived threats to US corporate interests. In line with that imperial tradition, in 1995 Senator Jesse Helms and Representative Dan Burton got the US Congress to pass their aptly entitled Cuba Liberty and Democratic Solidarity Act. Its stated aim is to restore democracy in Cuba. To that end it gives some US citizens the right to sue foreign companies that do business in

Cuba on land the government confiscated from former Cubans. US sugar, rum (i.e., Bacardi), and tobacco interests lobbied for the bill. When Cuba shot down two Cuban exile planes in February 1996 President Clinton's hand was forced, especially since it was an election year, to sign the Helms-Burton Act into law. In consequence, such foreign firms as Sherritt, Redpath Sugar, Cemex (Mexico), BAT (UK), and Pernod (France) all face the risks of becoming litigation targets of aggrieved US firms. The likely result would be costly out-of-court settlements, whereby these firms would gain a piece of the profits. But other firms with no special claims on Cuba still cannot trade with Cuba. So one effect of Helms-Burton has been to privilege some US firms against others.

Many American citizens have their doubts about Helms-Burton, just as they question the 30-year US trade embargo against Cuba. The National Association of Manufacturers opposes it, fearing that unilateral sanctions could threaten US export markets and investments. Internationally illegal actions by Washington, furthermore, make it easier for Castro to attack the US in international forums like the United Nations and further delay reform. Helms-Burton forbids conduct that is legal under both Canadian and Cuban law for Canadian firms. It extraterritorially extends US law beyond US borders, in violation of fundamental principles of international law and free trade. To quote one European official, 'This is as extraterritorial as you can get.'

Territoriality is a fundamental principle in international law, closely linked to sovereignty. Within a State's borders its laws alone hold sway. No State may legislate actions beyond its borders (except, to a limited degree, for its own citizens). But this is not the first time the United States has imposed its will extraterritorially. Previous examples include the Anti-Trust, Trading with the Enemy, and Foreign Corrupt Practices Acts. Helms-Burton, understandably, has been vigorously opposed by Canada, the G7, Europe, and most South American nations. Inasmuch as Helms-Burton imposes narrow political values on the conduct of foreign firms operating in foreign nations, it exemplifies 'the Righteous American' problem, namely, of assuming that US values are superior to those of other nations.

In addition, Helms-Burton's main assumption is false. Cuba did not refuse to negotiate compensation for foreign firms for expropriated property. Rather, the United States refused to negotiate. Wayne S. Smith, former director of Cuban affairs in the State Department until 1977, states that 'It is simply not true to say Cuba has been unwilling to discuss compensation. . . . Cuba fully recognized its obligation to compensate . . . and indicated its willingness to negotiate. Indeed it had already reached compensation agreements with most other countries.' Smith should know. He was the US representative in Havana until he resigned over disagreements with the Reagan administration in 1982, when the US opened discussions with Cuba but did not take the Cuban offer seriously.

After President Clinton signed Helms-Burton, Redpath Sugar of Montreal and Cemex of Mexico pulled out of Cuba. The US State Department formally accused Sherritt International of using Cuban property that belonged to a former US company, Moa Bay Mining. It alleged that Cuba expropriated it without compensation. But Moa is now owned by Citibank, which has not indicated that it wants to sue Sherritt.

Another firm, Consolidated Development, has filed a US$1 million lawsuit against Sherritt in Miami. There are over 5,900 such claims against foreign companies in Cuba registered with the US government, totalling US$95 billion.

In response, Canada has retaliated. Parliament amended the Foreign Extraterritorial Measures Act, which was originally passed in 1992 to deal with subsidiaries of American MNCs that refuse to trade with Cuba. The aim is to prevent Helms-Burton litigants from collecting on US court judgements in Canada and to allow Canadians to sue them in Canadian courts to recover any sums awarded by US courts. In response to the foreign opposition, President Clinton delayed full implementation of the law until at least mid-1997. The most predictable effect of Helms-Burton, therefore, has been to encourage litigation and to hurt US relations with friendly states. Helms-Burton, that is, has 'legalized' US/Cuba relations, extraterritorially.

Ethics in Foreign Investment

The Cuban case seems quite different from the Nigerian situation. Cuba is more developed and democratic and less corrupt than Nigeria. It has a functioning legal system and respects egalitarian values. Its economy is not nearly as corrupt as Nigeria's. And the American attempt to impose its laws extraterritorially raises ideological and imperial questions representing a throwback to the Cold War, which many thought had withered and died in 1990. In both cases, however, an underlying issue is the ethics of foreign direct investment.

For the businesses involved, there are three basic foreign investment options. (1) *Do business* in foreign nations; invest or stay. This is appropriate for most democracies and many developing nations. (2) The opposite, of course, is to *refuse to do business*. Do not invest, or leave. This applies to oppressive, corrupt, and unstable nations, whether developed or developing. (3) Finally, there is the qualified middle way of *conditional investment*. The principle here is that investment should not make things worse in the host nation, politically, socially, and economically, but should make things better. Thus, foreign firms should do what they can to respect civil and human rights and to further local socio-economic development. This suggestion of 'social trade' in international business rests on the exchange values implicit in all market transactions. They suggest that international business should promote trade and reciprocity among nations and discourage violence (i.e., threat values). As Montesquieu said, commerce should encourage peace. So foreign direct investment should bring socio-economic benefits and reduce oppression to host nations. Ethics in this sense is part of the bargain.

That is not to say international business decision-making is simple or easy. Both cases show the contrary to be the case. Rather, foreign firms need to make judgements about whether they can have any effect for the better in a host nation. 'Host nation', of course, means the communities affected and the people, not just a small political or economic élite. To the extent they can do business successfully, business judgement says to go ahead. To the extent a company's operation and presence make things better, it acts ethically. And some developing nations are evolving a legal framework and democratic institutions.[4] All in all, the more reciprocity between the guest corporation and the host nation, the more welcome the firm is and the more likely its stay is good for both parties. That, too, is good business.

On these grounds there seems to be a reasonable case for Sherritt and other firms to do business in Cuba, especially when combined with the growing international political pressure on Castro to democratize the government. On the other hand, there is no sign that foreign firms are discouraging the oppressive Abacha regime; nor is there clear evidence that their presence is a net contributor to advancing development and improving the socio-economic welfare of Nigerians. Neither ethically neutral investment in oppressive regimes nor extraterritorially imposing one's own laws is a constructive solution to the troubling ethical problems of international commerce.

Although the presence of foreign corporations in both nations is controversial, Shell and Sherritt have chosen the first option and decided to stay put. For Shell this represents historic practice. In the late 1980s Shell had resisted international pressure to leave South Africa; but the South African case showed that compliance with oppressive or morally dubious local laws is morally problematic.[5] None the less, neither company can credibly argue that its investment decisions are ethically or politically neutral. Controversy swirls around both situations. Both are moving up the issue life cycle. Both are certainly in the open debate phase of the issue cycle (see Chapter 8), but they are developing in different directions. At this time there are signs of some political accommodation on the Cuban issue. Here solutions seem possible. On the other hand, the Nigeria question smoulders, and threatens to approach the critical mass phase of the issue cycle. Here no solution is in sight. On the available evidence Nigeria is a dubious investment host, on both economic and ethical grounds.

Finally, conditional investment often makes sense. Frequently the picture is confused; and societies do change. Simply to say that companies should invest in democracy, support civil rights, and oppose oppression and corruption is too facile. Take South Africa. It is now a constitutional democracy, in part because of both international sanctions and the work of enlightened foreign corporations on the ground in the 1980s. So situations change. Civil rights in a nation may improve or worsen. Eastern Europe's emancipation from communism was sudden and largely unforeseen. Equally unexpected was the aftermath—many former Communist nations are now mired in a corrupt perversion of democracy and a criminal variant of capitalism. Investors therefore need to sense the direction of social, economic, and political change. Ethics may help in this project, as the next chapter suggests.

Many North American business people assume corruption and bribery are a way of life in developing nations and are often blind to the political corruption in their own societies. The campaign financing in the US political system, for instance, is hardly a model of international integrity. But various different problems are concealed under the label of corrupt payments. Extortion by violent criminals is common wherever there are organized mafias, for example, in eastern Europe, Northern Ireland, southern Italy, the drug-producing areas of Asia and South America, and the US inner cities. While the brunt of the extortion threat is faced by small businesses, it can infect the whole market, and often constitutes the basis for criminal gangs funding 'legitimate' businesses. Extortion is, in addition, a threat anywhere there is significant terrorism (including from the State). The fundamental issue is criminality and illegality. Such corruption represents a clear warning against investment. Corruption, however, does not always originate with the locals. Rather, an African government official who has dealt extensively with foreign multinationals felt Western firms are often the source of corruption.[6]

Sometimes We Are the Corrupt Ones

The Europeans and North Americans have been taking advantage of us for decades. [They] establish a joint venture and then strip the local company bare through transfer pricing, management fees and royalties. . . . I would like to find someone from the developed world I can trust. . . . You want to win all the time and you are so impatient you bribe.

On the other hand, voluntary payments like gifts, 'tips', and bribes form a continuum from legitimate payments to illegal bribery. Gifts such as business lunches are a normal part of businesses everywhere. Today, however, many companies are putting limits on gifts and hospitality.[7] Nortel's *Code of Business Conduct* suggests some tests:

* ❖   Is the gift related to the ordinary conduct of business?
* ❖   Is it moderate in cost?
* ❖   Is it legal?
* ❖   Does it imply any special favours?

All gifts, in addition, should be disclosed. In many poor countries officials expect small payments for government and other services, and agents are often used to help conduct business and negotiate contracts. Here ethical judgements are often murky. What is customary and accepted locally offers some guidance. But as the payments increase and are linked to other expected favours, then they verge on corruption. Bribery and extortion are, of course, illegal in most nations, but enforcement may be uneven and capricious.[8] The US Foreign Corrupt Practices Act not only requires companies to keep records and file reports on such payments to foreign governments and officials, it also prohibits any payments to foreign governments or officials intended to influence government policy, laws, or decisions. But the Act also allows for 'grease' or 'facilitating payments' to improve service from foreign government officials. They are often legitimate, given the low pay of public servants and general poverty of the country.

In navigating the murky waters of dubious payments, a good ethical rule is a combination of open disclosure/record-keeping, and integrity in company policy. Supporting corruption, after all, has its costs. It encourages dishonesty in the firm, can become an excuse for failure, and gives the company a name as a 'mark'. It is better to be known overseas as a company of integrity. A good rule is 'When in Rome do as the *better* Romans do.'[9]

Exploiting Children

Talk of global free trade still assumes old, morally neutral, *laissez-faire* notions. It remains resistant to requiring respect for civil and human rights in international commerce, despite growing evidence about unhealthy and exploitative work conditions in low-wage 'maquiladora' zones and even about child labour. On the contrary, the growth of child labour shows that international commerce cannot evade its obligations to support some form of social trade. Businesses should be wary of agreeing to terms of trade that violate human rights. Manufacturers and retailers should therefore try to avoid contracting with foreign suppliers whose labour practices are ethically unacceptable. A Honduras firm that supplies The Gap, a clothing retail chain, subcontracted its work out to a factory where children worked 13-hour days in harsh conditions for about $0.35 an hour. This contravened both local laws and The Gap's own stated policy against child labour.[10] The factory is in a maquiladora free trade zone. As information of this practice reached Europe, orders declined by US$14 million.

Children in Asia are kidnapped to toil in the carpet industry, where many are chained to the machines. Such sweatshops are straight out of Dickens's England. Businesses that source goods from suppliers using child labour and exploitative practices verging on slavery face a rising chorus of criticism. Anti-child labour activists have started to raid the factories to rescue the undernourished, exhausted children. A young Canadian, Craig Kielburger, has been active in the international battle against child labour.[11] Nor does child labour facilitate economic development. Rather, Kielburger explains, 'Child labour is keeping the Third World poor. Factory owners prefer to hire the children because they are cheap labour, easily intimidated, and won't organize trade unions to fight for better working conditions.'

There are one million child labourers in the Asian carpet industry. Malnourished four-year-olds load charcoal in Brazil. Worldwide, over 100 million children, many pre-teens, are similarly exploited. They often work over 12 hours a day in very unhealthy conditions. They don't go to school. They are poorly paid. Children do not choose to work in such conditions; nor do their families want them to. They only do it because their families desperately need the money. They are often forced to work and are beaten if they try to escape or complain to the authorities. One Pakistani boy had been shackled since he was four until he escaped, and then campaigned against slavery in the carpet industry. He was murdered at the age of 12 because of his influence as a labour activist.

A variety of social trade solutions are possible. Many of the retail companies that source goods from these factories rely on host nation laws against child labour, but the laws are often unenforced. India recently launched the Rugmark label, which certifies that no child labour was used. Regardless of a local government's ability or willingness to act, companies can still monitor their suppliers to ensure working conditions are up to standards, just as they do for quality and cost of the goods supplied. Firms like Levi Strauss, The Gap, Ikea, Adidas, and Wal-Mart are trying to ensure that their purchasing policies against child labour are being enforced, but this is not always easy. Reebok and Levi Strauss set a minimum age of 14 for child factory workers, and Wal-Mart, 15. Levi

Strauss buys from 600 suppliers in 59 nations. It has stopped doing business in China and Burma. In Bangladesh, however, it arranged for factories using child labour to pay the children's wages while they attended school and then to hire them back. In this way the children do not lose their jobs and the supplier keeps the Levi Strauss contract.

Volatile Finance

People should not be required by neo-conservative ideologues and dictatorial governments to abandon their intelligence and 'believe in' socially unregulated international trade. Free trade is not a matter of faith. Rather, trade, like any other social project, must prove worthy of our trust. In fact, free trade is a problem. Unregulated trade cannot of itself dampen the growing volatility in international finance.

The borderless world of global financial markets is far from rosy or stable. 'The whole idea of globalization', Michael Lewis, himself a former bond trader, has observed, 'was a canard. . . . It meant that money bounced more freely around the world.'[12] Lewis had reasons for concern. The track record of free international finance is not comforting. Asian financial markets are volatile. In December 1994 the Mexican peso was drastically devalued when short-term mutual and pension fund investors rapidly withdrew their money from Mexico because of its political crisis. The socio-economic damage caused by the massive flight of short-term portfolio finance capital included countless bankruptcies, rising unemployment, and the devalued peso. The US government had to mount a US$34 billion rescue operation.[13] A bank, in contrast, would have stayed on and rescheduled its loan. Foreign corporations with real assets on the ground would not, and could not, pack up and flee in a few hours.

One month later, in a 12 January 1995 editorial, the *Wall Street Journal* declared itself to be so concerned about fluctuations in the Canadian dollar and government debt that it termed Canada a Third World nation. The editorial writer turned out not to be an expert on the Canadian economy. It is noteworthy that the *Wall Street Journal* made no mention of persistently high Canadian unemployment in making its case; for that, you may remember, is on Wall Street a cause for optimism. High unemployment, as we saw in Chapter 4, means high share prices.

In February 1995, freely trading derivatives markets helped Barings Bank to lose £827 million and go bankrupt. The following year, in June 1996, Japan's huge Sumitomo bank suffered US$1.8 billion in losses due to unauthorized speculation on copper futures by one of its commodities traders.[14] The London Metal Exchange, a bastion of free trade, was consequently investigated by British regulatory authorities. Little was done to regulate its activities, however, and some feel the LME is a cosy old boys club. There is, it seems, some cause for witholding one's faith in free international financial markets. Certainly, to leave them unregulated implies an extraordinary willingness to trust in the wisdom of the financial community. It is far from evident that that is a good way to minimize the risks of further financial crises or snap judgements about 'Third World' economies.

Underlying these crises is a historically unprecedented development. In the last decade technological change, in the form of electronic communication flows, has multiplied the volume and velocity of financial information flows.[15] The result is that over $1.3 trillion in portfolio investment and currency transactions are now traded daily. Conventional trade in real goods and labour is but 1.4 per cent of international electronic financial transactions. But these enormous global financial flows are not stable. The unreal 'lightness of being' of electronic finance capital enables it to move about at whim, on the mere scent of a speculative gain, frequently based on a microscopically small numeric edge. Ask Barings. Instability in one nation is now transmitted to others at the speed of light. Unfortunately, millions of people may get hurt in the crossfire. Ask the Mexicans.

The global financial trading system appears to be fundamentally unstable and crisis-prone. Stabilization seems possible, without significant loss of efficiency, but governments do not seem willing to take appropriate action. In the 1995 Group of Seven meeting the Canadian government raised the idea of taxing international currency transfers as one way of stabilizing the world financial system and paying for the havoc it causes.[16] But the Germans said no, so the proposal was dropped. The Canadian proposal reflected an idea advocated by the 1981 Nobel Prize-winning economist, James Tobin. He was concerned that the flow of instantaneous currency and investment transactions is inherently unstable. Tobin's fears about instability were not allayed when a trader said to him, 'Sonny, my long run is the next ten minutes.'

Tobin's solution is elegantly simple and technologically feasible (for it is already in use on the Internet). He proposes a 0.5 per cent tax for every currency transaction. Thus, 1 per cent would come off the round-trip exchange. The same electronic media that enable instantaneous international communications and transactions could easily handle the tax metering. Instead of separate nations imposing the tax—and varying the rates and methods of enforcement—Tobin recommends that the tax be monitored by the International Monetary Fund. Payment of the tax would be a condition of receiving international financial support from it or the World Bank and of participation in international banking, trading, and investment systems. Tobin felt it could yield as much as US$500 billion in revenue a year. Those proceeds could be distributed to the World Bank, the UN, and participating nations. They could be used to help poor debtor nations like Mexico and close the development gap.

II New Tales about Social Trade

Talk about the new borderless world of free global trade and the disappearance of the State is premature, at best. Foreign investments by multinationals that show some commitment to civil rights and try to reduce the development gap exemplify the social trade approach. And three social trade development paths, discussed here, appear to be feasible: removing regulatory barriers to entrepreneurship; contracting with local manufacturers; and providing poor entrepreneurs with small loans.

Invest In Civility

Guicciardini's and Montesquieu's observations from centuries ago reflect an old maxim in international commerce. *Foreign merchants should respect local customs and laws.* Trade itself should foster interdependence, peace, and even democracy. Talk about the borderless world and the disappearance of the State is premature.

A better, social trade, approach is needed. Its underlying assumption is that all international commerce has socio-economic and political effects, and those impacts should be considered and managed better by international business. Increasingly, we have seen, ethical values are needed to help firms adequately evaluate which of the three options—*do business, don't do business*, or *invest conditionally*—is the best in deciding on any specific foreign investment opportunity. Indeed, many firms do consider socio-economic impacts, but mostly in terms of evaluating their own risks and rewards.

To nudge such considerations towards social trade and to clarify the values involved in such complex deliberations, two tests are required. Firstly, some civil rights indicators are useful, such as those presented in Table 9.1.[17] Secondly, a complementary set of economic development indicators will be presented in the next section.

Table 9.1: **Selected Democratic Indicators (1995)**						
Country	Elected Gov't	Free Speech	Political Prisoners	Political Violence	Fair Trial	Executed/ Sentenced to Death
Canada	Yes	Yes	None	No	Yes	0/0
U.S.A.	Yes	Yes	None	No	Yes	31/2870
China	No	No	1,000s	No	No	1,796/2,496
Cuba	No	No	600+	No	No	1/6
Guatemala	Yes	No	Yes	Yes	No	317/100+
Mexico	Yes	Yes	Yes	Yes	Y+N	70/100+
Nigeria	No	No	100s	Yes	No	150+/220
S. Africa	Yes	Yes	None	Yes	Yes	0/460
Vietnam	No	No	Yes	No	No	0/8

The civil rights indicators presented in Table 9.1 are only indirect measures of the extent of democratic values in a society, or, obversely, of its political oppressiveness and corruption. Civil rights, free elections, and other basic freedoms are fundamental to democracy. They must be real practices, rather than general value statements in constitutions. 'Political prisoners' implies that there are political crimes. 'Political violence' refers to State repression, terrorism, rebellion, and ethnic violence, as well as to executions and death sentences. Executions are extrajudicial as well as judicial, because of the great numbers of 'disappeared' persons (*desaperecidos*). The existence of due process and 'fair trials', as much as constitutions, show that the rule of law is accepted in the society. Despite concerns about legalization, a legal system, however poorly enforced, can constrain even dictatorial states. Despite oppressive politics, the criminal trial process may be fair. The South African judiciary during apartheid, for instance, made some notably independent judgements.

The indicators in Table 9.1, and others, suggest that the more democratic and constitutional a regime and the less violent and corrupt, the more legitimate and ethically preferred it is as a place to invest. Also, one hopes, it is more stable. Despite fashionable talk about globalization, there is a political dimension to international trade. Governments still set the investment and trade rules.

Direct investment involves a significant long-term commitment of real assets on the ground. The investment itself may change the situation in the host nation. MNCs should therefore consider the degree to which the rule of law and civil rights are rooted in the host society, both because it is ethically preferable and because such conditions may reduce investment risks. For similar reasons, as we will shortly see, companies should try to reduce the development gap through the benefits their investment transfers to the host nation.

Multinational corporations can influence support for social reform in host nations. Over half of the US MNCs operating in South Africa followed the Sullivan standards for non-racist operations, which were drafted in 1984 by the Black US minister, Leon Sullivan. His standards stipulated equitable business practices such as: equal and fair treatment, work conditions, training, and advancement for all their employees, Black and White. They advanced Blacks through the ranks into supervisory and managerial positions. They supported Black education, housing, health care, and business development. All these practices contributed to the eventual decline of apartheid. This represents the ethical case for conditional investment, even in less democratic regimes.

Civil rights have different meanings in different societies. The United States stresses individual freedom and equal opportunity, while Canada and European countries also value equity and group rights.[18] The core ethic, however, does not privilege the Western ethos of individual rights and freedoms, nor does it support without qualification Asian notions of social obligation, conformity, and hierarchy. Toyota Canada in its value statement, for example, sees itself as a 'company of the world', so it seeks to balance both (Western) individuality and (Eastern) teamwork. The Caux Round Table principles for international business ethics respect both Western and Eastern values, the dignity of the individual and the Japanese concept of *kyosei* or working together for the common good.

In sum, the more peaceful and democratic a nation the less risk there will be, by and large, in making the long-term commitment of direct investment. In addition, the more the development gap with developing nations is reduced, again, the less the risk. These two assumptions underly the concept of social trade.

Closing the Development Gap

Social trade involves reciprocity and exchange. It is always a two-way street. It is not a matter of charity, aid, or altruism. Here, that insight is extended to international commerce. One difference is that ethics take seriously the commitment to respect civil rights and to mutual benefits, not only for élites but also for local people, communities, and regions and ecosystems in host nations—in effect, care for the interests of stakeholders, both domestic and foreign. In this way social trade merges into a socio-economic concept of sustainable development.

Reciprocity is a central theme of the social trade approach to foreign direct investment. Through their investments foreign businesses from developed nations should do what they can to reduce the development gap with host nations. They certainly should not impose socio-economic harms on the host nation, such as exploitative work conditions, environmental destruction, and corruption. Various development indicators are used to help investing firms assess the home/host nation socio-economic development gap, especially in the developing world. A few are presented in Table 9.2: population, per capita GNP, literacy, infant mortality, longevity, and the United Nations Human Development Index rating.[19]

Table 9.2: **Comparative Human Development Indicators**							
	HDI*	Pop. (mn)	GNP (US$bn)	GNP per capita (US$)	Literacy %	Longevity (yrs)	Infant Deaths/ 1,000
Canada	0.951	28	575	20,670	99	78	7
U.S.A.	0.940	260	6,388	24,750	99	76	9
Chile	0.882	13.6	42.5	3,070	94	72	17
Mexico	0.845	88	325	3,750	88	70	35
Cuba	0.726	11	14	1,300	94	76	15.3
South Africa	0.649	42	118.1	2,900	65	63	53
Guatemala	0.580	9.7	11.1	1,110	55	65	58
Nigeria	0.401	112	32.9	310	51	52	84
Bangladesh	0.365	111.4	25.9	220	35	53	120

*HDI = Human Development Index

This is an incomplete set of indicators, but they do give an idea of the level of development in various nations in terms of literacy, health, and standard of living. Other measures are important, too:

❖   stable population dynamics
❖   general education

❖   women's autonomy
❖   access to appropriate technologies
❖   healthy communities
❖   healthy ecosystems
❖   sustainable resources.

Taken together, all these indicators show the need for a balanced, rich social trade approach to development. Using these measures we see a large development gap between societies with healthy economies, health care systems, democratic values, and less violence, like Canada and the US on the one hand, and other, less developed nations on the other. Nigeria, by these measures, is not only a corrupt and oppressive regime but also poor and undeveloped, despite its great resource wealth. On the other hand, Cuba is both less violent and less poor. Chile, a democratic regime, is also healthier economically.[20] Nor are these measures static. In many developing nations they have been declining recently, and in some they are rising.

Respecting civil rights, avoiding corruption, and reducing the development gap are all aims of social trade.[21] Social trade involves reciprocal exchange among all stakeholders: the foreign investor firm, local populations, communities and nations, allied firms (such as suppliers), and host and home nation governments. All should benefit, in varying degrees and ways, from the foreign direct investment relationship. Those benefits act as an economic incentive to do the right thing. This social trade view of foreign direct investment moves one well beyond the classic conflict between sovereign home nations and foreign multinational corporations and their powerful home governments. The nationality of the MNC, while important, is not the key consideration.[22]

MNC/host nation relations, then, should be based on welfare and reciprocity, not on hostility and conflict. MNCs offer poorer, developing host nations an opportunity to further their own socio-economic development. Progress along that path can be measured with the help of development indicators like those in Table 9.2. Not only do MNCs transfer resources such as capital, technology, goods, people, and knowledge from a home nation base (and often from other foreign subsidiaries) to the host nation economy. They can also help develop the skills of local employees and move them into technical and management positions, provide business opportunities for local suppliers, and, where appropriate, offer a world market mandate to some foreign subsidiaries. In return, they should reap a variety of benefits, such as lowered labour and production costs, higher profits and sales, and access to distant markets.

Organizationally, MNCs need to balance home base strategy and controls with responsiveness to local host nation values and welfare.[23] Even as they maintain their own integrity and see to their own welfare, foreign firms should try to become 'insiders' in each host nation, bringing benefits to the host economy and society and respecting local ways and values. So foreign firms and personnel need to avoid the twin extremes either of over-centralization and a home nation bias or of excessive decentralization and 'going native'. Akio Morita of Sony termed this balancing act 'global localization'. That, too, is part of social trade.

Social Trade Development Paths

Another aspect of social trade is to stress economic development over foreign aid. This does not mean that the only path to development is through State intervention and regulation. On the contrary, as we saw, legalizing business problems may all too often worsen them rather than solve them. This is one lesson from Hernando De Soto's research into poverty and the informal economy in Peru.[24] Most businesses operating on the streets of Lima, De Soto observed, were not legal. Lima's booming informal economy, like that in many developing nations, was extra-legal. How, he asked, did Peru's old, statist, highly regulated approach to development affect the urban poor?

To answer his question De Soto researched the regulations created by the State to regulate commercial licences and building permits, etc. He discovered an enormous mass of regulations representing an insuperable obstacle to creating legal business for most Peruvians. Obtaining a commercial licence of any kind typically involved over 200 steps and took more than a year. The costs of the legalization of economic growth were astronomical, amounting to 347 per cent of the profit of a typical small industrial firm. This regulatory morass suffocated the economic energies of entrepreneurial Peruvians. Legalization also had socially negative by-products, such as disrespect for the law, declining productivity and investment, technological stasis, inefficient taxation, and higher energy and transaction costs.

The legal system, De Soto showed, significantly affects development, for good or ill. Bad laws and invasive regulations frustrate and inhibit growth. Good laws enable development and justice. Without good laws people spend inordinate amounts of energy and time protecting themselves and their property and monitoring their business agreements. What Peru needed, De Soto concluded, were simpler and cheaper laws, especially in the civil, contract, and property fields. Such laws would reduce the transaction costs of entrepreneurship.

And Peruvians are self-reliant and entrepreneurial. All across Lima one finds enterprising Peruvians selling goods and services. As an old Peruvian proverb has it, 'En la republic peruana, cada uno no hace que de la gana' (In the Republic of Peru everyone acts for gain)! Years of observation of the bustling informal economy on the streets of Lima showed De Soto in detail how Peruvians manoeuvred around government regulations. They took over unused land to build their homes, moved onto the streets to sell their wares, and drove their own buses and taxis. Peruvians developed their own solutions to their own problems. They relied on themselves to make a living, not the State.

De Soto's aim, it should be emphasized, was not to create a free market for rich capitalists. It was to end poverty. But the path to a just economy is not to give away the wealth of the affluent to the poor. A better path is to remove the legal impediments that prevent the poor from creating wealth by means of their own entrepreneurial energy. The best solutions to the problems of poverty and injustice, De Soto believes,

are those that stem directly from the actual experience of the poor, from the barriers that they face and the institutions that they lack. The experience in

Peru [is] that it is not the elimination of the entrepreneurial class that the poor want. On the contrary they want the state to remove the obstacles that it has constructed that handicap their entrepreneurial efforts.

A similar insight underlies the 'Trade Not Aid' approach of The Body Shop and other like-minded firms.[25] The path to development, Anita Roddick insists, must involve 'helping people find the right tools, and the right approach to develop themselves'. It is not to import and impose one's own preconceived development plan. In this spirit, The Body Shop has sourced about 2 per cent of its supplies through purchases from small local suppliers in developing nations. Body Shop policy guidelines specify respect for local cultures and traditional skills, healthy and safe working conditions, the use of renewable materials, environmental conservation, and long-term sustainable trade relationships. While several projects have failed (shea-butter from Ghana and Brazil nuts from the Kayapo in the Brazilian Amazon), some seem to have worked out satisfactorily, such as sourcing paper from Nepal and foot massagers from India. The Body Shop Canada sources sweetgrass gift baskets from Aboriginal communities in New Brunswick.

Similar concerns motivated Muhammed Yunus, a Bangladeshi economist, to ask how most people could become poorer in a country that received over US$25 billion in aid.[26] His answer, like DeSoto's and Roddick's, was that the old megaproject model of development did not seem to help much. It often harmed agriculture, depopulated rural regions, and overcrowded the cities. In today's economy, Yunus feels, access to credit is a human right. A 'trickle-up' micro-investment approach to development therefore might do better than the old large-scale trickle-down approach to economic development. So he worked out a new way of financing local small-scale development in poor nations. In 1976 Yunus founded the Grameen Bank in Dhaka. It has lent about US$1 billion in small loans to impoverished Bangladeshis who needed some capital to escape poverty. Its micro-lending/self-reliance approach has now served over 2 million borrowers in Bangladeshi villages, distributing about US$35 million a month. The poor, Yunus says, are his new professors and the villages his new campus: 'At first people said it was a crazy notion. Now, many accept that the best way to fight poverty is to involve and empower the poor by lending them the smallest amounts of money.'

The 'People's Bank' concept has been copied in 33 nations, developed as well as developing. Average loans are $65; no collateral is required. About 95 per cent of the clients are women, and 97 per cent repay their loans, an extraordinary success rate. Yunus has raised US$20 billion for people's banks across the world. In Canada the Calmeadows Institute of Toronto has developed and applied Yunus's approach. Calmeadows developed a micro-lending project in the slums of La Paz, Bolivia, which was so successful that it became a full-fledged bank, Banco Solidario SA. Shared support and entrepreneurship are successful ways to develop less affluent neighbourhoods and communities. They are, Yunus quipped when he was in Canada recently, 'much better than lending to the Reichmanns'.

Through a similar micro-lending fund, Partnerships Assistance for Rural Development, Calmeadows has dispersed over $1 million in small loans in Toronto,

Nova Scotia, Vancouver, and 18 Aboriginal communities. In such projects borrowers form 'peer groups' and vouch for each other's loans—all at market-level interest rates. (The default rate is an impressively low 4 per cent, in contrast to the typical 20 per cent loss rate for new ventures.) This replaces the need for traditional collateral and reduces administration. The group, acting like a bank, vets potential borrowers and raises matching funds. Calmeadows and associated banks more than match every dollar the peer group puts into the capital pool. The aim is to help small entrepreneurs whose capital requirements fall below the threshold of conventional bank loans. Many clients are women seeking to develop small businesses.

Summary

Chapter 9 has shown that the old tales of foreign firms supporting oppressive regimes or of powerful home nations imposing their laws on foreign firms and nations do not represent an ethically appropriate model of foreign direct investment. Nor should global trade involve child labour or other forms of exploitation. The crisis-prone instability of international finance can and should be curbed, e.g., by the Tobin tax proposed by economist James Tobin. So the hard old ways of socially 'free' trade need to be constrained.

In Part II the new and better, seemingly soft, ways of social trade were introduced. Foreign direct investment can and should, it was argued, support civil rights and help host nations along their development path. The social trade path, moreover, as Hernando DeSoto, The Body Shop, and Muhammed Yunus have shown, involves local entrepreneurship and trade rather than aid. Business ethics, as we have seen, are often a matter of ethical values emerging from within the heart of business itself. But that, Chapter 10 shows, may be the path to the future.

Chapter 10

Foresight Ethics

Fortune is the arbiter of half our actions, but . . . it lets us control roughly the other half. . . . A ruler who trusts entirely to luck comes to grief when his luck runs out.

Niccolo Machiavelli, *The Prince*

Elijah predicted of the Children of Israel, 'you will be a light unto the nations.' Today our prophets are just as likely to predict, 'you will sell computer chips, or armaments or banking services to the nations.'

Max Dublin, *Futurehype*[1]

What Ship?

Our ship finally nears the end of its voyage. But where is it going? What is its name? A warning: the ship's name will tell us where it ends up. If it is full of the latest electronic gadgets and has a small, stressed-out crew, most of whose mates were laid off last year by a multimillionaire CEO awash in stock options, call it the AT&T Temp. But if the crew shows signs of independence and intelligence they will revolt at the way they're treated. Label that ship the Bounty. If you name it the Titanic, then an old story of conspicuous consumption and technological hubris forewarns us of an icy doom. Call it the Exxon Valdez if you'd like an exemplar of high environmental risk and uninnovative hull design from a very large corporation, but it's heading for shipwreck in northern waters. Maybe it's a brand new spaceship, full of high-tech electronic gear, but the captain has not been told of a weak seal in his rocket fuel system. That ship was NASA's Challenger.

All these old ships are so hard they will shatter on the reefs of the problems they themselves cause. I am old-fashioned. I prefer to name our ship a new Santa Maria, or NASA's Apollo. I want a ship that reliably explores routes to a new and better world. It is staffed with good officers and a well-paid, productive crew. It is fully supplied, and enjoys the latest clean and efficient technologies and the best computers and communications. That ship is going to new and better places. On it, the best of times become more likely than the worst of times, for it is fuelled by ethical values. Before we attempt to foresee where we're going, however, we need to restore ourselves and tap the resources we have stocked up along the way. So let's review where we've been.

Where We've Been

Hard Like Water began by rejecting the myth of an irreconcilable opposition between business and morality. Polarizing business and ethics is more likely to worsen problems businesses face than to solve them.[2] A polarized mind-set, Robert Reich states, merely locks people into endless 'cycles of righteous fulmination, first against corporate malfeasance and then against government intervention and back again. [They] enable us to keep at bay [the] troubling questions [of] how a complex economy is to be organized, and how responsibilities should be divided between the public and private realms.'

Instead, we set out on a new voyage, one that would show how ethical values are found inside business itself, and how those seemingly soft values had the power to change the way business is done. Indeed, it is no accident that in *Hard Like Water* the first core value is life itself. Like water, ethical values are often soft, gentle, and delicate at first. They help channel nutrients through the socio-economic organism, fostering their growth. Life forms may seem soft and tender; but in reality they are strong, like water itself. Young trees break through cement sidewalks. Gentle rivers reduce mountains to valleys. When heavy rains swell rivers into full flood they can wash away towns, a reality that needs no emphasis along Quebec's Saguenay River, in North Dakota and southern Manitoba, or along North America's Pacific coast.

Accordingly, we took a mini-voyage in each chapter. We started with old tales of hard, bad business practices and then moved to new tales about doing business in a better, more ethical fashion. We left behind the old stories about the highly leveraged auctioning of R.J.R. Nabisco, high-risk speculation at Barings, the autocratic groupthink organization, unnecessary deaths at Westray, failure-prone breast implants, tin-can oil tankers, a regulation-free PCB warehouse at St Basil le Grand, Quebec, and morally neutral foreign investments in oppressive nations.

Instead, fuelled by the core ethic, we sailed in search of new and richer ideas. Part One explored the core ethic, introducing a new element in each chapter. Each represented a general ethical tool or technique that could be used in many other spheres of business than the one described in the chapter:

❖   The Prologue introduced the *four core values: life, welfare, communication*, and *civil rights*, and the *five performance maxims: do no harm, solve the problem, enable informed choices, seek the common good*, and *act, learn, improve*.

❖   Chapter 1 presented a *more socially inclusive business ownership* system and a *stakeholder map* to help improve stakeholder relations.

❖   Chapter 2 showed the importance of *risk-minimizing, ethical problem-solving* to modern management and its roots in a wide range of socio-economic intelligences.

❖   Chapter 3 made the case for *high-feedback, low-risk organizational cultures*, in which *reciprocal exchange values* play a central role. A business, it suggested, is a community of interests.

Building on the expanded core ethic introduced in Part One, Part Two journeyed further still. Chapters 4 and 5 continued the theme of the first three chapters, of exploring the ways ethics can improve the quality of stakeholder relations inside a business. Chapter 6 linked internal with external stakeholders. Chapters 7 to 9 took our journey well outside the firm's boundaries. Each chapter introduced a new ethical tool or technique, but it was relevant mostly to the sphere of business operations or organizations described in that chapter:

❖ Chapter 4 argued for *more inclusive employee relations* based on productivity sharing, responsible pruning, equity, and employee participation in corporate governance.

❖ Chapter 5 showed that a *reciprocal exchange/informed choice ethic* lies at the heart of the market and leads to good value in products and services, honest, equitable marketing, and a social market.

❖ Chapter 6 presented an *innovation ethic*, in which management makes ethical choices in developing new technologies, aided by a technology life cycle and risk-minimizing redesign ethic. It also showed the need for private intellectual property in information stocks and common property in communication flows.

❖ Chapter 7 showed how the *environmental performance measures* and *indirect socio-economic indicators* correlated in good environmental performance, and then described what a proactive environmental management system involves.

❖ Chapter 8 presented the social performance spectrum, involving *co-operative business/government relations* and *proactive issues management*, notably in developing mutually beneficial relations with Canada's Aboriginal peoples and Quebec. Integrating economic and social performance suggested *a new business paradigm, the social market.*

❖ Chapter 9 extended the social market to a *social trade* approach, in which foreign investment respects civil rights and helps reduce the development gap, notably by supporting local entrepreneurs.

These are some of the new tales that indicate the slow but distinctly emergent evolution of ethical values in firms and markets and their growing acceptance. But now we must turn to thoughts about the future.

Where We're Going

Every chapter of *Hard Like Water* has been a mini-voyage. In each we have travelled from the old tales of the past to new tales of better ways of doing business. But we still remain at sea about the future. We face a cacophony of opposing visions. Some proclaim an ultimately beneficent and progressive view of technological and economic change. Some contrarians are concerned about futurist groupthink. Peter Drucker's view in *Post-Capitalist Society*, for instance, is based on the shift to new electronic communication technologies and a promising knowledge-based economy.[3] He calls for more accountable corporations, however, and rejects simplistic talk of the decline of government, stressing the need for 'strong, effective government', especially in the form of transnational political institutions. So his optimistic bias is tempered by the need for ethics in business and politics.

But many worry that the twenty-first century portends doom. Indeed, all around us today we hear tales of growth in unemployment and underemployment, amoral corporations, technological change, population explosion, environmental catastrophe, ethnic violence, and political anarchy. Voices are tinged with insecurity and fear. In a 1995 Decima poll, Canadians were apprehensive about 'a grim future with jobs even harder to find and social support more diminished'.[4]

We are, in the view of many, in the midst of deep and widespread civilizational and natural change; but we do not know where it, or we, are really going. Arnold Toynbee, the great historian of civilization, warned us that civilizations that do not adequately and creatively respond and solve the problems facing them will assuredly die. The challenge of responding to the problems we face is demanding and hard, for 'Ease is inimical to civilization.' Toynbee also noted that 'Civilizations come to birth in environments that are unusually difficult and not unusually easy.'[5] So we must identify the problem we face and act to solve it. That problem is civilizational in scope, as Homer-Dixon, Boutwell, and Rathjens argue. But they also caution that no future scenario is inevitable.

Ecological and Social Crisis

Renewable resources are linked in nonlinear feedback relations. The overextraction of one resource can lead to multiple, unanticipated environmental problems and sudden scarcities when the system passes critical thresholds. . . . Unequal access to resources combines with population growth to produce environmental damage. This phenomenon can contribute to economic deprivation that spurs insurgency and rebellion.

Ted Homer-Dixon, J. Boutwell, and G.W. Rathjens[6]

Homer-Dixon, Boutwell, and Rathjens suggest that the warning signs of crisis are already evident. In some respects the future expectations are a mix of both gloom and doom. The futurist John Naisbitt, for example, suggests that contrary trends are developing simultaneously: centralization and decentralization, globalization and local autonomy, cultural universalism and tribalism.[7] Conor Cruise O'Brien observes, somewhat optimistically, that talk of the breakdown of civilization is exaggerated, for 'worlds that fall apart can come together again.' Charles Dickens himself observed that the best and worst of times happen simultaneously, but in different places and to different people. The more one tries to foresee the future, the more the ancient cyclical concept of time makes sense. It is evident already in the boom/bust cycles of Canada's resource-based economy and may be emerging in our volatile international financial markets. We saw it in both the technology and issue life cycles discussed in Chapters 6 and 8. Each followed an S curve, life-cycle pattern. Both show the limits of a simple linear notion of time and trend-driven forecasting, whether the vector is pointed up or down. But any trend line can be a section of a curve. Faith in the linear extrapolation of a trend, whether up or down, assumes you know where you are in the appropriate cycle.

Clearly, foresight is a difficult art. Philosophers and scientists both agree that nobody knows the future. Like the weather, civilizational change is complex and unpredictable, a bewildering mix of system and chaos.[8] So foretelling the future is a guess. It is more like fortune-telling than scientific prediction. You tell the paying customer what he wants to hear. Attempts to anticipate what will evolve in the twenty-first century reflect present observations, current interests, and past realities much more than they demonstrate any prophetic intuition.

What remains true is that we must be alert and respond to any warnings of potential crisis, just as Machiavelli cautioned when he wrote, 'If the first signs of trouble are perceived it is easy to find a solution; but if one lets trouble develop, the medicine will be too late because the malady will have become incurable.'[9] Machiavelli likened fortune to a river prone to periodic flooding. If we take the appropriate precautions, we can minimize the damage the river causes. Through intelligent foresight and practical courage, he felt, we can to some extent shape the future, but we must also adapt to changing circumstances.

One lesson Machiavelli and ethics both teach is that a primary aim of foresight should be to minimize the risk of critical damage. Not until you have avoided shipwreck and reached port will you know whether you have sailed well. Given the current insecurity and uncertainty, this message is fitting. Indeed, not a few businesses today, and most of their employees, feel that survival is a priority. Accordingly, companies, Peter Schwartz suggests, need to determine what 'the small, specific signals' of oncoming problems might be and must scan for them. By responding to them at once and acting to solve them, companies can prevent disaster. They can prevent problems from evolving into full-blown crises. So responsiveness to early warnings and acting to minimize the risks of crisis are key means of organizational, and civilizational, survival.

As information becomes scarce, moreover, values play more of a role in our deliberations and beliefs. Indeed, the foresight of ancient prophets, Max Dublin noted, rested on their 'moral intelligence' and insight into human nature. Foresight is an ethical skill as much as a cognitive practice. Where we are going in the future, then, depends on the values and information that guide our present choices.

One way a company can plan and prepare for the future is to formulate a small set of possible scenarios.[10] Pierre Wack, the father of scenario planning, aptly compared it to sailing uncharted waters and shooting the rapids (i.e., Machiavelli's river). One should, however, suspend belief in all scenarios, including (especially) the official—usually optimistic—view, and remain open to the pessimistic possibility that worst nightmares may come true. One should therefore spell out the best- and worst-case outcomes in relation to the company's goals, ethical values, known trends, emerging issues, potential opportunities, and stakeholder perceptions. Good information, it should be noted, is not enough, for the future is unpredictable. One must also clarify the values used to develop each scenario. Ethics then can play an important role in scenario planning. Following the corporate social performance spectrum proposed in Chapter 8—hostile, legalistic, accommodative, leading edge—I suggest the following four scenarios for ethical foresight:

1. *Resist*: more of the same, deny reality; refuse to change.
2. *Comply*: follow required procedures; do what we must or are told to do.
3. *Adapt*: cope; accommodate change; mitigate harmful impacts and costs.
4. *Lead*: innovate; respond to early warnings; nip problems in the bud.

Wherever possible the scenario chosen should reflect the ethically preferred outcome. The goal should be to reach the most ethically desirable port of call. There is no algorithm for ensuring one makes it there safely. Even though Jeremy Rifkin feels that the current economic system is in decline, he also foresees the possibility of a great social transformation, for, he adds, 'The future lies in our hands.'[11] Each choice enters the river of time and shapes the gradually evolving future. There is no pre-set plan, no inevitable change, no predetermined paradigm shift. The overall direction of change will be the result of the innumerable choices we make now, and of the information, values, and intelligence that guide our current choices. This includes business decisions.

The daunting challenges we face today demand a creative response on the part of businesses. They should opt for the fourth scenario. It calls for ethical choices, in each company, by countless business people. *The result may be the ethical renewal of business, based on social management, the social market, social innovation, and social trade.* Social management involves accessing the whole range of human intelligences in identifying and solving the socio-economic problems businesses face. The social market can lead entrepreneurs to create new businesses and jobs that can help solve social problems. This may involve new forms of technology and all manner of socially creative services: health care, education, research, the arts, advocacy, helping the dependent, the sick, and the elderly, rehabilitating communities and ecosystems, and foreign suppliers and trade projects.[12] There certainly is no lack of social problems awaiting innovative solutions. Businesses can and should work with governments and stakeholders to help societies better prepare for the twenty-first century. In international investment and commerce, finally, this fourth and leading way becomes the social trade path to locally based, self-reliant development.

These new tales, all told in the previous chapters, are only hints of what the future might be, depending on how business people respond to the challenges they face. If businesses reassert the hard old ways, then the future will not be promising. If the choices companies make tell new tales, then there is hope that ethics can revitalize business. To the extent that soft, small seedlings are watered and nourished, they will become strong and can break through the hard crust of the old ways of doing business, and contribute to the evolution of a better world. If Russia could abandon communism, business can, and should, reform capitalism.

For ethics in business is hard like water. It is powerful because it is so soft and so alive. Rivers reduce mountains to valleys, and tempestuous seas toss huge ships about like corks. But because of the soft, gentle rains, food grows, flowers blossom, and countless animals and humans live their lives. Water enables the unending, reciprocal exchange of goods that benefits all living forms. It is to nature what ethics is to the market. The power of water was understood by the ancient Chinese philosopher, Lao Tzu, who said in the *Tao Te Ching*: 'The reason why the river and the sea are able to rule a hundred valleys is that they take the lower position.'[13]

Glossary of Key Terms

The Core Values

Life: One should care for both human and natural life. One should not deliberately put the life of employees, customers, or others at risk, or wantonly destroy natural habitats and life forms.

Welfare: One should care for the material, psychological, social, and cultural well-being of people, and for a healthy environment. One should practise reciprocity in one's dealings, bringing benefits to all parties involved.

Communication: One should take care to communicate honest, trustworthy information to others in one's social and business relationships. While one should not lie or deliberately deceive others, one is not obligated to disclose everything to anyone.

Civil Rights: One should care for fundamental individual and group freedoms (of speech, religion, and association), and for basic political and legal rights; one should treat others fairly, regardless of their gender, race, culture, or religion, and seek to allocate resources equitably.

The Core Maxims

Do no harm: One should not cause people unacceptable physical or socio-economic harms or destroy natural ecosystems and life forms.

Solve the problem: One should identify the ethical problem and search for and implement the best achievable solution to the problem.

Enable informed choice: In making decisions one should access the best available information and/or supply it to others.

Seek the common good: One should care for the good of the whole organization or group over time, and not just one special part of it to the exclusion of others.

Act, learn, improve: In conducting one's affairs one should seek to attain the best achievable level of ethical performance, learn from experience, and strive to do it better next time.

Other Elements

The stakeholder map (ch. 1) helps one to see how those stakeholders most directly at risk from a problem or a decision have the greatest claim to share in solving the problem or making the decision.

The risk matrix (ch. 2) not only shows how to classify risks but also indicates that minimizing risks means avoiding unacceptable and worrying risks and moving from tolerable to acceptable levels of risk.

Exchange values (ch. 3) involve reciprocity or a mutual transfer of benefits. In other words, such values offer a win/win situation. They are preferable to win/lose *threat values* as a basis for interconnecting people over time in durable organizations and social relationships.

An ethical organizational culture (ch. 3) is one based on encouraging feedback and minimizing risks.

Notes

Abbreviations

BWK	=	*Business Week*
CEM	=	*The Corporate Ethics Monitor*
FP	=	*The Financial Post Magazine*
GM	=	*The Globe and Mail*
GW	=	*The Guardian Weekly*
HBR	=	*Harvard Business Review*
JBE	=	*Journal of Business Ethics*
NWK	=	*Newsweek*
TS	=	*The Toronto Star*
WSJ	=	*Wall Street Journal*

Prologue: Ethics in Business

1. Reich, 1988: 18.
2. This view, typical of classic philosophers like Aristotle and Plato, has been reaffirmed in modern feminist ethics; see Gilligan, 1993: 19 ff.
3. R. Solomon and K. Hansen, *It's Good Business* (New York: Atheneum, 1985): 5.
4. See *GM*, 7 Sept. 1996. I have been teaching business ethics since 1981, and am also the Forum editor of the *Corporate Ethics Monitor*.
5. See Donaldson, 1989: chs 5, 6; De George, 1993: ch. 1. On care, see Martin Heidegger's *Being and Time*. The performance maxims reflect the North American pragmatism of Charles Pierce (see his *Lectures on Pragmatism*).
6. See Kropotkin, 1955, 1968.
7. Reich, 1988: 238; also see M. Sahlins, *Stone Age Economics* (New York: Aldine, 1972): 178–82.
8. In Toffler, 1986: 224.
9. On dilemmas, see Cavanaugh and McGovern, 1988; Pastin, 1986: ch. 1; Jackall, 1989. The stress on dilemmas reflects the influential adversarial legalistic paradigm of moral reasoning.
10. See Plato's *Republic*, 417; Aristotle's *Nicomachean Ethics: II to V.*
11. See A. Molho, ed., *Economic Foundations of the Italian Renaissance* (New York: Wiley, 1969); Di Norcia, 1980.
12. See John Locke's *Second Treatise on Government*; Karl Marx, *The Communist Manifesto*; John Stuart Mill, *Lectures on Political Economy*; Max Weber, *The Protestant Ethic and the Spirit of Capitalism*; Adam Smith, *The Theory of Moral Sentiment* (Oxford: Clarendon Press, 1976); and

also Bowie and Beauchamp, 1996: ch. 9; De George, 1993: chs 6, 7; Di Norcia, 1980; Donaldson and Werhane, eds, 1996: Part II; Etzioni, 1988; Robinson, 1983; Sen, 1987; Solomon, 1992: Part I; Thurow, 1980.

13. I eschew the jargonistic term 'deontology', it being Anglicized Greek for 'duty theory'. On Kant, see his *Metaphysics of Morals* and *Critique of Practical Reason*, published in 1788 and 1785 respectively, and his important essay, 'What is Enlightenment?'

14. See Benedict, 1946; Lao Tzu, *Tao Te Ching*. These notions underlie the growing critique of the weaknesses of Western society in the Far East, notably by Lee Kuan Yew, the former prime minister of Singapore.

15. Solomon, 1992: Part II, reframes the virtue ethic in modern economic terms.

16. On economics and ethics, see Robinson, 1983: ch. 3; C. Dyke, *Philosophy of Economics* (Englewood Cliffs, NJ: Prentice-Hall, 1981): 30 ff. For critiques of utilitarianism, see J.S. Mill, *On Utilitarianism*; Sen, 1987: ch. 2; Etzioni, 1988: ch. 2.

17. Gilligan, 1993: 173. Gilligan criticizes conventional moral theory for assuming the strange idea of the separate self combined with an abstract, and male, rationality as a moral ideal (1993: ch. 3). For these reasons she rejects Lawrence Kohlberg's theory of moral development.

Chapter 1: Owning Values

1. R.S. Saul, 'Hostile Takeovers', *HBR* 63, 5 (Sept.-Oct. 1985): 20; Drucker, 1982a: 35, 37.

2. On Renaissance business, see Origo, 1988: chs 3, 4, 5.

3. When US business is being discussed all amounts are stated in US dollars. The first reference will always begin with 'US$'. Sources for the RJR buy-out are Burroughs and Helyar, 1990; *NYT* articles from Oct. 1988 to Apr. 1989; *WSJ* company background brief at \www\wsj.com; on Kohlberg Kravis and Roberts, see Bartlett, 1992. The Kohlberg quote is on p. 214.

4. In December 1988 Drexel Burnham Lambert and Michael Milken, the firm's junk bond expert, were found guilty of securities violations and fraud. The firm is now bankrupt. See C. Bruck, *The Predator's Ball* (New York: Penguin, 1989).

5. Jensen, 1989: 61–74; Jacobs, 1991: 61 ff., 114, 120, 130 ff.; Di Norcia, 1988a.

6. See Jacobs, 1991: 120 ff.; Di Norcia, 1988a; Reich, 1983: ch. 8; Thurow, 1980: ch. 8; *BWK* 17 Feb. 1986; *The Economist*, 13 June 1992.

7. Reich, 1983: 141, 157.

8. Lewis, 1989: 162. Also see Jacobs, 1991: 15, 22 ff.

9. *GM*, 19 Jan., 27, 28 June 1996; 8 Dec. 1995; on the Vancouver Stock Exchange, see *GM*, 19 Jan. 1996; 4 May 1993.

10. Jacobs, 1991: chs 1, 4.

11. Burroughs and Helyar, 1990: 241.

12. *FP*, 4, 11, 18 May 1996; Jacobs, 1991: 19 ff.; *GW*, 22 Aug. 1993.

13. See *GM*, 7 July, 29 Dec. 1995; 8 Jan., 5 Feb. 1996; *BWK*, 29 Apr. 1996; Jacobs, 1991: 128 ff.

14. Alexander, 1990: 11; Stewart, 1995: Appendix; *GM*, 9 Oct., 20 Dec. 1995; 15, 21 Feb. 1996; *The Economist*, 1 Aug. 1992: 63.

15. Stewart, 1995: chs 9, 10.

16. John Grisham, *The Rainmaker* (New York: Dell, 1994): 67.

17. J.M. Wainberg and M.I. Wainberg, *Duties and Responsibilities of Directors* (Toronto: CCH Canada, 1984): 2 ff., 10, ch. 4; *FP* 4 May 1996; Gillies, 1992: ch. 1.

18. Gillies, 1992: 46 ff., 278 ff., ch. 2; Berle and Means, 1968: 336; *FP*, 4, 11, 18 May 1996. Also see I. Fefergard's columns on boards in *CEM* 6, 1 (Jan.-Feb. 1994): 14; 6, 5 (Sept.-Oct. 1994): 78; 6, 6 (Nov.-Dec. 1994): 95; D. Olive, *CEM* 7, 5 (Sept.-Oct. 1995): 78.

19. Thain's article is in *Business Quarterly* 59, 1 (Autumn 1994): 77–86; also see D. Olive, 'Senate Hearings on Corporate Governance', *CEM* 7, 6 (Nov.-Dec. 1995): 94; M.B.E. Clarkson, 'Redefining the Corporation', *CEM* 8, 2 (Mar.-Apr.): 31.

20. The Canadian Corporate Board Act unfortunately speaks of directors as 'managing' firms, as does Gillies, 1992: 62. For a less intrusive notion of the directors' relation to management, see *NYT*, 16 Jan. 1994. On Zimmerman, see *GM*, 2 July, 22 Feb. 1996; Watson quote from *FP*, 11 May 1996.

21. See *FP*, 4, 11, 18 May 1996.

22. Sources for the franchise story are Lorinc, 1995; *GM*, 9 Oct. 1995; *TS*, 16 Nov. 1996; *TS*, 27 Nov. 1994; Lorinc, 1995: ch. 4. On Loeb, see *Sudbury Star*, 7 July, 7 Aug., 12, 29 Oct. 1996, and a letter in the Apr. 1997 *Canadian Business*. On Provigo, see *FP 500*, 1996. Loeb is a division of Provigo, a large Montreal retail food corporation with 155 supermarkets in Quebec. It had $5.7 billion in revenues and 18,000 employees in 1995. Its 1995 net income, at $40.7 million, yielded a relatively low 0.71 per cent profit; but its return on equity was 18.7 per cent and return on assets, 23.6 per cent.

23. Jacobs, 1991: ch. 2. If, as the law pretends, corporations were really persons, then the market in corporate ownership would resemble slavery. See R. Manning, 'Dismemberment, Divorce and Takeovers', in Poff and Waluchow, eds, 1991: 97–102. But the legal pretence is a fiction (see Chapter 3).

24. Macpherson, ed., 1978: 9.

25. See Freeman, 1984: ch. 1; Wood, 1989: ch. 3.

26. See Di Norcia, 1988a. Unless otherwise stated, 'stakeholders' means *direct* stakeholders only. On jobs as assets or property right, see Drucker, 1982b: ch. 31.

27. See Clarkson and Deck, 1995.

28. One way of saying this is to see the direct/indirect and internal/external distinctions as fuzzy sets rather than hard compartments or crisp distinctions. See Bart Kosko, *Fuzzy Thinking* (New York: Hyperion, 1993).

29. Di Norcia, 1989c. On Hiram Walker, see *TS*, 11 July, 3, 4 June, 6, 13 Sept., 8 Oct., 11 Nov. 1986.

Chapter 2: Managing Values

1. Machiavelli, 1988: ch. 21; Toffler, 1986: 10.

2. Sources for the Barings saga are Rawnsley, 1995: 8; *GW*, 10, 29 Oct. 1995; *NYT*, 24 Dec. 1995; *GM*, 11 Sept. 1995; Galbraith, 1993: 54 ff.; on derivatives, see Rawnsley, 1995: 100

ff.; *GM*, 8 Mar. 1996.

3. Rawnsley, 1995: 130.

4. *GW*, 10, 29 Oct. 1995.

5. For which Deutsche Bank got a Christmas prize: the *New York Times* Financial Follies of the Year Award. See *NYT*, 24 Dec. 1995.

6. *GM*, 11 Sept. 1995.

7. See Stewart, 1995: 126–31, and chs 6, 7.

8. Brooks, 1995: 17, 71; Stewart, 1995: 147; J. Gaa and C.H. Smith, 'Auditors and Financial Statements', in Poff and Waluchow, eds, 1991: 138–56.

9. See L. White, *The S&L Debacle* (New York: Oxford University Press, 1991); Stewart, 1995: 103 ff.

10. Galbraith, 1993: chs 2, 3.

11. Toffler, 1986: 49–70; quote, p. 58.

12. M. Hammer and J. Champy, *Re-engineering the Corporation* (New York: HarperBusiness, 1993): 2, 5; also see chs 3–5; Shapiro, 1995: ch. 15 and the 'Fad Surfer's Dictionary of Business Basics', which is worth the price of the book; *GM*, 31 Jan. 1996. The old friend is Doug Williamson, a former Dean of Science at Laurentian University,

13. Roderick quote from O'Toole, 1985: 145; on the old guard, see O'Toole, 1985: 27 ff.

14. M. Friedman, 'The Social Responsibility of Business is to Increase its Profits', in Poff and Waluchow, eds, 1991: 41 ff.

15. Sources for Table 2.2 are: *Financial Post*, 1996; *BWK*, 13 May 1996; on manipulating profit numbers, see Jackall, 1989: 178.

16. O'Toole, 1985: 143. The Communists, he adds, often demanded higher profit rates than market systems, but they were disguised as taxes and other imposed costs.

17. Drucker, 1982a: 37 ff.; also see Peters and Waterman, 1982: ch. 2.

18. Packard, 1995: 83–7.

19. See *Financial Post*, 1996. Throughout *Hard Like Water*, the ethics performance tables of the *Corporate Ethics Monitor*, from 1990 to June 1996, are used for Canadian corporate data; the quote is from Drucker, 1972: 12.

20. See Ohmae, 1982: 155 ff.; Thurow, 1984: ch. 8. On excellence, see Peters and Waterman, 1982, whose view is still compelling; and Solomon, 1992: ch. 16, though his focus is primarily on the individual.

21. Bell Canada, *Code of Business Conduct*, 1996: Module 3.

22. Reich, 1988: 198.

23. 'Lex Service Group Ltd case, part D: The Reading Pallets', in Matthews, Goodpaster, and Nash, 1991: 180–2.

24. See Ackoff, 1978; Nash, 'Ethics without the Sermon', in Andrews, ed., 1989: 243–56.

25. On vigilant decision-making, see Janis and Mann, 1977: ch. 3, 262; Alexander, 1990: 16 ff.

26. See March and Olsen, 1982: ch. 2.

27. Ackoff, 1978: 189. Just as Janis and Mann and Nash integrate decision-making and problem-solving, Ackoff relates problem-solving to systems theory. Underlying this section is a problem of special interest, namely, how to integrate all these approaches.

28. McLuhan, 1967: 37; see Peters and Waterman, 1982: ch. 2.

29. Source for Table 2.3 is Mintzberg, 1973: 59 ff.; on the hard/soft paradox, see Peters and Waterman, 1982.
30. Messick and Bazerman, 1996; *GM*, 22 Feb. 1966; cf. Mintzberg, 1973: 97.
31. Mintzberg, 1973: 52. On role conflicts, see Toffler, 1986; Bowie and Duska, 1990: ch. 1; Derry, 1987; Liedtka, 1989; Kram, Yeager, and Reed, 1989.
32. Bird and Waters, 1985, 1986.
33. See Gardner, 1983: 60–9. Peters and Waterman, 1982: part II; D. Goleman, *Emotional Intelligence* (New York: Bantam, 1995). One might add 'emotional intelligence' to this list, too, Daniel Goleman argues.
34. Mintzberg, 1973: 52–3, 97.

Chapter 3: Organizing Values

1. Grossman, 1988: 39, 35; Morgan, 1986: 13; also see Hirschmann, 1970.
2. Sources for this section are Jackall, 1989; quotations from 16, 171, 178–80.
3. See Michalos, 1995: ch. 4; Bowie and Duska, 1990: ch. 4.
4. The Quinn story is from *NYT*, 9 Oct. 1994; on loyalty and voice, see Hirschmann, 1970; Grossman, 1988.
5. Toffler, 1986: 244.
6. Walton, 1988: 176–93 ff. See also Freeman and Gilbert, 1988: 170; Derry, 1987; Liedtka, 1989; Kram, Yeager, and Reed, 1989; Solomon, 1992: part II. For critiques of individualism, see Etzioni, 1988; Sen, 1987; Daly and Cobb, 1989.
7. Nielsen, 1989. Only a few states, including Michigan, have passed laws to protect employees who report violations of state or federal laws from wrongful dismissal. So most whistle-blowers lose their jobs and can't find another one.
8. Sitkin and Bies, eds, 1994: 21; also see Morgan, 1986: ch. 2.
9. See Gillies, 1992: 22 ff.; Jacobs, 1991: 78–94 ff. On the sentencing guidelines, see E. Waitzer, *CEM* (July-Aug. 1992).
10. Janis, 1971.
11. See Boulding, 1970: 49 ff., 108 ff., 232 ff. The book also includes his essays on spaceship earth and on knowledge as a commodity.
12. Morgan, 1986: chs 2, 7.
13. Toffler, 1986: 28; Pastin, 1986: 200 ff.
14. Deal and Kennedy, 1982: 107–8; also Morgan, 1986: 17; Pastin, 1986: ch. 7; Toffler, 1986. Table 3.2 modifies Deal and Kennedy's own matrix, but it respects their basic insight of generating it by combining risk and feedback values.
15. Pastin, 1986: 129. See Ouchi, 1982: ch. 1; also see Morgan, 1986: ch. 5, on the Organic-Collective Organization.
16. See Stewart, 1995: chs 8, 9.
17. Packard, 1995: chs 9–11; Peters and Waterman, 1983: 75, 122 ff., 289; quote from p. 244.
18. *NYT*, 29 Apr. 1994.
19. See Janis, 1971: 76; Janis and Mann, 1977: chs 7, 8, 14; Morgan, 1986: ch. 4.
20. Corporate personality was legally recognized even before Canadian women were deemed persons in 1929, or US Blacks in the 1860s!

21. See Shapiro, 1995: 44 ff.; Peter French, 'The Corporation as a Moral Person', in Poff and Waluchow, eds, 1991: 85–90.
22. Deck, 1997.
23. Clarkson and Deck, 1992, 1995.
24. See Shapiro, 1995: chs 1, 2; Pastin, 1986: ch. 2 (on ground rules) and ch. 8.
25. The total number surveyed was 212. There were 44 positive responses (20.7 per cent); 28 questionnaires were answered (13.2 per cent); and 37 sent other materials (17.4 per cent). The codes received are all listed in the Bibliography. The questionnaire is available on request. Ranked lowest in the survey were environmental values (13), the future (11), shareholder relations and finance (10), and international values (9). Despite all the talk about shareholder rights and finance, they consistently came near the bottom.
26. Deck, 1997; also see *GM*, 15 Mar. 1996.

Chapter 4: Working Values

1. S. Adams, *The Dilbert Principle* (New York: HarperBusiness, 1996): 244; Thurow, 1980: 194, 206.
2. Origo, 1988: 80.
3. The main source for the Westray story is the official transcripts and exhibits from the Westray Mine Public Inquiry. My thanks to Ms Deirdre Williams-Cooper, the chief administrator, for her co-operation in enabling access to inquiry materials. Also see *GM*, 16 Jan. to 6 Aug. 1996; *Maclean's*, 19 Apr. 1993; 10 June 1996.
4. *GM*, 24 Jan. 1996.
5. *GM*, 8, 9 May 1996.
6. Sethi and Steidlmeyer, 1991: 230–41. Homicide is a broad notion. There are degrees of culpable homicide, from criminal negligence and manslaughter to murder, but there is also defensible homicide, as in unavoidable accidents and self-defence.
7. See McGregor, 1960: ch. 3; on theory Y, see ch. 4.
8. See *Report of the Royal Commission on the Health and Safety of Workers in Mines,* James M. Ham, Commissioner (Toronto: Attorney-General of Ontario, 1976).
9. A. Leblanc, 'Safety First', *GM*, 24 Jan. 1995.
10. Sources are, in order, Rifkin, 1995: 3; Bragg et al., 1996; *GM*, 30 Aug. 1991; 11 Jan. 1993; June 1995; 19 Sept. 1995; 20, 23 Mar. 1996.
11. Chrominska, 1996.
12. Patricia Norman, 'Downsizing and Organizational Performance: Empirical Evidence', paper presented at the 1995 Academy of Management meeting, Vancouver.
13. A. Downs, 'The Wages of Downsizing', *Mother Jones* (July-Aug. 1996). Also see A. Sloan, 'The Hit Men', *NWK*, 26 Feb. 1996; Canadian data from Craig and Solomon, 1996: 56; J. Wells, 'Jobs: Government Cuts and Corporate Layoffs', *Maclean's,* 11 Mar., 1996; *NYT*, 3 Mar. 1994.
14. *NYT*, 3 Mar. 1996.
15. See David Olive, *GM Report on Business* (Sept. 1993): 11; F. Reicheld, 'Loyalty Crisis Linked to Bottom Line', *GM*, 6 Mar. 1996.
16. *WSJ*, 11 Apr. 1996; *GM*, 10 Apr. 1995; 13 Apr. 1996.
17. D. Toole, 'Bad job news just wasn't bad enough to make it good', *TS*, 5 May 1996; Greg Ip,

'Shareholders vs. job holders', *GM*, 23 Mar. 1996; A. Lindgren, 'Remember, behind company layoffs lie investors' demands', *GM*, 31 Mar. 1996.

18. On Dunlap and AT&T, see *NWK*, 26 Feb. 1996; Robert E. Allen, 'The Anxiety Epidemic', *NWK*, 8 Apr. 1996.

19. On stock markets, see *WSJ*, 11 Apr. 1996; *GM*, 9 Mar., 5 Apr. 1996; *TS*, 21 Mar. 1996. G.J. Church, 'What's going down', *Time*, 11 Apr. 1996. The Bertram quote is from *GM*, 23 Mar. 1996. Also see Robert Samuelson, 'Capitalism under Siege', *NWK*, 6 May 1996; Peter Cook, 'The Ungrateful Stock Market', *GM*, 5 Apr. 1996.

20. *NYT*, 3 Mar. 1996.

21. Shapiro, 1995: chs 14–16. On re-engineering, see *The Economist*, 2 July 1994; *GM*, 15 Aug. 1995.

22. H. O'Neill, P.M. Norman, and A.T. Ranft, 'Workforce Reductions and Market Valuation', paper presented at the 1995 Academy of Management meeting, Norman, Okla.; *GM*, 3 Jan., 23 Mar. 1996.

23. Peters and Waterman, 1982: 44.

24. L. Greenhalgh, A.T. Lawrence, and R.I. Sutton, 'Determinants of Work Force Reduction Strategies in Declining Organizations', *Academy of Management Review* 13, 2 (1988): 241–54; D. Israelson, 'Corporate Backfiring', *TS*, 2 June 1996; *The Economist*, 3 Sept. 1994.

25. The Economist, 3 Apr. 1993.

26. Len Brooks, 'Downsizing versus Ethical Renewal', *CEM* 8, 1 (Jan.-Feb. 1996); David Nitkin, 'Layoffs, Loyalty, Life and Labour', *CEM* 3, 1 (Jan.-Feb. 1991); L.T. Perry, 'Least-Cost Alternatives to Layoffs in Declining Industries', *Organizational Dynamics* 14, 1 (1986): 48–61.

27. See D.S. Perkins, 'What can CEOs do for displaced workers?' *HBR* (Nov.-Dec. 1987): 90–3. On a similar approach at Boeing, see C. Van Deusen, 'Downsizing: A Model for Collective Effort among Community, Government, Management and Labor', in J.M. Logsdon and K. Rehbein, eds, *Proceedings of the 7th Annual Conference, International Association of Business and Society*. Santa Fe: University of New Mexico: 608–10.

28. Packard, 1995: 132 ff.

29. Chrominska, 1996.

30. K. Onstad, 'The Sound of One Mouse Clicking', *Canadian Business Technology* (Winter, 1996): 66–72.

31. Rifkin, 1995: chs 2, 4, 6; Kellogg quote on p. 27.

32. *Maclean's*, 14 Mar. 1994; Craig and Solomon, 1996: 175; Rifkin, 1995: 224 ff.

33. Thurow, 1980: 194, 206.

34. Ethical performance survey data from 472 corporations: *CEM*, 1990 to June 1996. On unions, see Craig and Solomon, 1996: 193 ff.

35. *BWK*, 1 Aug. 1994.

36. *NYT*, 18 Sept. 1994.

37. Beck, 1992: chs 4, 8, p. 149.

38. Reich, 1993: Part 3.

39. Macpherson, 1973: ch. 3, p. 109; Solomon, 1992; Peters and Waterman, 1982: ch. 8; Aristotle, *Nicomachean Ethics*: Book II.

40. Drucker, 1993: 83 ff., part 3; on education and work, see pp. 215, 218.

41. Bunder, *BWK*, 17 Apr. 1989.
42. Ohmae, 1982: 207.
43. See Nightingale, 1982: 217 ff.
44. Drucker, 1993: ch. 3.
45. Nightingale, 1982: app.; *GM*, 1 June 1992; D. Crane, *TS*, 19 Apr. 1992; Crispo, 1978.
46. Craig and Solomon, 1996: 69 ff.
47. *GM*, 2 Aug. 1991; 29 Feb. 1992; Craig and Solomon, 1996; quotes from *GM*, 1 June 1992 (Ostroski); Craig and Solomon, 1996: 6 (Girard).

Chapter 5: Marketing Values

1. Ogilvy, 1985: 96; Drucker, 1982a: 37.
2. Sources for the tobacco industry tale are Hilts, 1996; Hilts, *NYT*, 16–18 June 1994; Smith and Quelch, 1992: 87–111; Sethi and Steidlmeyer, 1991: 338–52; *GM*, 22 Mar. 1996; 22, 25 Sept. 1995; *BWK*, 23 Dec. 1996. Quotes are from Hilts: p. 1 (Buffet), p. 64 (Yeaman and Johnson), p. 123 (Tisch), p. 29 (Green); *NWK*, 25 Mar. 1996 (Texas attorney general); *NYT*, 18 June 1994 (Project Truth).
3. On P&G, see Matthews, Goodpaster, and Nash, 1991: 377–83; Beauchamp, 1989: 87–95.
4. Smith and Quelch, 1992: 31 ff.; J. Dobson, 'Reconciling Financial Economics and Business Ethics', *Business and Professional Ethics* 10, 4 (1992): 23–41. On ethics and economics, see Sen, 1987; Thurow, 1984; Daly, 1991; Etzioni, 1988. On communications media theory, see Innis, 1972; Di Norcia, 1986, 1990. Chapter 6 will explore information age ethics.
5. *GM*, 2 July 1996; on the Lopez case, see *BWK*, 25 Mar., 16 Dec. 1996; *GM*, 12 Dec. 1996, 11 July 1995; *NWK*, 9 Dec. 1996.
6. See Ohmae, 1982: 21 ff., 100 ff.; R. Petersen, *Small Business: Building a Balanced Economy* (Toronto: Porcepic, 1977): ch. 2; R. Kao, *Entrepreneurship and Enterprise Development* (Toronto: Holt, Rinehart and Winston, 1989): ch. 1; Drucker, 1982a: chs 1, 2 16–21, 25; Reich, 1983: 145–50 ff.
7. Gordon Sharwood, CEO, Sharwood Company, letter to the author, 2 Jan. 1996.
8. Peters and Waterman, 1982: chs 6, 10. On excellence and quality, see ibid., 171 ff., 223 ff.; Aristotle, *Nicomachean Ethics*, Book II; Solomon, 1992: ch. 13. Also see Packard, 1995: chs 5, 6. References are to Nortel's 1995 *Code of Business Conduct* and Provigo's 1995 *Code of Ethics*.
9. *GM*, 10 Jan. 1996.
10. *NYT*, 30 Jan. 1994.
11. EthicScan Canada, *The Ethical Shoppers Guide* (Toronto: Broadview Press, 1992); on the 1974 Equal Credit Opportunity Act, see *NYT*, 19, 22 Jan. 1994.
12. See Arens, 1996: ch. 4; Smith and Quelch, 1992: 20–9, ch. 1; Bowie and Beauchamp, 1996: 201–15.
13. Arens, 1996: ch. 3.
14. Ogilvy, 1985: chs 2–4; Arens, 1996: 90, 94.
15. Arens, 1996: chs 1, 4, p. 218. Arens is the source of much of the information presented about contemporary advertising methods, media, agencies, costs, and ethical problems.
16. Arens, 1996: ch. 1, 180 ff. For contrast, see Michalos, 1995: ch. 8; Velasquez, 1992: 292 ff.

17. See Craig and Solomon, 1996: 273 ff.
18. Arens, 1996: 65, ch. 7 case; Poff and Waluchow, eds, 1991: chs 46–8.
19. Arens, 1996: 44–9 ff.
20. Section 1, *Code of Advertising Standards,* The Canadian Advertising Foundation, 1991. The voluntary code is supported by many advertising and marketing trade associations. In 1995 there were 764 consumer complaints to the Canadian Advertising Foundation, down from 908 in 1994. Of the complaints, 183 were upheld.
21. Unsolicited mailing I received in Aug. 1996 from The Angel Inspiration Center in Nepean, Ontario. Since I am no longer a theology *aficionado* I presume the Center divined my address from other, more secular, subscription lists.
22. Arens, 1996: 42 ff.
23. See, for example, Aristotle's *Rhetoric.*
24. Arens, 1996: 21 ff., 175 ff., 360; Ogilvy, 1985: 96, 99; Padulo quote from conversation with the author, 23 Feb. 1996.
25. Hilts, 1996: 67–70, 78–83.
26. Galbraith, 1958: ch. 11; Poff and Waluchow, eds, 1991: chs 43, 44; McLuhan, 1967: 82; *GM*, 20 Nov. 1996; Leiss, 1976: 13 ff.
27. Arens, 1996: 17–23 ff.
28. Arens, 1996: 109–19; McLuhan, 1967: 97; C.B. Macpherson, *The Political Theory of Possessive Individualism* (Oxford: Oxford University Press, 1962); Polanyi, 1964: 40, 57.
29. *NYT*, 17 Apr. 1994.
30. Ogilvy, 1985: 93, 99; Arens, 1996: 410; *GM*, 12, 22 July 1995.
31. Arens, 1996: 378; *NWK*, 11 Sept. 1995; *GM*, 12 Oct. 1995.
32. Arens, 1996: 64, 498 ff.
33. *NYT*, 6 Oct. 1994.
34. *GM*, 12 Oct. 1995; *GW*, 17 Feb. 1995.

Chapter 6: Technical Values

1. Franklin, 1990: 115; Machiavelli, 1988: ch. 21. On the grand, Calvinist, theory of techno-logical determinism, see J. Ellul, *The Technological Society* (New York: Random House, 1964): 21 ff., 79; George Grant, *Technology and Empire* (Toronto: Anansi, 1969). But their simplistic abstractions neglect the complexity of technological change; see Di Norcia, 1984, 1990.
2. On medical devices, see Regush, 1993: ch. 4. Sources for the breast implant story are Regush, 1993: chs 5, 6; *WSJ*, 3 June 1996; *BWK*, 12 Dec. 1996; *NWK*, 12 Dec. 1996; *GM* 16, 27 May 1995; *NYT*, 16 May 1995; 17 June 1994. On the Swansons, see J.A. Byrne, 'Informed Choice', *BWK*, 2 Oct. 1995. On the litigation, see J. Nocera, 'Fatal Litigation' and 'Dow-Corning succumbs', *Fortune*, 16, 30 Oct. 1995: 60–82, 137–58. Quotes are from Regush, 1993: 193 (1989 memo); *GM*, 22 Dec. 1995 (Supreme Court).
3. See J.N. Clarke, *Health, Illness, and Medicine in Canada*, 2nd edn (Toronto: Oxford University Press, 1996): 378–81.
4. Dunford, 1987: 513 ff. A phenomenon, he adds, that is largely ignored in research on com-petitive strategy.
5. Layton, 1986: ch. 3. On nuclear reactors, see Perrow, 1984: 38 ff., 179–88, 207–8, 349–50.

On oil tankers, see Perrow, 1984: ch. 6; also see C. Freeman, 1986: 45.

6. Tapscott, 1995: 2; emphasis added.

7. Galbraith, 1967: ch. 6; Boulding, 1970: 144. But the technostructure is not part of any new *industrial state,* for the new economy is based on electronics, not machines, and the technological revolution is more socio-economic than political. Its emergence was presaged by Boulding (1970), and more latterly by Drucker (1982, 1993), Beck (1992), and Reich (1993).

8. See Morison and Hughes, 1988: 3, 158. On engineering versus commerce, see Layton, 1986; J. Stevenson, 'Regulation, Self-regulation and Deregulation, The Case of the Engineers', in Poff and Waluchow, eds, 1991: 156–70.

9. For the DC–10 story, see Matthews, Goodpaster, and Nash, 1991; Donaldson and Gini, eds, 1996: 135–41. On the *Challenger*, see D. Vaughan, 'Autonomy, Interdependence and Social Control', *Administrative Science Quarterly* 35 (1990): 225–57; Poff and Waluchow, eds, 1991: ch. 16.

10. See Hilts, 1996: 196–203.

11. Forester, ed., 1989: chs 8, 9; Hirschorn in Forester, ed., 1989: 301.

12. Francis, 1986: 78; Franklin, 1990: 118; Trist, 1981; also see Drucker, 1993; Forester, ed., 1989: 304.

13. Packard, 1995: chs 7, 8 (re the maverick, p. 107); Peters and Waterman, 1982: 177.

14. See Boulding, 1970: 141–75. He was well ahead of his times. He wrote about the knowledge economy and allocating intellectual resources almost 30 years ago. Also see Mason, Mason, and Culnan, 1995: 53, an excellent study of ethics in information management.

15. The theory of communications media was originally developed, with extraordinary foresight, by two Canadian thinkers, Harold Innis and Marshall McLuhan. See Innis, 1964, 1972; McLuhan, 1964: esp. chs 32, 33, on electronic communications media; Di Norcia, 1986, 1990.

16. Bell Canada, *Code Of Business Conduct,* 1996: 45; Xerox, 1987: 16; see Mason, Mason, and Culnan, 1995: 253 ff.

17. Hewlett-Packard, 1993.

18. *GM,* 10 Feb., 1 May 1996; *BWK,* 5 May 1996.

19. *NYT,* 29 Aug. 1994.

20. Mason, Mason, and Culnan, 1995: 68–71.

21. Innis, 1972: 124 ff.; see Di Norcia, 1986, 1990.

22. Barlow, 1994; also see Mason, Mason, and Culnan, 1995: 10, 272.

23. *Sudbury Star,* 16 Sept. 1995.

24. See Mason, Mason, and Culnan, 1995: 19; on givers, etc., see 28ff. I would add knowledge producers to make the list complete.

25. On Equifax, see Mason, Mason, and Culnan, 1995: 9 ff., 37 ff.; *NYT,* 9 Feb. 1995; June 1996 *WSJ* Backgrounder Brief at www\wsj.com; on Citibank, see *GM,* 28 May 1994.

26. *GM,* 28 May 1994; 20 June 1996.

27. In Mason, Mason, and Culnan, 1995: 278 ff.; for other codes, see pp. 271 ff.

28. *GM,* 9 Apr. 1996.

29. C. Stoll, *The Cuckoo's Egg* (New York: Pocket Books, 1989): 329.

30. Ibid.; for IBM, see *BWK,* 17 June 1996.

31. Tapscott, 1995: 22.
32. W.A. Maker, 'Money and Truth: Science and the Public Good', paper presented at Science and Culture Conference, Trent University, Peterborough, Ont., 11 May 1997.
33. Dahlman, 1980; Di Norcia, 1986.
34. M.L. Tushman and P. Anderson, 'Technological Discontinuities and Dominant Designs', *Administrative Science Quarterly* 35 (1990): 604–33; J. Corn, *Imagining Tomorrow* (Cambridge, Mass.: MIT Press, 1986).
35. Betz, 1987: ch. 7; Di Norcia, 1994.
36. Mason, Mason, and Culnan, 1995: ch. 7; Innis, 1964: 190–5; Innis, 1972: chs 6, 7; Di Norcia, 1986.
37. Freeman, 1986: chs 1, 8, pp. 150, 176–80.
38. NYT, 3 Feb. 1991; also see Hauser and Clausing, 1988; on 3M, see Peters and Waterman, 1982: 224–34.
39. Betz, 1987: 68.
40. On variability in risk assessment, see Brunk, Haworth, and Lee, 1991; R. Meehan, *The Atom and the Fault* (Cambridge, Mass.: MIT Press, 1984): chs 7, 8; S. Krimsky and A. Plough, *Environmental Hazards: Communicating Risks as Social Process* (Dover, Mass.: Auburn House, 1988): ch. 7.
41. A. Wildavsky, *Searching for Safety* (New Brunswick, NJ: Transaction Press, 1989): 77 ff. and ch. 2. Due to limited space, these comments are somewhat simplistic. They ignore problems like unpredictable 'normal accidents' in complex systems like nuclear reactors; see Perrow, 1984.
42. Freeman, 1986: 26; Papanek, 1985: 235–47.

Chapter 7: Natural Values

1. Welford and Gouldson, 1993: 2.
2. Sources for the *Exxon Valdez* story: *NYT*, 25–31 Mar. 1989; *BWK*, 3 Jan. 1993; 17 Apr., 18 Sept. 1989; 6 Aug. 1990; *NWK*, 18 Sept. 1989; *GM*, 1 Apr., 16 May 1989; *GW*, 9, 16, 23, 30 Apr. 1989. On Exxon, see *WSJ*, 25, 26 June 1996, and www\wsj.com; Donaldson and Gini, eds, 1996: 107–19. Quotes are from *NYT*, 31 Mar. 1989 (Yost); *San Francisco Chronicle*, 6 Aug. 1995 (Pesci). On shipping risks and the *Braer* spill, see Perrow, 1984: ch. 6; *GM*, 7, 8 Jan. 1993.
3. *GM*, 28 Aug. 1995.
4. On Pollution Probe and Greenpeace, see *GM*, 8 Jan. 1996, 27 June 1989; D. Jones, 'Enviro-Scare Tactics', *Globe and Mail Report on Business*, June 1996: 95–6; *Maclean's*, 17 July 1989; Di Norcia, 1989d; Stephen Dale, *McLuhan's Children: The Greenpeace Message and the Media* (Toronto: Between the Lines, 1996).
5. The Body Shop, *Environmental Statement 1996* (Watersmead, UK: Body Shop International, 1996). Also see Falconbridge Ltd, *Report on the Environment* (Sudbury, Ont., 1995); D. D'Aguiar, ed., *Safety, Health and Environment Annual Review 1995* (Sudbury, Ont.: Inco Ontario Division, 1995); E.B. Eddy, *A Question of Balance: Second Report on Sustainable Development*, 1994. While one has to allow for the PR aspect of such reports, they can offer the careful reader a fair amount of information about environmental performance in business.

6. See D. Dewees, 'The Regulation of Sulphur Dioxide in Mining', in Doern, ed., 1991: ch. 6; Di Norcia, Cotton, and Dodge, 1995.

7. See Di Norcia, 1996.

8. CCPA, 1994; also see Environment Canada, *State of the Environment Report* (Ottawa: Supply and Services, 1991).

9. P. Muldoon and M. Valiante, *Zero Discharge* (Toronto: Canadian Environmental Law Association, 1989): 19; see Macdonald, 1991: ch. 12.

10. On chlorine in pulp and paper mill effluents, see N.C. Bonsor, 'Water Pollution and the Canadian Pulp and Paper Industry', in Doern, ed., 1991: 155–88. Di Norcia, 1996; Di Norcia, Cotton, and Dodge, 1993; Fred C. Munro, Manager, Technical Services, E.B. Eddy, *Espanola Mill Division: AOX Elimination Report Summary*, 9 May 1994; Dick Erickson, Vice-President, Manufacturing and Technology, Weyerhauser Company, *Closing up the Bleach Plant: Striving for a Minimum-Impact Mill*, 1994.

11. B.Z. Mausberg, *A Brief on the Pulp and Paper Industry: Chemical Warfare in Ontario* (Toronto: Pollution Probe, 1991); for Greenpeace's view, see R. Krosea, 'Dioxins, PCBs and the Chlorine Industry', in *Proceedings: 4th Conference on Toxic Substances* (Montreal: Beauregard, 1990): 70–7. On British Columbia, see *GM*, 22 Feb. 1996.

12. B. Hull, *Effluents from Pulp Mills using Chlorine* (Conference Board of Canada, 1992).

13. See Beckenstein et al., 1996: ch. 4.

14. J.H. Carey, P.V. Hodson, K.R. Munkittrick, and M.R. Servos, *Recent Canadian Studies of the Physiological Effects of Pulp Mill Effluent on Fish* (Ottawa: National Water Research Institute and Great Lakes Laboratory for Fisheries and Aquatic Sciences, Supply and Services Canada, Feb. 1993); *GM*, 22 Feb. 1996.

15. See Weyerhauser Company, *Meeting the Challenge of 'No Effect' Pulping and Bleaching*, n.d. My thanks to Lou Vargas and Dick Erickson of Weyerhauser for their help.

16. On all three of which EthicScan produced largely favourable environmental review reports in 1991 for the four-year, $84,000 Environmental Values and Technological Innovation University of Sudbury research project. The team included Barry Cotton and John Dodge as well as myself.

17. See *NYT*, 3 Feb. 1991; 3M, *Outline of 3M Quality Environmental Management Program*, n.d.

18. See Minor, Bradley, and Neuber, 1990.

19. Volkswagen Research and Development and Public Relations, *Recycling at Volkswagen*, n.d. My thanks to Siegfrid Hohn for the information.

20. See Cairncross, 1993; Carson and Moulden, 1991; *GM*, 25 June 1992.

21. Ernst & Young, *Study of the Ontario Environmental Protection Industry* (Toronto: Queen's Printer, 1992); *GM*, 4 June 1996.

22. Daly, 1991; Paehlke, 1989: 124 ff.

23. National Roundtable on the Environment and the Economy, *Building Consensus for a Sustainable Future: Guiding Principles* (Ottawa: Canadian Roundtables, 1993).

24. Much of this material is from the Environmental Values and Technological Innovation project case study report on *Environmental Values At Falconbridge*, submitted to the company in 1995; also see Di Norcia, Cotton, and Dodge, 1995.

25. See J.M. Gunn, ed., *Restoration and Recovery of an Industrial Region* (New York: Springer-Verlag, 1995); T. Pender, 'The Mining Industry Gets a Grip on Toxic Water', *Sudbury Star*, 10

July 1995.

26. Both Falconbridge and Inco allowed me to read internal audit reports and related docu-
    ments. Given the sensitivity of such materials I am not at liberty to quote them. I would like
    to thank Bob Michelutti at Falconbridge and Larry Banbury at Inco for their co-operation in
    this area.
27. See Di Norcia, Cotton, and Dodge, 1993.
28. See T. Schrecker, 'Risks versus Rights', in Poff and Waluchow, eds, 1991: 333–52.
29. Ontario Ministry of Mines and Northern Development, *Rehabilitation of Mines: Guidelines*
    (Toronto, 1991); *ICME (International Council on Metals and the Environment) Newsletter* 2, 1
    (1995).
30. Macdonald, 1991: 12 ff., 195 ff., ch. 10.
31. Boulding, 1970: 235. Markets, however, have limited value in costing and reducing current
    pollution flows. See Cairncross, 1993: chs 3, 4.

Chapter 8: Social Values

1. Roddick, 1991: 16; and course material obtained from Dr Clarkson.
2. On the St Lawrence, see *GM*, 22 Nov. 1991; 15 Dec. 1992; 21 Jan., 2 Feb. 1993. On St Basil
   le Grand and PCBs, see *GM*, 25 Aug. to 12 Sept. 1988; *GM*, 31 Aug. 1996.
3. In Donaldson and Werhane, eds, 1996: 211–12.
4. See Polanyi, 1964.
5. Keynes, 1963: 321.
6. *OECD in Figures*, 1996 supplement to *OECD Observer* no. 200 (June-July 1996); also see
   Cameron and Finn, 1996.
7. Boulding, 1970: 275–87.
8. C. Lindblom, *Politics and Markets* (New York: Harper, 1977): Part II.
9. Preston and Post, 1975: 3; Gillies, 1981.
10. Mintzberg, 1996. The top 10 federal and provincial Crown corporations and co-operatives
    are listed in 'The 1000 Top Private Companies', *Globe and Mail Report on Business*, July 1996.
11. De Soto, 1989: 238.
12. Boulding, 1970: 17.
13. Clarkson, 1988, slightly abbreviated.
14. See the data on 472 Canadian firms in the ethics performance tables in *Corporate Ethics
    Monitor* from 1990 to June 1996. Also EthicScan, *The Ethical Shoppers' Guide,* and the May-
    June 1996 edition of *Business Ethics*.
15. See Wood, 1991; Meznar et al., 1991; Epstein, 1987; Wartick and Cochrane, 1985;
    Mintzberg, 1984.
16. Heath and Nelson, 1986: 13.
17. Issue cycles follow a classic S curve; see Stanbury, 1986: 213 ff.; Di Norcia, 1994.
18. See Donaldson and Gini, eds, 1996: 128 ff.
19. Stanbury, 1986: 211. The literature on media ethics is growing fast. Far fewer media orga-
    nizations have ethics codes than do businesses; and the media rank well below business in
    social respectability. See N. Russell, *Morals and the Media* (Vancouver: University of British
    Columbia Press, 1994): ch. 1.

20. Beauchamp, 1989: 247–59; Bowie and Beauchamp, 1996: 606–8.

21. Steele, 1992. On the NDP, see T. Walkom, *Rae Days* (Toronto: Key Porter, 1994): ch. 11.

22. See Perrow, 1984: 196–203; R. Killman and I. Mitroff, *Corporate Tragedies* (New York: Praeger, 1984); Sethi and Steidlmeyer, 1991; Papanek, 1985: chs 4, 6.

23. See Berger, 1977; Sloan and Hill, 1995.

24. On Quebec, see *GM*, 16 Feb., 4 Oct., 1 Nov. 1995; 17 Jan. (Bouchard quote), 12 June 1996; *Maclean's*, 7 Dec. 1995; Barrett, 1996; Di Norcia, 1981, 1985.

25. *TS*, 14 Apr. 1996.

26. On McDonald's, see *TS*, 13 Oct. 1988; *Mother Jones*, July-Aug. 1990.

27. Sources are Roddick, 1991; The Body Shop, 1996a, 1996b, 1996c; Hanson, 1996; J. Entine, 'Shattered Image', *Business Ethics* (Sept. 1994): 23-8; J. Entine, 'Rain Forest Chic', *Globe and Mail Report on Business*, Oct. 1995; EthicScan, *The Body Shop Canada: Corporate Social Profile*, June 1995; *GM*, 27 Apr. 1990; 15 Mar. 1995; 3 Jan. 1996; *Dow Jones Business News*, 2 May 1996; C.P. Wallace, 'Body Shop Shape Up?' *Fortune*, 15 Apr. 1996; *Women's Wear Daily*, 12 Apr. 1996; *GW*, 19 Jan. 1996; *Animal People*, Nov. 1994. The quotes are from Roddick, 1991: 24, 27, 19, 16; Hanson, 1995: 5, 2; and *Georgia Straight*, 11 Aug. 1996 (Nader). Thanks to Jon Entine for supplying some material.

28. The Body Shop, Entine reports, paid US$3.5 million to the owners of the original The Body Shop stores in California for the rights to the The Body Shop trademark in the US, Japan, and Israel (July 1996 communication to the author).

29. See P. Begoun, *Don't Go To the Cosmetics Counter Without Me* (Vancouver: Raincoast, 1994); Debra Lynn Dadd, *Nontoxic, Natural and Earthwise* (Los Angeles: Tarcher, 1994).

Chapter 9: International Values

1. In J.B. Ross and M.M. McLaughlin, eds, *The Renaissance Reader* (New York: Viking, 1973): 190; Montesquieu, *The Spirit of the Laws*, 1748: section XXIII.

2. Sources for the Nigeria tale are J. Hammer, ' Nigerian Crude', *Harper's*, June 1996: 58–66; *BWK*, 8 July 1996; R. Hough, 'Nightmare in Lagos', *Canadian Business*, Sept. 1995: 116–24; *GW*, 19, 26 Nov., 17 Dec. 1995; 14 July 1996; *GM*, 22 May, 22 July 1996; 12–20 Nov. 1995. Quotes are from Hammer (Achebe, Mitee); *GW*, 17 Dec. 1995 (Ofonih, Ake); *GW*, 19 Nov. 1995 (Saro Wiwa).

3. Sources for the Cuba tale are *GM* articles from 12 Mar. 1995 to 16 Nov. 1996; A. Kingston, 'Our Manager in Havana', *Globe and Mail Report on Business*, Dec. 1995; *Financial Post*, 1–3 June 1996. On Guatemala, see Donaldson, 1989: 11 ff. On 'the Righteous American', see De George, 1993: 15 ff. On extraterritoriality, see Neale and Stephen, 1989: ch. 1. Smith quote is from *GM*, 8 July 1996.

4. See De George, 1993: 192 ff.

5. See Di Norcia, 1989b; Donaldson, 1989: ch. 8.

6. H. Lane and D. Simpson, 'Bribery in International Business', in Poff and Waluchow, eds, 1991: 390–7; quote on p. 395.

7. See Copeland and Griggs, 1985: 169 ff.; Arens, 1996: 233; *GM*, 5 June 1996.

8. See *GM*, 10 June 1996; *GM*, 9 Oct. 1995; Copeland and Griggs, 1985: 178; *GM*, 14 Feb. 1994; *NYT*, 4 Feb. 1994. On the Foreign Corrupt Practices Act, see Matthews, Goodpaster,

and Nash, 1991: 485–92; De George, 1993: 102 ff.; Copeland and Griggs, 1985: 130 ff., 164–70, ch. 9.

9. Lane and Simpson, in Poff and Waluchow, eds, 1991: 397.

10. See *London Daily Telegraph*, 22 Jan. 1996; *GM*, 20 Nov., 11, 17 Sept., 22 July 1996; *TS*, 12, 26 Nov. 1995; *BWK*, 29 July 1996; *Maclean's*, 11 Dec. 1995; *NYT*, 23, 29 Nov., 5 Dec. 1994; 11 Sept. 1995.

11. *GM*, 26 Nov. 1995; *TS*, 26 Nov. 1995.

12. Lewis, 1989: 197, chs 8, 9. On the traders' gambling culture, see Rawnsley, 1995: ch. 9; Philips, 1994: ch. 4; *TS*, 15 Jan. 1995. On the *Wall Street Journal* and Canada, see *WSJ*, 11, 20 Jan. 1995; *GM*, 12, 24 Jan. 1995; *Maclean's*, 23 Jan. 1995.

13. David Crane, in *TS*, 11, 13 June 1995; *GM*, 12 Jan. 1995.

14. *BWK*, 1 July 1996; *GM*, 20 June 1996.

15. *GM*, 9 July 1996.

16. See *GW*, 25 June 1995; 17 July 1994; 'A Sinking Feeling', *Time*, 20 Mar. 1995; *GM*, 10 Mar. 1995; Tobin, 1995.

17. Amnesty International, *Report 1996* (Amnesty International U.S.A., 1996).

18. See De George, 1993: 52 ff.; also see Copeland and Griggs, 1985: ch. 4; Donaldson, 1989: ch. 5. On obligation in Japanese culture, see Benedict, 1946: ch. 3.

19. Sources for Table 9.2 are United Nations Development Programme, *Human Development Report 1996* (New York: Oxford University Press, 1996): ch. 2; John W. Wright, ed., *The Universal Almanac* (Kansas City: Andrews and McMeel, 1996); Q.H. Stanford, *Canadian Oxford World Atlas* (Toronto: Oxford University Press, 1992).

20. United Nations, 1996: ch. 2; *GM*, 17 July 1996.

21. See De George, 1993: ch. 3; Donaldson, 1989: ch. 3; Cavanaugh and McGovern, 1988: ch. 8, 99 ff.

22. See Reich, 1993; A. Rotstein, 'When the U.S. was Canada's Japan', *HBR* (Jan.-Feb. 1989): 38–43; Ohmae, 1990: ch. 1.

23. See Prahalad and Doz, 1988: 99 ff.; C.A. Bartlett and S. Ghoshal, *Managing Across Borders* (Cambridge, Mass.: Harvard Business School Press, 1989): 59 ff., 64 ff., 131 ff.

24. See De Soto, 1989, esp. ch. 5, 151 ff. De Soto's views have been very influential throughout South America and the developing world.

25. Roddick, 1991: 180, 185; Body Shop, 1996c; Hanson, 1996: 20; *GM*, 3 Jan. 1996.

26. *GM*, 11 Feb. 1992; 23 Oct., 23 Nov. 1995; M. Cannon, 'The People's Bank', *Globe and Mail Report on Business*, Oct. 1995; *TS*, 23 Nov. 1995; *Financial Post*, 19 July 1995; also material from the Calmeadows Institute.

Chapter 10 Foresight Ethics

1. Machiavelli, 1988: ch. 25; M. Dublin, *Futurehype: The Tyranny of Prophecy* (New York: Viking, 1989): 13.

2. Reich, 1988: 210 ff.

3. Drucker, 1993: chs 6, 7.

4. *Maclean's*, 1 Jan. 1996. For opposing demographic views, see D.K. Foot and D. Stoffman, *Boom, Bust and Echo* (Toronto: McFarlane, Walter and Ross, 1996); P.R. Ehrlich and A.H.

Ehrlich, *The Population Explosion* (New York: Simon and Schuster, 1990).

5. A. Toynbee, *The Study of History* (Oxford: Oxford University Press, 1962): 88, 140.

6. 'Environmental Change and Violent Conflict', *Scientific American*, Feb. 1993: 38–45.

7. See J. Naisbitt, *Global Paradox* (New York: Avon, 1994): ch. 1; C.C. O'Brien, *On the Eve of the Millennium* (Toronto: House of Anansi, 1995): 70.

8. J. Gleick, *Chaos* (New York: Penguin, 1986); M. Waldrop, *Complexity* (New York: Simon and Schuster, 1992).

9. Machiavelli, 1988: ch. 7, 103 ff. Interestingly, Machiavelli contrasted *fortuna* with *vertu*, which combines practical intelligence and moral courage.

10. Wack, 1985; P. Schwartz, *The Art of the Long View* (New York: Doubleday, 1991): 198, 170 ff., 208 ff.

11. Rifkin, 1995: 293. Also see Paul Kennedy, *Preparing for the Twenty-First Century* (New York: Random House, 1993); R.L. Heilbroner, *Business Civilization in Decline* (New York: Norton, 1976). For more optimistic expectations, see Drucker, 1993; Tapscott, 1995; A. Toffler, *The Third Wave* (New York: Bantam, 1970); F. Feather, *G Forces* (Toronto: Summerhill Press, 1989); D. Cohen and G. Stanley, *No Small Change* (New York: Macmillan, 1993).

12. For converging, ethical views of a 'social future', see Franklin, 1990: ch. 6; Rifkin, 1995: Part V; Papanek, 1985: Part II; Drucker, 1993: ch. 9; Freeman, 1986: chs 9, 10.

13. Lao Tzu, *Tao Te Ching*, trans. D.C. Lau (New York: Penguin, 1963): 159.

Bibliography

Ackoff, Russell. 1978. *The Art of Problem Solving*. New York: Wiley.

Air Canada. 1993. *Corporate Policy Guidelines on Business Conduct*. Ville St Laurent, Que.

Alberta Natural Gas Company Ltd. n.d. *Code of Business Ethics*. Calgary.

Alexander, I. 1990. *Foundations of Business*. Oxford: Basil Blackwell.

Andrews, K.R., ed. 1989. *Ethics in Practice: Managing the Moral Corporation*. Boston: Harvard Business School Press.

Arens, W.F. 1996. *Contemporary Advertising*, 6th edn. Chicago: Irwin.

Barlow, J.P. 1994. 'Everything You Know about Intellectual Property Is Wrong', *Wired* (March).

Barrett, M. 1996. 'Architects of Our Future' (Notes for remarks for the Annual Meeting of the Bank of Montreal). Calgary, 15 Jan.

Bartlett, S. 1992. *The Money Machine: How KKR Manufactured Power and Profits*. New York: Warner.

BCE. n.d. *Codes of Conduct*. Montreal.

Beauchamp, T. 1989. *Cases in Business Ethics and Society*, 2nd edn. Englewood Cliffs, NJ: Prentice-Hall.

Beck, Nuala. 1992. *Shifting Gears*. Toronto: HarperCollins.

Beckenstein, A.R., F.J. Long, and T.N. Gladwin. 1996. *Stakeholder Negotiations: Essays in Sustainable Development*. Chicago: Irwin.

Bell Canada. 1995. *Competitive Business Practices Training*. Toronto.

Bell Canada. 1996. *Code of Business Conduct*. Montreal.

Benedict, R. 1946. *The Chrysanthemum and the Sword*. New York: Meridian.

Berger, T. 1977. *Northern Frontier, Northern Homeland: The Report of the Mackenzie Valley Pipeline Inquiry*, vol. 1. Ottawa: Supply and Services Canada.

Berle, A., and G. Means. 1968. *The Modern Corporation and Private Property*, rev. edn. New York: Harcourt, Brace.

Betz, F. 1987. *Managing Technology*. Englewood Cliffs, NJ: Prentice-Hall.

Bird, F., and J. Waters. 1985. 'Everyday Moral Issues Experienced by Managers', *JBE*: 373–84.

Bird, F., and J. Waters. 1986. 'The Moral Dimension of Organizational Culture', *JBE*.

Body Shop, The. 1996a. *1996 Approach to Ethical Auditing*. Watersmead, UK: The Body Shop International.

Body Shop, The. 1996b. *Our Agenda*. Watersmead, UK: The Body Shop International.

Body Shop, The. 1996c. *Social Statement 1995*. Watersmead, UK: The Body Shop International.

Boulding, K. 1970. *Beyond Economics*. Ann Arbor: University of Michigan Press.

Bowie, N., and R. Duska. 1990. *Business Ethics*, 2nd edn. Englewood Cliffs, NJ: Prentice-Hall.

Bowie, N., and T. Beauchamp. 1996. *Ethical Theory and Business*, 5th edn. Englewood Cliffs, NJ: Prentice-Hall.

Bragg, R., L. Uchtelle, N.R. Kleinfield, S. Rimer, E. Kolbert, K. Johnson, A. Kleimer, D.E. Sanger, and S. Lohr. 1996. 'The Downsizing of America', *NYT*, 3–9 Mar.

Brooks, L. 1995. *Professional Ethics for Accountants*. St Paul, Minn.: West Publishing.

Bruncor Inc. (NB Tel). 1994. *Code of Business Ethics*. Saint John, NB.

Brunk, C., L. Haworth, and B. Lee. 1991. *Value Assumptions in Risk Assessment*. Waterloo, Ont.: Wilfrid Laurier University Press.

Burroughs, B., and J. Helyar. 1990. *Barbarians at the Gate*. New York: Harper.

Cairncross, F. 1993. *Costing the Earth*. Cambridge, Mass.: Harvard Business School Press.

Cameron, D., and E. Finn. 1996. *10 Deficit Myths*. Ottawa: Canadian Centre for Policy Alternatives.

Canada Post Corporation. 1994. *A Selection of Corporate Policies*. Ottawa.

Canadian Chemical Producers Association (CCPA). 1994. *Responsible Care 1994. A Total Commitment*. Ottawa.

Canadian Pacific Ltd. 1991. *Code of Business Conduct*. Montreal.

Carson, P., and J. Moulden. 1991. *Green is Gold*. New York: HarperBusiness.

Cavanaugh, G., and A. McGovern. 1988. *Ethical Dilemmas in the Modern Corporation*. Englewood Cliffs, NJ: Prentice-Hall.

Central Credit Union. 1993. *Human Resources Policy Manual: Code of Ethics*. Toronto.

Chrominska, S.D. 1996. 'Falling Down: Avoiding the Pitfalls of Restructuring', paper presented to Ethics and Restructuring Conference at Wilfrid Laurier University, Waterloo, Ont., 25 Oct.

CIBC Corporation. 1994. *Where We Stand. The Core Values of the CIBC Corporation*. Toronto.

Clarkson, M.B.E. 1988. 'Corporate Social Performance in Canada, 1976–86', *Research in Corporate Social Performance* 10: 241–65.

Clarkson, M.B.E., and M. Deck. 1992. 'Effective Codes of Ethics', The Clarkson Centre for Corporate Social Performance and Ethics, University of Toronto Faculty of Management.

Clarkson, M.B.E., and M. Deck. 1995. 'A Risk Based Model of Stakeholder Theory', University of Toronto Faculty of Management.

Coca Cola Beverages Ltd. 1992. *Code of Business Conduct*. Toronto.

Copeland, L., and L. Griggs. 1985. *Going International*. New York: New American Library.

Craig, A.W., and N.R. Solomon. 1996. *Industrial Relations in Canada*. Scarborough, Ont.: Prentice-Hall Canada.

Crispo, J. 1978. *Industrial Democracy in Western Europe*. Toronto: McGraw-Hill Ryerson.

Dahlman, C. 1980. *The Open Field System and Beyond*. Cambridge, UK: Cambridge University Press.

Daly, H. 1991. *Steady State Economics*. Washington: Island Press.

Daly, H., and J. Cobb. 1989. *In the Common Good*. Boston: Beacon Press.

Deal, T.E., and A.E. Kennedy. 1982. *Corporate Cultures*. Lexington, Mass.: Addison-Wesley.

Deck, Michael. 1997. *Business Ethics Survey Report*. KPMG (Feb.).

De George, Richard. 1993. *Competing with Integrity in International Business*. New York: Oxford University Press.

Derry, R. 1987. 'Moral Reasoning in Work-related Conflicts', *Research in CSP* (JAI Press): 25–50.

De Soto, H. 1989. *The Other Path*. New York: Harper.

Di Norcia, V. 1980. 'Calvin and Kropotkin', in R. Fitzgerald, ed., *Comparing Political Thinkers*. Sydney, Australia: Pergamon.

Di Norcia, V. 1981. 'Le fédéralisme, l'état, et la démocratie', *Printemps* (avril): 167–84.

Di Norcia, V. 1984. 'Beyond the Red Tory: Rethinking Canadian Nationalism', *Queen's Quarterly* 91, 3 (Winter): 83–98.

Di Norcia, V. 1985. 'Social Reproduction and a Federal Community', in R. Martin, ed., *Critical Perspectives on the Constitution*. Winnipeg: University of Manitoba Press: 196–210.

Di Norcia, V. 1986. 'Of Stone, Books and Freedom', *Visible Language* 20, 3: 344–54.

Di Norcia, V. 1988a. 'Mergers, Takeovers and a Property Ethic', *JBE* 7: 109–16.

Di Norcia, V. 1988b. 'The Hard Problem of Management Is Freedom, Not the Commons', *Business and Professional Ethics*, 6, 3: 57–71.

Di Norcia, V. 1989a. 'An Enterprise/Organization Ethic', *Business and Professional Ethics* 7, 3–4: 61–79.

Di Norcia, V. 1989b. 'The Leverage of Foreigners: Multinationals in South Africa', *JBE* 8: 865–71.

Di Norcia, V. 1989c. 'Let's Restructure Labour, Too!' in M. Hoffman, ed., *The Ethics of Organizational Transformation*.

Di Norcia, V. 1989d. 'Activism or Action? The Pollution Probe Controversy', *CEM* 1, 5 (Sept.): 77–8.

Di Norcia, V. 1990. 'Communications, Power and Time: An Innisian View', *Canadian Journal of Political Science* 23, 2 (June).

Di Norcia, V. 1994. 'Ethics, Technology Management and Innovation', *Business Ethics Quarterly* 3, 3 (July): 235–52.

Di Norcia, V. 1996. 'Environmental and Social Performance', *JBE* 15: 773–84.

Di Norcia, V., B. Cotton, and J. Dodge. 1993. 'Environmental Performance and Competitive Advantage in Canada's Paper Industry', *Business Strategy and the Environment* 2, 1 (Winter): 2–7.

Di Norcia, V., B. Cotton, and J. Dodge. 1995. 'Mining Technology and the Environment', in T.C. Hynes and M.C. Blanchette, eds, *Sudbury '95. Mining and the Environment*, vol. 1: 239–48.

Doern, B., ed. 1991. *Getting It Green*. Toronto: C.D. Howe Institute.

Dofasco Inc. 1984. *Code of Business Conduct*. Hamilton, Ont.

Donaldson, T. 1982. *Corporations and Morality*. Englewood Cliffs, NJ: Prentice-Hall.

Donaldson, T. 1989. *The Ethics of International Business*. Oxford: Oxford University Press.

Donaldson, T., and A. Gini, eds. 1996. *Case Studies in Business Ethics*. Englewood Cliffs, NJ: Prentice-Hall.

Donaldson, T., and P. Werhane, eds. 1996. *Ethical Issues in Business*, 5th edn. Englewood Cliffs, NJ: Prentice-Hall.

Drucker, P. 1972. *The Concept of the Corporation*. New York: New American Library.

Drucker, P. 1982a. *The Practice Of Management*. New York: Harper.

Drucker, P. 1982b. *The Changing World of the Executive*. New York: Times.

Drucker, P. 1993. *Post-Capitalist Society*. New York: HarperBusiness.

Dupont Canada Inc. 1982. *General Company Procedures: Business Ethics*. Toronto.

Dunford, R. 1987. 'Suppressing Technology', *Administrative Science Quarterly*: 512–25.

Epstein, E.M. 1987. 'The Corporate Social Policy Process: Beyond Business Ethics, Corporate Social Responsibility and Responsiveness', *California Management Review* 29, 3: 99–114.

EthicScan. 1990–6. 'Ethical Performance Tables', *Corporate Ethics Monitor*.

Etzioni, A. 1988. *The Moral Dimension*. New York: Free Press.

Financial Post. 1996. 'FP 500', *FP*.

Forester, Tom, ed. 1989. *Computers in the Human Context*. Cambridge, MA: MIT Press.

Francis, Arthur. 1986. *New Technology at Work*. Oxford: Oxford University Press.

Franklin, U. 1990. *The Real World of Technology*. Toronto: CBC Enterprises.

Freeman, C. 1986. *The Economics of Industrial Innovation*. Cambridge, Mass.: MIT Press.

Freeman, R.E. 1984. *Strategic Management: A Stakeholder Approach*. London: Pitman.

Freeman, R.E., and D. Gilbert. 1988. *Corporate Strategy and the Search for Ethics*. Englewood Cliffs, NJ: Prentice-Hall.

Galbraith, J.K. 1958. *The Affluent Society*. Boston: Houghton Mifflin.

Galbraith, J.K. 1967. *The New Industrial State*. New York: New American Library.

Galbraith, J.K. 1993. *A Short History of Financial Euphoria*. New York: Penguin.

Gandalf Technologies Inc. n.d. *Gandalf: Our Vision*. Nepean, Ont.

Gardner, H. 1983. *Frames of Mind*. New York: Basic Books.

Gillies, J. 1981. *Why Government Fails*. Halifax: Institute of Research and Public Policy.

Gillies, J. 1992. *Boardroom Renaissance*. Toronto: McGraw-Hill Ryerson.

Gilligan, Carol. 1993. *In a Different Voice*, 2nd edn. Cambridge, Mass.: Harvard University Press.

Grossman, B. 1988. *Corporate Loyalty*. Toronto: Penguin.

Hanson, K.O. 1996. *Social Evaluation: The Body Shop International 1995*. Watersmead, UK: The Body Shop International.

Hauser, J.R., and D. Clausing. 1988. 'The House of Quality', *HBR* (May-June): 63–73.

Heath, R.L., and R.A. Nelson. 1986. *Issues Management*. Newbury, Calif.: Sage.

Hewlett-Packard Company. 1993. *Standards of Business Conduct*. Palo Alto, Calif.

Hilts, P. 1996. *Smokescreen: The Truth behind the Tobacco Industry Cover-up*. Lexington, Mass.: Addison-Wesley.

Hirschmann, A.O. 1970. *Exit, Voice and Loyalty*. Cambridge, Mass.: Harvard University Press.

Innis, H.A. 1964. *The Bias of Communications*. Toronto: University of Toronto Press.

Innis, H.A. 1972. *Empire and Communications*. Toronto: University of Toronto Press.

Jackall, Robert. 1989. *Moral Mazes*. New York: Oxford University Press.

Jacobs, M. 1991. *Short-Term America*. Cambridge, Mass.: Harvard Business School Press.

Janis, I. 1971. 'Groupthink', *Psychology Today* (Nov.): 43–6, 74–6.

Janis, I., and L. Mann. 1977. *Decisionmaking*. New York: Free Press.

Jensen, J.M. 1989. 'The Decline of the Public Corporation', *HBR* (Sept.-Oct): 61–74

Keynes, J.M. 1963. *Essays in Persuasion*. New York: Norton.

Killman, R., and I. Mitroff. 1984. *Corporate Tragedies*. New York: Praeger.

Kram, K., P.C. Yeager, and G.E. Reed. 1989. 'Decisions and Dilemmas', *Research in Corporate Social Performance* 11: 55–92.

Kropotkin, Petr. 1955. *Mutual Aid*. Boston: Porter Sargent.

Kropotkin, Petr. 1968. *Ethics: Origin and Development*. New York: Blom.

Layton, E.T., Jr. 1986. *The Revolt of the Engineers*. Baltimore: Johns Hopkins University Press.

Leiss, W. 1976. *Limits to Satisfaction*. Toronto: University of Toronto Press.

Lewis, M. 1989. *Liar's Poker*. New York: Penguin.

Liedtka, J. 1989. 'Managerial Values and Corporate Decision Making', *Research in Corporate Social Performance* 11: 21–54.

Lorinc, J. 1995. *Opportunity Knocks*. Scarborough, Ont.: Prentice-Hall Canada.

Macdonald, D. 1991. *The Politics of Pollution*. Toronto: McClelland & Stewart.

McGregor, D. 1960. *The Human Side of Enterprise*. New York: McGraw-Hill.

Machiavelli, Niccolo. 1988. *The Prince*. Q. Skinner and R. Price, ed. and trans. Cambridge: Cambridge University Press.

Mcintyre, Alasdair. 1981. *After Virtue*, 2nd edn. South Bend, Ind: University of Notre Dame.

McLuhan, H.M. 1964. *Understanding Media*. New York: McGraw-Hill.

McLuhan, H.M. 1967. *The Mechanical Bride*. Boston: Beacon Press.

Macpherson, C.B. 1973. *Democratic Theory: Essays in Retrieval*. Oxford: Oxford University Press.

Macpherson, C.B., ed. 1978. *Property*. Toronto: University of Toronto Press.

Manulife Financial. 1977. *Code of Business Conduct and Conflict of Interest Statement*. Toronto.

March, James, and J. Olsen. 1982. *Ambiguity and Choice in Organizations*. Oslo: Universitetsforlaget.

Mason, R.O., F.J. Mason, and M.J. Culnan. 1995. *The Ethics of Information Management*. Newbury, Calif.: Sage.

Matthews, J.B., K. Goodpaster, and L. Nash. 1991. *Policies and Persons: A Casebook in Business Ethics*, 2nd edn. McGraw-Hill.

Messick, D., and M.H. Bazerman. 1996. 'Ethical Leadership and the Psychology of Decision Making', *Sloan Management Review* (Winter): 9–22.

Meznar, M.B., J.J. Chrisman, and A.B. Carroll. 1991. 'Social Responsibility and Strategic Management: Toward an Enterprise Strategy Classification', *Business and Professional Ethics* 10, 1: 47-66.

Michalos, A. 1995. *The Pragmatic Approach to Business Ethics*. Newbury, Calif.: Sage.

Minor, G., W.P. Bradley, and F. Neuber. 1990. *Profiting from Pollution Prevention*, 2nd edn. Toronto: Pollution Probe.

Mintzberg, H. 1973. *The Nature of Managerial Work*. New York: Harper and Row.

Mintzberg, H. 1984. 'The Case for Corporate Responsibility', *Journal of Business Strategy*: 3–15.

Mintzberg, H. 1996. 'Managing Government and Governing Management', *HBR* (May-June): 75–83.

Moore Corporation Ltd. 1990. *Business Conduct: A Policy Statement*. Toronto.

Morgan, G. 1986. *Images of Organization*. Newbury, Calif.: Sage.

Morison, C., and P. Hughes. 1988. *Professional Engineering Practice: Ethical Aspects*, 2nd edn. Toronto: McGraw-Hill Ryerson.

Motorola Canada Ltd. 1993. *Motorola Code of Conduct*. North York, Ont.

Muldoon, P., and M. Valiante, 1989. *Zero Discharge*. Toronto: Canadian Environmental Law Association.

National Roundtable on the Environment and the Economy. 1993. *Building Consensus for a Sustainable Future: Guiding Principles*. Ottawa: Canadian Roundtables.

Naylor, T. 1987. *Hot Money and the Politics of Debt*. Toronto: McClelland & Stewart.

Neale, A.D., and M.L. Stephen. 1989. *International Business and National Jurisdiction*. Oxford: Clarendon Press.

Newfoundland Power. 1996. *Mission Statement*. St John's, Nfld.

Nielsen, R. 1989. 'Changing Unethical Organizational Behaviour', *Academy of Management Executive* 3, 2: 123–30.

Nightingale, D.V. 1982. *Workplace Democracy*. Toronto: University of Toronto Press.

Norman, P. 1995. 'Downsizing and Organizational Performance: Empirical Evidence', paper presented at the annual meeting of the Academy of Management.

Northern Telecom. 1995. *Acting with Integrity. Nortel's Code of Business Conduct*. Mississauga, Ont.

Ogilvy, D. 1985. *Confessions of an Advertising Man*. New York: Atheneum.

Ohmae, K. 1982. *The Mind of the Strategist*. New York: Penguin.

Ohmae, K. 1990. *The Borderless World*. New York: HarperBusiness.

Ontario Hydro. n.d. *Code of Conduct for Employees*. Toronto.

Origo, I. 1988. *The Merchant of Prato*. New York: Penguin.

O'Toole, J. 1985. *Vanguard Management*. New York: Doubleday.

Ouchi, W. 1982. *Theory Z*. New York: Avon.

Packard, D. 1995. *The HP Way*. New York: HarperBusiness.

Paehlke, R. 1989. *Environmentalism and the Future of Progressive Politics*. New Haven, Conn.: Yale University Press.

Papanek, V. 1985. *Design for the Real World*. Chicago: Academy Chicago.

Pastin, M. 1986. *The Hard Problems of Management*. San Francisco: Jossey-Bass.

Perrow, C. 1984. *Normal Accidents: Living with High-Risk Technologies*. New York: Harper.

Peters, T., and R. Waterman. 1982. *In Search of Excellence*. New York: Harper.

Petro-Canada. 1994. *Code of Business Conduct*. Calgary.

Philips, K. 1994. *Arrogant Capital*. Boston: Little, Brown.

Placer Dome Inc. n.d. *The Corporation's Mission*. Vancouver, BC.

Poff, D., and W. Waluchow, eds. 1991. *Business Ethics in Canada*, 2nd edn. Scarborough, Ont.: Prentice-Hall Canada.

Polanyi, K. 1964. *The Great Transformation*. Boston: Beacon Press.

Prahalad, C.K., and Y.L. Doz. 1988. *The Multinational Mission: Balancing Local Demands and Global Vision*. New York: Free Press.

Preston, L., and J. Post. 1975. *Private Management and Public Policy*. Englewood Cliffs, NJ: Prentice-Hall.

Provigo. 1995. *Code of Ethics*. Montreal.

Quaker Oats Company. n.d. *Code of Ethics*. Peterborough, Ont.

Rawnsley, J. 1995. *Total Risk: Nick Leeson and the Fall of Barings Bank*. New York: HarperBusiness.

Regush, N. 1993. *Safety Last*. Toronto: Key Porter.

Reich, R. 1983. *The Next American Frontier*. New York: Times.

Reich, R. 1988. *Tales of a New America*. New York: Random House.

Reich, R. 1993. *The Work of Nations*. New York: Knopf.

Rifkin, J. 1995. *The End of Work*. New York: Tarcher/Putnam.

Robinson, J. 1983. *Economic Philosophy*. New York: Penguin.

Roddick, A. 1991. *Body and Soul*. New York: Crown Trade.

Sahlins, M. 1972. *Stone Age Economics*. New York: Aldine.

Sen, A. 1987. *On Ethics and Economics*. Oxford: Basil Blackwell.

Senge, P. 1990. *The Fifth Discipline*. New York: Doubleday.

Sethi, P., and P. Steidlmeyer. 1991. *Up Against the Corporate Wall*, 5th edn. Englewood Cliffs, NJ: Prentice-Hall.

Shapiro, E. 1995. *Fad-Surfing in the Boardroom*. Lexington, Mass.: Addison-Wesley.

Sitkin, S.B., and R. Bies, eds. 1994. *The Legalistic Organization*. Newbury, Calif.: Sage.

Sloan, P., and R. Hill. 1995. *Corporate Aboriginal Relations: Best Practice Case Studies*. Toronto: Hill Sloan Associates.

Smith, N.C., and J.A. Quelch. 1992. *Ethics in Marketing*. Chicago: Irwin.

Solomon, R.C. 1992. *Ethics and Excellence*. New York: Oxford University Press.

Stanbury, W.T. 1986. *Business-Government Relations in Canada*. Toronto: Methuen.

Steele, S. 1992. 'The New Sovereignty', *Harper's* (July): 47–54.

Stelco. 1994. *Code of Conduct and Ethics*. Hamilton, Ont.

Stewart, W. 1995. *Belly Up: The Spoils of Bankruptcy*. Toronto: McClelland & Stewart.

Stoll, C. 1995. *Silicon Snake Oil*. New York: Doubleday.

Syncrude. n.d. *Vision and Values Guiding Principles* [and selected policies]. Fort McMurray, Alta.

Tapscott, D. 1995. *The Digital Economy*. New York: McGraw-Hill.

Thurow, L. 1980. *Zero Sum Society*. New York: Penguin.

Thurow, L. 1984. *Dangerous Currents*. New York: Random House.

Toffler, B. 1986. *Tough Choices*. New York: Wiley.

Toyota Canada Inc. 1995. *Guiding Principles*. Scarborough, Ont.

Trist, Eric. 1981. *The Evolution of Socio-Technical Systems*. Toronto: Ontario Quality of Working Life Centre, Government of Ontario.

United Nations. 1996. *UN Human Development Report*. New York: Oxford University Press.

VanCity Credit Union. 1995. *Mission Statement*. Vancouver.

Velasquez, M. 1992. *Business Ethics, Concepts and Cases*, 4th edn. Englewood Cliffs, NJ: Prentice-Hall.

Wack, P. 1985. 'Scenarios: Uncharted Waters and Scenarios: Shooting the Rapids', *HBR* (Sept.-Oct. and Nov.-Dec.): 73–89, 139–50.

Walton, C. *The Moral Manager*. Cambridge, Mass.: Ballinger.

Wartick, S., and P. Cochrane. 1985. 'The Evolution of the Corporate Social Performance Model', *Academy of Management Review*: 758–69.

Welford, R., and A. Gouldson. 1993. *Business Strategy and The Environment*. London: Pitman.

Wood, D.J. 1989. *Business and Society*. Boston: Little, Brown.

Wood, D.J. 1991. 'Corporate Social Performance Revisited', *Academy of Management Review* 16, 4: 691–718.

Xerox Canada Inc. 1987. *Business Conduct Guidelines*. North York, Ont.

Index